Foundations of Managing British Olympics

FRONTIERS OF MANAGEMENT HISTORY

Edited by: Dr Alex G. Gillett, University of York, UK; Dr Kevin D. Tennent, University of York, UK

Frontiers of Management History focusses on new and emerging scholarship on management history, presenting innovative methodological approaches to study history, and new or disruptive ways of thinking about and theorising management and business history. The books within the series combine the craft of the business historian with the methodology of the social scientist, to offer interdisciplinary perspectives on the management history field, alongside theories, frameworks, critiques, and applications for practice. Featuring a wide range of theoretical, empirical, and historiographical contributions concerned with organisations from various sectors, the series creates a new space in which to engage a new generation of historians and social scientists, to contribute to the future direction of business, organisational, and management history.

Previous volumes:

London Transport: A Hybrid in History 1905–1948
By James Fowler

The Red Taylorist: The Life and Times of Walter Nicholas Polakov
By Diana Kelly

The Emergence of Modern Hospital Management and Organisation in the World 1880s–1930s
By Paloma Fernández Pérez

Strategy and Managed Decline: London Transport 1948–87
By James Fowler

Collective Entrepreneurship in the Contemporary European Services Industries: A Long Term Approach
Edited by Paloma Fernández Pérez and Elena San Román

Foundations of Managing British Olympics: Institutions Through Time

BY

ALEX G. GILLETT
University of York, UK

AND

KEVIN D. TENNENT
University of York, UK

emerald
PUBLISHING

United Kingdom – North America – Japan – India – Malaysia – China

Emerald Publishing Limited
Emerald Publishing, Floor 5, Northspring, 21-23 Wellington Street, Leeds LS1 4DL.

First edition 2025

British Library Cataloguing in Publication Data
A catalogue record for this book is available from the British Library

ISBN: 978-1-80262-096-2 (Print)
ISBN: 978-1-80262-095-5 (Online)
ISBN: 978-1-80262-097-9 (Epub)

Printed and bound by CPI Group (UK) Ltd, Croydon, CR0 4YY

INVESTOR IN PEOPLE

To Skylar, Griffin and my family (A. G. G.)

To Leah and my family (K. D. T.)

Contents

List of Tables

List of Abbreviations

AAA	Amateur Athletic Association (England)
AAC	Amateur Athletic Club
AAU	Amateur Athletic Union (USA)
AFA	Amateur Fencing Association
AGA	Amateur Gymnastic Association
ARA	Amateur Rowing Association (England)
ASA	Amateur Swimming Association (England)
BOA	British Olympic Association
BOAC	British Olympic Association Council
CoE	Church of England
FA	Football Association (England)
FIFA	Fédération Internationale de Football Association
FNOC	French National Olympic Committee
IFAB	International Football Association Board
IPB	International Peace Bureau
IOC	International Olympic Committee
LAC	London Amateur Athletics Club
LCC	London County Council
MCC	Marylebone Cricket Club
MWOS	Much Wenlock Olympian Society
NCAA	Northern Counties Athletic Association
NCU	National Cyclist's Union (England)
NOA	National Olympic Association
NOC	National Olympic Committee
NPRS	National Physical Recreation Society
NSA	National Skating Association
OCOGs	Organizing Committees for the Olympic Games
RFU	Rugby Football Union
SAGB	Swimming Association of Great Britain
USFSA	Union des Sociétés Françaises de Sports Athlétiques (Union of French Athletic Sports Societies)

About the Authors

Alex G. Gillett is a Senior Lecturer at the School for Business and Society, University of York, UK, where he has worked since 2011. His research interests are in longitudinal and historical research, particularly in the business and administrative history of sport, as well as in marketing. His research is also concerned with organisational networks that involve balancing for-profit and not-for-profit objectives. He is Co-editor of the Emerald book series Frontiers of Management History.

Kevin D. Tennent is Reader in Management at the School for Business and Society, University of York, UK, where he has worked since 2012. His research interests include the application of historical methods in business and management studies, and governance and strategy with a specific interest in the sport and transport fields. His publications include contributions to *Management Learning*, *Public Management Review*, *Economic and Industrial Democracy*, *International Journal of Project Management*, *Business History* and *Management & Organizational History*. He has been an Associate Editor of the *Journal of Management History* since 2020. He is Co-editor of the Emerald book series Frontiers of Management History.

Acknowledgements

We'd like to thank the archivists who helped to support the project and without whose expertise historical research would be impossible:

- Paul Dudman and Monna Matharu of the University of East London Library Archives for their help and guidance in accessing the collections of the British Olympic Committee.
- Hamda Gharib and colleagues in Special Collections welcomed us at the Cadbury Research Library, University of Birmingham, where the Amateur Athletic Association archives are held.
- Tracking Lord Desborough's story took us to two different counties – the staff of both Buckinghamshire Archives and Hertfordshire Archives and Local Studies (HALS) were enormously helpful
- The archivists of the IOC Study Centre in Lausanne were extremely generous with their time and very supportive of our research – they have also kept us in their community over the years.
- The archivists at FIFA in Zurich were also supportive and extremely accommodating when we visited them some years ago.
- Alex Jackson of the National Football Museum continues to support and encourage our work and facilitated our access to the museum's unique archival collections in Preston.

The historian of migration Drew Keeling gave us some helpful ideas on how to look at the costs of transatlantic shipping in the 1900s.

Numerous colleagues have given helpful feedback over the years including the reviewers and participants of the BAM Management and Business History Track when we presented an early draft of the book.

We'd also like to thank our colleagues at the School for Business and Society here at the University of York for their interest, ideas, and feedback over the years – including those involved in the Centre for Contemporary Business History and Society, and the CEGBI Summer Conference where we presented an early draft of some of the ideas in the book.

Chapter 1

Introduction

Main Themes

This book sets out to chart how the British contributed to the development of the Olympic Games as an institution and how they did this through the development of competitive sport through the 19th and early 20th centuries. Starting from the 18th century, the 'Grand Tour' to Europe awakened a new interest in classical Greece and Rome which reawakened interest in the concept of the ancient Olympic Games as a show of physical strength and prowess. This came together in the 19th century with the developing ideology of muscular Christianity, originating from the playing fields of England's public schools, stressing the physical as well as mental development of the young men who would enter public life. These men, once they moved into university and into employment in a range of professional and clerical roles, from the military to banking, continued these values through the organisation of amateur sport, which in time became a regularised system for competition. Sport was cleaned up and pursued for its own sake, with monetary prizes banned, and the ethical problems arising from betting sidelined, although this did not prevent business-like values from entering the system in terms of governance. This structure and moralising ethos partly inspired the French man Baron de Coubertin to form the International Olympic Committee (IOC), a move he finally undertook in 1892. We demonstrate that the British remained involved in this process which involved building and reinforcing what became known as 'the classic Olympic system' (Chappalet, 2023, pp. 785–786), a structure of interlocking distributed responsibility based on the collaboration of the Organizing Committees for the Olympic Games, National Olympic Committees, and National and International Sports Federations. This structure started to form and settle in the mid-1900s where this volume concludes, with the British on the verge of hosting in London.

The early Olympiads were ambitious projects which aimed to serve as pacifist meeting places for young people from a range of nations. From the start, they emulated the established World's Fair, or exposition movement, building on a 19th-century tradition of entertainment based on the grand spectacular. Even at Athens in 1896, the stadium was refurbished at great cost, and a new velodrome was constructed. The World's Fairs saw governments, including the British, sponsor official pavilions, and fostered a sense of peaceful international competition – the Olympics embraced this concept and would in time eclipse the World's Fairs.

Foundations of Managing British Olympics: Institutions through Time, 1–4

doi:10.1108/978-1-80262-095-520251001

This book attempts to explore the British contribution among those of other nations and place it in historical context, one which it is tempting to dismiss as ad hoc. For instance, the British missed competing in St Louis 1904, and at Paris in 1900 competitors had not even realised they were taking part in an Olympic Games. Nevertheless, the organisation of multi-sport tournaments involving unpaid athletes with only (mostly) steam railways, ships, post, and telegraph as the available transport and communication technologies was an impressive undertaking which required organisational skill on an international scale. Britain was among the world's most developed countries, and its amateur sporting enthusiasts collaborated with those of other countries and contributed with aplomb. They were self-organising and though having political connections, participated without government funding and attempted to avoid drawing on philanthropy or patronage. This book is the management and organisational history of Britain's participation in that process which created lasting structures that continue to have a meaning that resonates in the 21st century.

As we discuss what we consider to be key influences and milestones in the journey towards 1908, we make no apologies for the Anglo-centrism in our choice of events and influences, but wherever possible we have couched these in the broader geographic context. For example, our account would not be complete without some details of what are now regarded as being the first three editions of the Games in Athens, Paris, and St Louis, the Intercalated Games also in Athens, of the earlier 18th-century Greek games (and smaller-scale events elsewhere in Europe) and pseudo-Olympics in the United States, nor the great influence of France and particularly of French aristocrat Pierre de Coubertin. However, throughout the respective chapters we relate this to the British experience, context, and sporting institutions, and to the folk-history and Victorian history of Olympic revivals in England. We do not seek to deny the existence nor the influence or importance of traditions and institution elsewhere on Olympic history, but we hope that our readers also understand that to compile a complete geographic account of the genesis of the modern Olympic Games, it would require a book of its own and would be a diversion from the what this book is trying to achieve: A long range narrative of the background to the Olympics hosted in the British Isles, against a backdrop of international movements.

Sources and Methods

The research was conducted using an interpretive archival approach, in which we looked for traces of the British Olympic past from an eclectic range of sources. Our aim was to construct a narrative organisational history (Popp & Fellman, 2017) of the precursors to and formation of the British Olympic Association with the emphasis on building a historiographical contribution (Tennent, 2021) emphasising historical integrity over theoretical veracity on this occasion (Maclean et al., 2016; Tennent & Gillett, 2024) but with the potential to illuminate future theory building. Following Tennent and Gillett (2023), we considered carefully the organisations and personalities that we would need to research and used the CLUMOP mnemonic to identify useful collections. We present the results in Table 1.

Table 1. CLUMOP Archival Repositories Consulted.

Category	Repository	Purpose	Coding
Corporate	IOC Study Centre, Lausanne, Switzerland	BOA-IOC Correspondence, Rome and London 1908 files	IOC
Local authority	Buckinghamshire Archives, Aylesbury, UK	Correspondence of Lord Desborough	BA
	Hertfordshire Archives and Libraries, Hertford, UK	Correspondence of Lord Desborough	HALS
Universities	University of East London Library Archive, London, UK	British Olympic Association Collections – BOA Council minutes and correspondence	BOA
	University of Birmingham (UK) Cadbury Research Library – archive and manuscript collections	National Athletics Archive - Amateur Athletic Association minutes, financial records, and rulebooks	AAA
Museums and libraries	National Football Museum Archive, Preston, UK	Football Association Council minute books	FA
Others	N/A	N/A	N/A
Public	N/A	N/A	N/A

Source: Tennent and Gillett (2023, p. 110).

Consistent with the approaches of Nix et al. (2023) we also consulted several digital archives including Gale's Primary Sources for national and regional newspaper sources – not just high-profile papers such as the *Times*, *Daily Telegraph* and *Morning Post* but the many regional and local titles now held by the British Library Newspapers collection, which carried syndicated reports of events and give us an insight into what ordinary people read. The House of Commons Parliamentary Papers and Foreign Office reports were also useful. The reports, official and unofficial of the 1896, 1900, and 1904 games held by the LA'84 Foundation, were helpful for organisational details about those competitions. Similarly valuable were the reports published by the Royal Commissions who organised the official British presence at the various World's Fairs. Published travelogues and memoirs by people such as Baron de Coubertin, Theodore Andrea Cook, and Burton Homes gave a sense of what it was like to beat the events and we have drawn on these where appropriate – we approached these as primary sources, and as such they appear in the footnotes.

When constructing our narratives we were careful to do so in a reflexive way, thinking carefully about issues of change over time, causality, context, complexity, and contingency (Andrews & Burke, 2007). To do so, we attempted to be historically conscious, and thence be reflexive of method in both the first and second orders, considering carefully not just the institutions and practices of sporting figures and organisations but also our relationship to them by carefully identifying and questioning narrative silences (Decker, 2013; Tennent et al., 2020). The narrative was inherently international and took us across many countries and settings – not just the United Kingdom and the complex identities within but also Greece, the United States, and France, among others, as well as throwing up questions about the relationship between *fin-de-siecle* Europeans and the rest of the world. As British authors ourselves we were conscious of the dangers of constructing a hagiography and were mindful to evaluate historical actors by weighting them against the standards and constructs of the period.[1] In building a managerial and organisational history, we have therefore attempted to evaluate the story with contemporary standards of ethics, governance, and organising in mind, unlocking these constructs for a contemporary perspective.

[1]As is usual in historical writing we have not provided contemporary conversions for monetary amounts because these figures generally make more sense in their historical context. We recommend measuringworth.com if you wish to generate modern equivalents.

Chapter 2

On the Shoulders of Zeus: Ancient Olympia, 'Modern' Revivals, and an Embryonic Olympic Movement

Abstract

We first briefly introduce the origins of the Olympic Games in ancient Greece, as they emerged from earlier funeral games which existed from at least the 13th-century BC. A four-year cycle of games known as 'The Olympiad' which ran for nearly 1,200 years evolved, and which symbolised the rise of a new ethic centred around leisure. Our narrative then moves to Britain in the early-modern era, where folk sports and entertainments had already emerged, and from the 17th century the term Olympic started to be applied to festivals which involved sports, sometimes with other classical allusions, the earliest case perhaps being the Cotswold Olympics held from about 1612 to 1642. We then explore other international attempts at Olympic revivals before considering the origins of formalised sports in Britain's public schools and elite universities through the ideology of muscular Christianity, which also emphasised classical revivalism. Finally, we consider the emergence of the Shropshire-based Much Wenlock Olympian Class, which would prove to be perhaps the most inspirational precursor event, organised by Dr William Penny Brookes.

Keywords: Ancient Olympics; classical Greece; Grand Tour; Olympic revivalism; sport history

Introduction

In this chapter, we chart the background to the 'modern' Olympic movement. We agree with MacAloon (2006a, p. 339) who wrote that tracing the early history of the Olympic Games is 'delightful and compelling, but also rather complicated', crossing 'the boundaries of various academic disciplines: history, anthropology, sociology, psychology, literary criticism and classical studies'. Synthesising the

Foundations of Managing British Olympics: Institutions through Time, 5–17

doi:10.1108/978-1-80262-095-520251002

complex literature and primary sources relating to the historic roots and emergence of the 'modern' Olympic movement is difficult and presenting it in a compelling but honest narrative is not easy. The chronology is important, but events and the individual's interconnect. Important ideas and influences appear here and there, disappear, and then re-emerge in a different time or place. This makes a strict chronology tricky without losing the thread and it is not always possible to 'prove' links or causalities between events in, for example, Britain, Greece, the United States, and France. However, we explain similarities and influences, the evidence for relationships between these where they exist.

We begin by identifying the roots of the Olympic story as first emerging in ancient civilisation located in what is now Greece. We discuss the trend for 'Olympic' revivals in western Europe, particularly in 19th-century England, which coincided with shifts in society, perhaps all though not entirely due to innovations in transport and the industrial revolution, and by the 'discovery' (for Britain) and later excavation (mainly a German initiative) of the original site of Olympia. We discovered a great volume of scholarship on these subjects as well as on some of the key individuals and organisations involved, the intersecting and evolving histories of global politics, sport, culture, science, and humanity.

Ancient Roots

> Our culture and leisure behaviour, in part, are rooted in the past. They are founded on a history of what people in the past have done, and on customs and traditions handed down over the centuries. (Torkildsen, 2005, p. 11)

> Sports are often associated with the past; our sports heritage is made up of instantly-recognized names. (Torkildsen, 2005, p. 44)

The above quotations are taken from Torkildsen, who did much to establish the profession of leisure centre manager in the United Kingdom through the late 20th century. He was concerned not just with practice but with the pedagogy of leisure management, and in his explanation of sport and leisure, charts a grand narrative which ties it fundamentally to the evolution of society.

A formational era in the history of Western society was that of ancient Greece. Many city-states hosted local sports events, often through a civic gymnasium, the place where citizens would exercise to promote good health, alertness, and physical fitness (Spivey, 2005, p. 32). The first recorded events, written in Homer's Iliads, were the Mycenaean funeral games, which can be traced to the 13th-century BC and involved combat sports such as chariot race, boxing, wrestling, a footrace, and spear-throwing, between warring Greek societies (Dickie, 1984). Perhaps the best know local events are the later Panathenaic Games of Athens, which began after 566 BC, in which young men nominated by their voting wards, were judged on appearance and on physical and equestrian activities (Spivey, 2005, p. 65).

More significantly, in terms of scale and of date established were the Olympian or Olympic Games that took place cyclically every four years, this cycle being

'The Olympiad'. An important part of political, religious, and cultural life, the Games were held in the summer, at the development known as Olympia. The first recorded instance was the 776 BC edition (Spivey, 2005), but it is thought that they likely began earlier and ran to at least 393 AD, a period of around 1,200 years. The cycle of the Olympiad began with the Pythian Games, held in Delphi and dedicated to the God Apollo. In the second year were held the Nemean Games, at Nemea and dedicated to Zeus. Thirdly, the Isthmian Games were held at Corinth and dedicated to Poseidon. Year four was the culmination; Olympic Games (Polley, 2011).

These early Olympic Games were thus one part of a religious festival, dedicated to Zeus, King of the Gods (IOC, 2021a) or Jupiter as he was known to the Romans, who would eventually conquer the Greek empire in the second-century BC. The site of Olympia, situated near Elis, had been developed to include religious temples and sports facilities with the areas for spectators. But it had been a religious centre since at least the Bronze age, perhaps even Neolithic times (MacAloon, 2006b; Polley, 2011).

Until the Roman era, all free Greek males were allowed to take part, regardless of their social standing, although many were soldiers. Contrastingly, women could neither compete nor attend the Games. Events included combat sports such as boxing (but without weight divisions/classifications), wrestling, pankration (a hybrid of boxing and wrestling), as well as chariot racing, long jump, javelin and discus, and running (IOC, 2021a). In contrast to the modern Olympics, ball games were absent, being considered of relevance only to children and women, and 'had no role in the classical conventions of male athleticism, itself shaped by military needs and the adoration of certain forms of fitness' (Walvin, 1994, p. 12).

The emergence of the original Olympic Games coincided with the rise of a 'leisure ethic' which Torkildsen (2005, p. 12) defines as 'the intelligent use of free time was the purpose of life. The natural life of man was collective, life in the community. The ideal was the perfection of civil life and political life'. The 'proper life' was good citizenship and good citizens were created out of leisure and education. However, this leisure ethic also presented an opportunity for commerce and sport, public entertainment and competitions were increasingly commercialised or even professionalised; as Van Nijf (2004) states, any claims that Greek Olympic sport was purely amateur is an inaccurate claim made by 19th and early 20th century revisionists.

Prior to Roman occupation, those who were victorious in their sports received non-monetary recognition, usually an olive branch or a statue of themselves dedicated within the site. However, in later centuries, competitors arrived from across the Roman Empire. Many had been sponsored to train and compete, with the incentive of being rewarded with wealth and status if they were successful in their events. Participation in the games was still only available to free men, and they were not open for participation nor for spectating of women, slaves, or those who were disrespectful to the Gods. Despite the competitive, in some regard violent nature of the sports, which were based on activities useful for war, peace was an important principle: The Olympic truce required for 'all wars and disputes within the Hellenic world be suspended, and all competitors granted safe passage to Olympia' (Polley, 2011, p. 13).

During Roman occupation, ceremonial life (contests and festivals) initially continued to be a major preoccupation of city inhabitants (Van Nijf, 2000). Events were also important for networking or displaying status; professional associations were present at banquets and processions and had reserved seats in the stadia of the cities. Professional associations can thus be seen as taking their place in the hierarchy of status groups which made up the Greek cities under Roman rule (Van Nijf, 2023). Olympic Games thrived under Roman occupation, being symbolic of Hellenic culture, and although athletics were not an important part of Roman life, upon contact with the Greek world, Romans were attracted to Olympic Games as spectators and participants and Emperors positioned themselves as benefactors or protectors of this aspect of Greek culture. At the end of the first century, Domitian established Greek Games in Rome, and Hadrian, during his reign 117–138 AD, re-established the Panathenaic Games to Athens, introduced others, and tuned the city into his conceptualisation of Greek cultural identity (Van Nijf, 2004).

Despite being a culturally significant ritual lasting several hundred years, it is understood that the ancient Olympic Games were eventually discontinued in 393 AD by the Roman Emperor Theodosius the Great, a Christian who banned Greece's pagan landmarks and ceremonies, including the Zeus dedicated Olympic Games and Olympia development (Baker, 2008) although other Greek sports festivals continued. Olympia was burned down by decree of Theodosius the younger, and thereafter suffered natural disasters, looting, and dismantling (Polley, 2011).

The Written Word, Folk Sport, and British Interest in Olympia

For many years much of what we might think of as education was an activity of monasteries (Ferzoco, 2000). The ability to read and write was the preserve of the very wealthy and powerful, or those occupied by religion, such as monks who hand-wrote religious documents such as bibles. However, medieval universities began to resurrect classical education in the 12th and 13th centuries, including Latin and Greek languages. Latin was internationally used and served as a common language for society's leaders.

In the aftermath of social upheaval caused by the Black Death of 1349, the feudal and clerically dominated Middle Ages gradually gave way to the renaissance, the reformation, and the age of enlightenment. Society became more secular and greater emphasis was placed on appreciation of the arts and of logic and reasoning. The Olympics had been mentioned explicitly in certain classical literature, by philosophers, poets, geographers, and historians, whose lifetimes coincided within the age of the Olympics (Spivey, 2005 names Pausanias and Philstratos as examples). The invention of the printing press in the 1400s had been an important innovation and must have stimulated interest in the written word, as well as making more books and now pamphlets more widespread and relatively affordable. Increased demand led to, or at least coincided with, translations into English (and other European languages) of some works hitherto only available in editions handwritten in Greek or Latin.

The religious Puritan movement of the 16th and 17th centuries capitalised upon the opportunities presented by the printed word, to publish denunciations of festivity and activities which they considered Popish, pagan, or out of step with their own narrow interpretation of Christianity. Puritans cast judgement on some of the popular sport, leisure, and recreation practices of the British people, some of which had roots in folk traditions and pre-protestant or even pre-Christian traditions, although Holt (1990) posits this was mostly when they occurred on Sunday, which was considered sacred, rather than the persecution of fun for its own sake. In 1617, King James I issued a *Declaration of Sports*, to Lancashire and in 1618 nationally. Also known as *The Book of Sports* it listed explicitly his views about the activities that could be undertaken, giving permission for some pass-times including archery, dancing, leaping, and vaulting. Significantly he also allowed May celebrations including Morris dancing and May-poles, which the puritans were against (Tait, 1917). Reissued by Charles I in 1633 as *The King's Majesty's declaration to his subjects concerning lawful sports to be used*, including the same main text but with new introduction and conclusion adding wakes and ales (countryside festivals) (Govett, 1890), it was rejected by the Puritans, who had gained power in Parliament, which ordered it be publicly burned in 1643, just months after the outbreak of Civil War (Polley, 2011).

At around this time, in the Cotswolds area of Southwest England, lived Robert Dover, a country lawyer (Haddon, 2004). Dover established a local annual event *The Cotswold Games*, probably in or around 1612 (Anthony, 1997). Born into a Catholic family in Norfolk and educated at Cambridge and London, Dover eventually moved to the Cotswolds to work. It is thought that there he would have attended the rural Whitsantide celebrations, which would have been similar to myriad others throughout the British Isles at this time. However, Dover developed the games into something much grander, perhaps in defiance of the puritanism of the age.

The event included a large rotating model castle, large enough to house two working cannons, and included folk-sports such as armed and unarmed combat (from fighting and throwing poles, sword and dagger fighting, to shin-kicking, jumping, and hare chasing) as well as feasting and frivolity (Haddon, 2004; Polley, 2011). Haddon (2004) identifies that board games such as *Chess, Irish,* and *Cent* were also played. Dover added classical amusements such as a 'blind Homer and a turf Troy town' (Haddon, 2004, p. 219) and at some point featured a 'Homeric harpist' to 'give them "an Olympic character" and to attract the gentry to these essentially plebeian festivals' (Brailsford, 1969, cited by MacAloon, 2006b, p. 512). This annual event is important to our narrative, because they are perhaps the first recorded event in Britain to be attributed with the word 'olympics' (or 'Olimpicks'/'Olympicks' to use the archaic spelling). The events apparently drew great crowds, where social classes intermingled in the pursuit of recreation and fun (Polley, 2011, pp. 22–23).

The 'Olimpick' moniker was arguably bestowed not by Dover, but by the poet Michael Drayton (Burns, n.d., cited by Haddon, 2004, p. 53). By adopting the word, Dover could also secularise his games, which may have been important if, for example, they had taken over a traditional Church feast or 'ale'. The games would now appear pagan rather than Roman Catholic, which was preferable now that the latter was outlawed, even at a time when Protestant Puritanism was rising (Haddon, 2004).

The Cotswold games were held annually through the early decades of the 17th century and seem to have had greater significance than the usual local fayres and festivities. They were well known by people who might not normally have paid attention to sport. This could have been because, as evidence shows, they had royal support which itself drew on the common belief (although not shared by the puritans) that sporting festivals were traditional and expressions of Englishness, as important to England as sport had been to the ancient Greeks. Indeed, the word 'Olympic' became the way to describe many well-organised sporting events in England (Radford, 2012, p. 161).

The outbreak of the English Civil War in 1642 appears to have been the end of the Cotswold Olyimpicks, which otherwise seem to have been popular. Polley (2011) claims there is no evidence to indicate that they were resuscitated when the conflict ended in 1651, or after the restoration of the monarchy in 1660. However, Haddon (2004, pp. 164–165) points to a poem of 1740 that bemoans the deterioration of the Games and of a novel of 1773 which refers to a 'heathenish assembly … on the Cotswold hills, called Dover's meeting'. Whether or not this evidences a true revival/continuation of Dover's Olimpicks, or rather that the name had been attributed to the latest reincarnation of the feast day, is unclear. Certainly, Dover's Meetings involving backsword contests and wrestling were recorded in the 19th century, although there does not seem to have been much Hellenic revival in them. There was also a donkey race, cock fighting, bowling, and jingling (a game involving blind-folded participants trying to avoid another wearing bells).

In 1845, these games were organised by a local publican, who paid £5 for the hosting rights, but made money back from letting out space for stalls, booths, and presumably sold drinks too (Haddon, 2004). This does not seem to have gone well, apparently 'From 1846 onwards, the games, instead of being as they originally were intended to be decorously conducted, became the trysting place of all the lowest scum of the population which lived in the districts lying between Birmingham and Oxford' (Vyvyan, 1878, cited by Haddon, 2004, p. 170). A few years later, the land on which the games were held was distributed between local farmers and landowners, and 'the Olympick flame was snuffed out for the second time' (Haddon, 2004, p. 173).

But genuine interest in the ancient Olympics of Greece had not ended with the English Civil War, as the classical revival was just beginning. Through the mid-1600s to the mid-1800s, upper-class young gentlemen by around the age of 21 would undertake *The Grand Tour*, which served as an educational rite of passage encompassing classical antiquity and the renaissance, to observe and experience first-hand the culture, art and antiquities of continental Europe, especially those of Italian, Roman, Greek, and French origin. It was also customary for such gentlemen to join or form clubs, which served as a social network and a platform for entertainment, with associated opportunities for political capital, business contacts, and in some cases, for the pursuit of knowledge. As the English public schools emerged they emphasised the teaching of Greek, Latin, and classical civilisation which reinforced the interest of young members of the British ruling class in legitimating themselves through classical revivalism (Chaney, 2014).

In 1723, a French Benedictine named Bernard de Montfoucon advocated excavating Olympia followed by German art historian and archaeologist Johann Joachim Winckelman, who never reached it in-person.[1] However, action came when The Society of Dilletanti, a group dedicated to sponsoring the study of ancient Greece and Rome, commissioned an expedition to Asia Minor and Greece undertaken as of August 1765, to collect and observe what remained there of classical antiquity. The brief did not explicitly ask the expedition to locate or investigate Olympia, but they managed to do so. The approximate location and what was there seems to have been known, to the local population at least (Spivey, 2005) but it does not yet seem to have been knowingly visited, investigated, or recorded by anyone from Britain, or elsewhere in western Europe. The reports of the entire expedition took around a decade to complete and publish beyond the society, of which Olympia was but one part. There hadn't been much to see although the report of the Greek leg of the expedition, published in 1776, mentioned finding brickwork and a hollow where a stadium might have been, but that much of the site was submerged in water (Chandler, 1776; Polley, 2011). This excavation, in which Oxford don Richard Chandler 'rediscovered' Olympia, appears to have been important in encouraging further intellectual interest in the concept of the games and the potential for their revival. Also potentially important, at least in Great Britain, was the topographic mapping by Lord Stanhope in the early 1820s, although in France, the discovery of Olympia was attributed to the Morea expedition of 1828–1829 and to Albert Blouet, who excavated part of the Temple of Zeus and famously brought to the Louvre fragments of its Heracles metopes (MacAloon, 2006b, p. 505).

Olympic Revivals Gain Momentum

MacAloon (2006b, p. 512) suggests precedents for reviving the Olympic Games 'are known from the United States, England, France, Sweden, Germany and Greece' a point made too by Koestner (1974, cited by Driega, 1997) and by Ruhl (1997). MacAloon cites a letter to the scientist Josiah Willard of Harvard dated 1788 that mentions an 'eventual rebirth of the Olympic Games in America' at which athletes 'must practice Greek exercises' (MacAloon, 2006b, p. 512). As well as the report of the Dilletanti sponsored exhibition (Chandler, 1776) the latter years of the 18th century also spawned, in 1793, *Gymnastik für Jugend* authored by the German gymnastics education pioneer Guts Muths, which included a long section on the Olympic Games. MacAloon (2006b, p. 512) elaborates 'by the time the second edition was published in 1804, he was flirting with the idea of a revival'.

---

[1]Lambros, S., & Politis, N. G. (1896). *Official report of the 1896 Olympic games: Part 1* (English/German ed., p. 15). International Olympic Committee. Retrieved January 29, 2025, from https://www.olympic-museum.de/o-reports/olympic-games-official-report-1896.php.

It was, however, a pan-Scandinavian game that provides the first serious attempt of the 19th century at re-creating the ancient Olympic Games, and it included wrestling, high jump, pole vault, rope climbing, gymnastic exercises, and long- and short-distance running. There were two editions, in 1834 and 1836. The second edition added competitions for the best reading of compositions having to do with the Olympic Games, but the games ended after these two attempts (MacAloon, 2006b).

Circuses and shows referencing the Olympic tradition existed in at least the mid-1800s in the United States, and typically exhibited chariot races and other activities such as gladiatorial contests said to have occurred during the reign of Emperor Nero. These circuses and travelling revues seem to have been carnival, an entertainment spectacle, part of show-business. However, the word 'Olympic' was also used by an athletic club in San Francisco, California, United States, during the 1860s, which held public displays of activities such as fencing and trapeze acts. This club, in the 1890s, notably hosted a pseudo-Olympic Games, which converged the spectacle and re-enactment of the earlier travelling shows with the legitimacy of a real athletic club, to recreate Greco-Roman events in a 290-foot-long arena. The games were paired with a Fair and a pamphlet was produced containing details of the programme and in which advertising space was sold, to help ensure the financial success of the venture. A key objective of the games appears to have been the pursuit of financial gain to sustain the club. Sports and other performances incorporated some ancient inspired events, and the entire programme included among its activities, running, discus, jumping, Greco-Roman wrestlers, javelin, boxing, pankration, tug-of-war, gladiatorial contests such as bareback sword fighting on specially trained cavalry horses, and chariot racing, as well as the burning of incense and performance of odes (Rozmiarek et al., 2023). But as we shall see, it was in England, and also in Greece, that revivals of the Olympic Games gained most momentum throughout the 19th century. It mainly was those, perhaps also with some influence from the San Franciscan Olympic Club's activities, that would have a direct influence on the eventual genesis of the global Olympic institution the *International Olympic Committee* (Chapter 4).

Organising Sport in Britain

MacAloon (2006c, pp. 422–424) identifies the English public schools as having played an important part in the social history of modern sport, appropriating and transforming the rural/folk-games and amusements into sports played by the British gentry and aristocracy. This led to several versions or codes of some sports. One of the earliest examples is rowing, which can be found at Winchester in the middle 1700s, but was also popular on the Thames and the Tyne from the 18th and 19th centuries, attracting crowds of thousands of people (Holt, 1990). The demise of professional rowing could be pinned on the prestige of the 'public school, Varsity and Henley events' which began after the school's began to adopt them around 1800 as well as the 'declining economic importance of the watermen themselves' (Holt, 1990, p. 22). The sport is today most famously associated with the more formal university boat races which began in 1829, thereafter becoming 'a notable activity at those public schools blessed with suitable riverine courses' (MacAloon, 2006c, p. 424).

Cricket, a popular boys' game in the South-East of England since at least the 16th century, became an established adult game popular across social classes (MacAloon, 2006c, p. 422), including, for example, factory workers in Birmingham (Holt, 1990) as well as social elites (Stone, 2022). As with most formal sports at this time, the upper-classes preferred to play and compete among themselves, to an extent motivated by the potential for gambling, and there is evidence of the game having been played among the pupils of Harrow by at least 1768. The game then appeared at Rugby school, and others. The Marylebone Cricket Club was founded by public-school graduates in 1787, becoming a leading governing body and codifier of cricket (and later lawn-tennis), and regular games between the universities of Oxford and Cambridge began in 1827 (MacAloon, 2006c, p. 422).

Another game formalised via the public schools, universities, and alumni was football. Originally a mob game often played between villages and with many local variations, perhaps a variation of a ball game introduced following the Norman invasion and often associated with festivals such as Shrove Tuesday celebrations (Hornby & Inglis, 2007). Having been adopted and refined by the public schools, the myriad rules were eventually consolidated and codified in 1863 as a set of Laws, so that they could be played more easily between schools, universities, and their alumni (Hughes, 2009; Sanders, 2010).

These are perhaps the earliest significant examples but by no means an exhaustive survey, or demonstrating the ways in which sport evolved through folk and rural games, were refined through the education system, and later developed by the alumni. Many of whom continued to play beyond their school and university years, some taking on the role of sports administrators. The successful way in which sport and sports administrators were developed is sometimes thought to stem from the culture or pedagogy of *muscular Christianity* which emphasised the participation in physical activities as being a fundamentally important component of the education of young males alongside an academic education. This was considered important for the development of 'manly' leaders of a high state of spiritual, moral and physical development who would be able to sustain the British Empire, as well as encouraging broader physical and mental health through the population (Watson et al., 2005, p. 2). Muscular Christianity may be considered part of the Broad-Church movement of the Church of England (CoE). This movement of the mid-1800s positioned the CoE as less narrow in its doctrine, and based upon a breadth of learning, and applied to some elements of the CoE's more liberal members who 'welcomed progress in science and in the textual criticism of the Bible' and 'became the medium through which the Church gradually regained contact with the modern forces in the world' moving it away from the pure fundamentalism and evangelism which is now more associated with the earlier half of the century (Winn, 1960, p. 66).

An important moment in British cultural history is the book *Tom Brown's School Days* authored by the English lawyer, judge, politician, and author Thomas Hughes. Hughes, in his legal career, improved the position of co-operative societies to form limited companies, and published a manual for running them.

This liberalisation or hybridisation of the legal position of business perhaps also later helped community-based organisations such as football clubs and athletic societies to also do so. As an author of fiction (or semi-fiction), Hughes' story of *Tom Brown* was a semi-autobiographical and based upon his own education at Rugby School and its headmaster, who also possessed the same Christian name, *Thomas Arnold*. Hughes writes of his character Brown as being enrolled 'in the brotherhood of muscular Christians' (Winn, 1960, p. 70). Arnold's approach as Headmaster clearly shaped Hughes interpretation of what that meant, although it is now understood that Arnold did in reality not place much importance on athletics. By today's standards his strict personality and belief that all boys under the age of thirteen were 'wicked' is now considered flawed. However, Hughes developed Arnold's teaching that a moral struggle is ongoing through life, by including sport in his story as a vehicle for teaching 'fight'. Winn suggests this was shaped by Hughes' understanding of England's ancient games as having been closely related to the Church, which held annual feasts of dedication to which each village sent its sporting champion. Hughes remembered these events from earlier in his own lifetime and 'seriously regretted their passing away' (Winn, 1960, p. 70). The passing of festival games appears to have corresponded to increasing industrialisation, urbanisation, and population concentration as rural people migrated to work in the new mills and factories. This corresponded with a change to the stratification of society with growing professional and middle classes, university graduates, and codification of sport into regional and then national varieties such as association football (Hornby & Inglis, 2007).

The Much Wenlock Olympian Class

Another proponent of the muscular Christian ideal of Physical Education as being in balance with intellectual endeavour was Dr William Penny Brookes. Educated in London, Dr Brookes returned to the town of Much Wenlock, Shropshire, where he took over his father's medical practice. He was interested in local sanitation and hygiene, and considered community matters important, contributing to education, transport, and botany while also becoming a magistrate in 1841 (Ashrafian, 2005).

Brookes was aware of the growing urban sprawl and associated mental, physical and moral effects of the industrial revolution (blast furnace men had until the 1840s worked 12 hour shifts, 7 days a week) as well as the challenges in agriculture; the lives and conditions of agricultural labourers could be hard, the corn laws which had previously protected United Kingdom farms from foreign imports had been introduced in 1815 but while their repeal in 1846 reduced the price of food for factory workers, it put economic pressure on UK agriculture, which had to adjust. Better living conditions and pay for agricultural workers was a possibility as the nation prospered but would be a long-term outcome, if they were to happen at all. But improvements to health could have a more immediate and direct impact (Beale, 2011).

Motivated by the opportunity to improve the lives and conditions of the area's agricultural and industrial working classes, Brookes in 1841 established Wenlock

Agricultural Reading Society with the collaboration of the Society of Arts (later Royal Society of Arts). A main feature was its lending library, and Brookes then added interest groups known as Classes, in art, music, botany, and eventually in 1850 added an Olympian Class. Public lectures were given in these various subjects, with emphasis on inclusivity, an important feature at a time when the English system of social class was more rigid than today (Anthony, 1997; Beale, 2011). It is the Olympian Class that is of most interest to our story, established

> for the promotion of the moral, physical, and intellectual improvement of the inhabitants of the town and neighbourhood of Wenlock and especially of the working classes, by the encouragement of outdoor recreation, and by the award of prizes annually at public meetings for skill in Athletic exercise and proficiency in Intellectual and industrial attainments. (Anthony, 1997, p. 18)

This contrasts with the Olympic Revivals occurring at around this time in the United States (Rozmiarek et al., 2023) which seem to have been focussed on travelling circuses and entertainment spectacles, or on membership athletics clubs, rather than on the education or societal benefit of Dr Brookes' initiative.

The Olympian Class involved Brookes own idiosyncratic and parochial mini-Olympic Games (Kent, 2008). Initially, Brookes was thinking locally and annually, unlike the four-year cycle and international scope of ancient Greece. The inaugural edition of *The Annual Wenlock Olympian Games* took place over two days, October 22–23, 1850. This first edition comprised nine events and cash prizes as well as laurel wreaths awarded to the winners, although at least three of these events were clearly more English than Hellenic, consistent with the country-fares and fund-raising church wakes of the time, which had over the centuries evolved into a sort of secular carnival rather than strict religious affair, as we previously detailed regards the Dover 'Olimpicks' of Chipping-Norton (Beale, 2011, p. 25; Young, 1996): Cricket, 14-a-side football and quoits (although Brookes, and the English more broadly, inaccurately associated quoits with the ancient discus). Additionally, there is little evidence in ancient scriptures that the Greeks or Romans competed at hopping on one leg in Olympia either. The remaining five events were more easily categorised as track and field (high jump, long jump, and adult as well as juvenile foot races) and thus probably a bit closer to what we might think of as being rooted more convincingly in the Hellenic era. Such track and field athletics, although commonplace and popularised today, were still 'embryonic' in England at this time (Beale, 2011, p. 25; Young, 1996, p. 9). These were a wholesome games; some of the more violent rural 'sports' previously associated with rural seasonal festivals and wakes popular among agricultural labourers such as cock-fighting and bull-baiting were outlawed by the Cruelty to Animals Act of 1835, and 'Any person guilty of drunkenness, or using profane or improper language, or otherwise misbehaving himself' would face the possibility of a fine, between 1 and 5 shillings (Beale, 2011, p. 25).

Dr Brookes was also delighted when Lord John Manners, a member of the Young England movement, arrived to spectate. The movement looked back to the feudal paternalistic past, a reaction to industrialisation. Manners had called for rest days in the form of National Holy Days for the working classes. At Wenlock, he offered a prize of £1 which the committee decided to award to the footrace, and he was applauded as 'The Labourer's friend, and the advocate of the good old English games' (Beale, 2011, p. 27).

After 1850, the Wenlock Games developed, its subscription more than doubling for its second year (Beale, 2011). More events were introduced, some for adults and some for children, some being open to residents, but others open to 'all England' (Polley, 2011, p. 42). For example, a hurdles race was introduced as a serious athletic competition, and more whimsically, perhaps as a throw-back to the old rural church wakes was a running race for old-women who competed for a pound weight of tea, costed at 5S to the organising committee (Beale, 2011; Polley, 2011). In 1852, the games became a one-day event, and although having begun in 1850 on the race-course, the exact location rotated in different years. In 1852, held in Windmill Field (named after the structure which overlooked from a nearby hill, a photograph depicting this is to be found in Polley [2011, p. 41]) the medieval pageantry was re-enforced with a procession of floral shields inscribed on their back with 'Success to the Olympic Games', perhaps partly inspired by a widely reported speech by a German archaeologist, Ernst Curtius, in January of that year (he would later carry out full excavations at Olympia later in the century). This wording is considered the first time that the Wenlock games were specifically described as 'Olympic' (Beale, 2011, p. 30).

From the beginning, Brookes had blended some degree of ceremony to the event, drawing on ideas (or interpretations) of mediaeval English or European, as well as some considered Hellenic, such as the awarding of laurel wreaths. There was a parade of competitors and committee before the event, and some pageantry and fuss made of the opening ceremony, involving flags, bell ringing, and a closing ceremony including the band, spectators and two winners of footraces held aloft wearing laurel crowns. Semantics are of academic interest: Brookes called these *Olympian Games* more frequently than *Olympics*, although both terms were used, the more frequent -ian suffix hints that Brookes was trying to emulate Olympic ideals into something new and different, rather than claiming a straight revival of the ancient Games (Young, 1996). In their first few years, despite including events open in theory to the entire nation, they remained relatively local, although travel and inter-regional sporting competition was becoming more feasible, as we shall see.

Chapter Summary

The Olympic Games were an ancient sporting event that seems to have emerged from funeral games and rotating religious festivals, in which men from across the Hellenic world competed through sport rather than war, although these sports were often rooted in combat or combat preparation. Olympic myth or wisdom is absorbed into British folk sport and festivals, although are subdued at least temporarily by the Puritan movement and English Civil War. By the 18th century, the Grand Tour and dilettantism are part of a cultural shift towards Romanticism and rekindled interest in ancient Greece including the Olympic Games.

Exploration and excavations are undertaken by British and French interests. Muscular Christianity in education and paternalism or progressive social ideas at least by the relatively rigid social structure of the time, see sport increasingly used to better the character and health of people. In Much Wenlock, Shropshire, an agricultural class spawned an annual event that would become a landmark in Olympic history.

Chapter 3

Emergence of Multi-sport Events in Britain and Abroad

Abstract

While sporting events remained localised in the mid-19th century, an industrialising world was seeking opportunities to showcase its achievements through large-scale events which could serve as meeting places, informing and educating the public about the world. We consider the emergence of the World's Fairs movement through the Great Exhibition, held in London's Hyde Park in 1851, an event that brought together 14,000 exhibits and drew 6 million visitors. Contemporaries drew comparisons between the event and the Olympic Games. Greece meanwhile emerged as an independent country in 1830. The fledgling state tried to re-assert its control of the concept of the Olympic Games and we chart the attempts of a Greek businessman, Evangelis Zappas, to do this with support from the Greek crown. In Britain, attempts at revivals continued too, and the Wenlock festival gave way to a series of National Olympic Festivals, culminating in the foundation of the National Olympic Association (NOA) in 1865. The same period was also when amateur sports started to organise in civil society away from the educational institutions. Self-reliant associations were founded which financed themselves through the subscriptions of sports clubs. This movement was epitomised by the formation of the Football Association (FA) in 1863, though would take hold especially in emerging disciplines such as rowing, swimming, athletics, and cycling, and developed into a network of amateur sporting associations, often with affiliated bodies in Scotland and Ireland as well as England. The Amateur Athletic Association (AAA), formed in 1880, epitomised many of these principles.

Keywords: Cotswold Olimpicks; Wenlock Olympics; National Olympian Association; Amateur Athletic Association; sport history

Foundations of Managing British Olympics: Institutions through Time, 19–47

Published under exclusive licence by Emerald Publishing Limited
doi:10.1108/978-1-80262-095-520251003

Introduction

We reported in the previous chapter how organised sport and the idea of the Olympic Games originated in ancient Greece and was encouraged even under Roman Rule, before its end in a broad move against pagan festivities. Olympic-styled revivals emerged again from English folk festivities before similarly being closed down by the puritanism that led to the Civil War during the mid-1600s. The rediscovery of ancient ruins in the 1700s during a period of increased interest in the Romantic stimulated archaeological excavations and another Olympic revival in the United Kingdom and abroad. Approximately 200 years after puritanism had oppressed sport and celebration in England, there had been industrial revolution, increased urbanisation, and movement to organise or coordinate sport, although this initially tended to be regional. Dr William Penny Brookes and the Wenlock Agricultural Society, a movement to improve education and hygiene in the Wenlock area of Shropshire, launched an Olympian Class as a way for local people to enjoy athletic games. He even made its events, which had prizes of monetary value, open to all in England, at least in theory (Young, 1996). The Wenlock initiative can be considered a progressive movement for its time typified by emphasis on community and the interaction between social classes. In this chapter, we explore the way in which sport began to organise nationally and attempts to create new and larger-scale institutions and events, some of which drew upon Olympic history, or at least a romanticised idea of it. We show these things as occurring in tandem with a movement to re-establish Olympic Games in the young nation of modern Greece and that the English and Greek movements interacted and supported each other. We draw particularly on secondary literature but also on contemporaneous sources including newspapers and also the archives of the AAA.

The Crystal Palace and the Great Exhibition

The Wenlock Olympian Games emerged at an exciting time for events and festivities to celebrate achievement and British achievements. Perhaps most notable of all at this time was the Great Exhibition of 1851. Britain possessed the largest empire in history, was the largest economy in the world, and was a significant global power, perhaps the foremost. Nevertheless, military efforts in Afghanistan between 1839 and 1842 resulted in British troops withdrawing in one of the worst defeats of the century. Increasing involvement in South Africa through the 1830s and 1840s had also brought the British into confrontation with the Boers, white settlers of Dutch origin. In India, where Britain had enjoyed a major presence through the rule of the East India Company since the 1600s, tensions would reach boiling point in the rebellion of 1857–1858 resulting in the nation's direct possession by the British Crown. There were tensions too at around this time in Canada, particularly between British and French colonists (see e.g. Cain & Hopkins, 1987).

Britain was a powerful nation; geographically, the British Isles were the origin of great innovation, even if the overseas empire was proving challenging to maintain. A shift from reliance on agriculture to industry was well on the way by the end of the 18th century; by around 1780, Britain could consider itself the most economically developed country in the world (Evans, 1996). Technological change in the making of textile machinery, iron making, and the invention of the steam engine came together with several comparative advantages, such as the availability of cheap coal and a pre-existing culture of mechanical skills to create the world's first industrial revolution (Owen, 1999). Regions and cities were able to specialise with the creation of industrial clusters (Wilson & Popp, 2003) in, for instance cotton textiles in Lancashire (Owen, 1999), steel, metallurgy, and armaments in Sheffield (Corker, 2023), and pottery in North Staffordshire (Lane, 2023). Industrialisation meant that real wages for workers were starting to increase, even if overall living standards were restricted by poor sanitation in growing cities (Gallardo-Albarrán & De Jong, 2021). By 1850, British GDP per capita was US$4,332 compared to France at US$2,545 and US$3,632 for the United States.[1] Britain's national population had surged too, from 8,565,000 in 1700 to 27,181,000 in 1850 (MPD Version 2023: Jutta & Leuiten van Zanden, 2024). Individual towns and cities saw considerable urbanisation, led by London which expanded from 959,000 people in 1801 to 2,252,000 by 1851 and 3,254,000 by 1871 (Evans, 1996, p. 430). When considering technological and economic progress at this time in British history, it is impossible to overstate the importance of the railways, which had begun to 'gather steam' in the North East of England in the 1820s but by the 1830s had expanded to include not just the hauling of minerals but also of human cargo. Railways spread nationwide, connecting towns and cities, reducing travelling times, and ushering in mass-transit on a scale more significant than even the canal system had allowed (Bagwell & Lyth, 2002).

Railways were also developed corporate forms based on managerial bureaucracy and distributed authority (Gourvish, 1972; Turner, 2013) a model emulated in other parts of the economy. The growth of industry and resultant urbanisation was particularly felt in locations where raw materials such as coal and iron ore could be mined or processed. One such Victorian boom town was Middlesbrough, which saw expansion from a few farmhouses in 1831 to a population of over 40,000 by 1871 (Evans, 1996), studied by Budd (2017) as a microcosm of sport in urban England during the latter years of the 19th century. With particular reference to sport, railways enabled games to be played in and between teams and individuals in other cities. Steamships, no longer restricted by the speed of the wind, allowed for faster and more reliable travel for athletes and teams around the world, with, for instance, an English cricket team touring Australia in 1861–1862 (Frost, 2002). At this point we must be careful to also acknowledge Holt (1990) who warns us to not oversimplify Victorian sport; urbanisation, connectivity and the organisation, codification, and perhaps sanitisation of sport by the administrative classes did not suddenly nor completely purge the nation of local sport, customs, or attitudes. Rural pastimes endured while local or regional contests continued to exist, while violent attitudes to sport as entertainment and gambling involving fighting between

[1]2011 US Dollars.

human beings or animals persisted in town and country. Industrial revolution, the development of transport, and technology and social progression happened, yes, but attitudes and culture did not change as suddenly, nor simultaneously and there were also regional and class divisions that should be acknowledged.

The middle of the 19th century was also an important time in the history of British organised public events and exhibitions; the mid-century provided a good opportunity to reflect on the nation and its Empire's place in the world. To showcase Britain's industrial and cultural strengths, and to galvanise its global position as a civilising force, the event to give its full grand title was the 'Great Exhibition of the Industry of All Nations' (Bonython & Burton, 2001) (hereafter *The Great Exhibition*) staged in May–October 1851. Such exhibitions became a 'recurrent feature of public life in western Europe and the United States from the mid nineteenth century' (Geppert, 2010, p. 7) and form a prominent theme throughout this book. Exhibitions are underexplored in business history literature (Declercq, 2022; Walker, 2024) but are worthy of study (Friedman & Jones, 2011) particularly because they 'represent manipulated environments and singular events at which diverse operations may be investigated' and illuminate 'interfaces between business, society, and especially culture' (Walker, 2024, p. 2). The Great Exhibition can be seen as part Britain's 'philanthropic landscape' in which voluntary giving was significant (Harvey et al., 2019) although Walker's (2024) analysis finds the financing and governance of the Exhibition to have been less dynamic and strategic than had previously been believed.

Precedents existed for such expositions. In Britain's neighbour and global rivals, France, regional and national exhibitions were an established phenomenon; the Napoleonic exhibitions of 1804 and 1806, and the industrial expositions that had operated since 1798 are important, but it was that held in 1849 which is deemed the most significant step towards what was proposed for London. The French event was expanded to give enhanced prominence to agriculture as well as industrial products (Courtin, 2016). This, the 'first of Republican France' was reported to have 'far surpassed in every way anything of the kind that had yet been attempted'. The area for buildings covered 221,000 feet, which is greater than previous French expositions but just one third of what was proposed in 1850 for Hyde Park the following year.[2] The Great Exhibition of 1851 predominantly focussed on showcasing technological innovation, manufacturing capabilities, and the trading and economic prowess of the nation, with space also dedicated to show the part played by other countries and works of art and cultural value. The potential of the event was to create an environment 'knitting likewise nations in bonds of peace and harmony by facilitating the interchange of their products'.[3] The idea for the event is credited to civil servant Henry Cole, who as founding director of the Victoria and Albert Museum is also attributed as the inventor and

---

[2]*The Illustrated London News*, 'The Great Exposition of the Industry of All Nations', Volume 17, Issue 455, 16 November 1850.
[3]*The Illustrated London News*, 'The Great Exposition of the Industry of All Nations', Volume 17, Issue 455, 16 November 1850.

sender of the first commercial Christmas card (V&A, n.d.). Although building upon the expositions of the European continent and regionally in the United Kingdom, The Great Exhibition of 1851 may be considered the first truly international exhibition or world exposition (Leapman, 2001).

The Great Exhibition was organised by commissioners appointed by the government and who were given royal permission to build in Hyde Park. The Commissioners of the Royal Exhibition were constituted by Royal Charter as a corporation with corporate personality with powers to 'sue and be sued, implead and be impleaded, and should have perpetual succession', though not with limited financial liability which created difficulty financing the exhibition (Walker, 2024). A number of well-known engineers were appointed to the board including Robert Stephenson and William Cubitt, as well as Prince Albert and John Shepperd, the Chairman of the East India Company.[4] Prince Albert had made a speech expressing belief 'the world had reached a stage where all knowledge and innovation we recognised as being the property of the international community as a whole, not something that needed to be protected by secrecy from the gaze of outsiders' and that the Exhibition would embody this ideal, to be funded by donations from localities rather than from Central Government funds (Leapman, 2001, p. 24). Conversely, we can also consider the Exhibition that was delivered as being very much a state encouraged enterprise designed to demonstrate the economic might and achievement of contemporary Britain and its colonies. Despite the prestige involved in making such donations the commissioners found that the public were reluctant to provide the £206,000 estimated expense of running the exhibition, with only £46,903 raised by May 1850 (Walker, 2024). Unable to secure a loan on the takings or a building yet to be brought into being, the Commissioners negotiated a credit facility with the Bank of England, ultimately of up to £227,500 which required guarantors including the Commissioners but also a cohort of wealthy London and provincial philanthropists, as well as suppliers to the project, to cover any loss (Walker, 2024).

Constructed of iron and glass and taking five months to build, the structure built in Hyde Park housing the event was formally named the *Palace of the Great Exhibition of the Works and Industry of All Nations* but popularised as the *Crystal Palace*, a punchier title attributed to the appropriately named satirical publication, *Punch* magazine.[5] The building was itself a product of its time, the ability to

[4]House of Commons Parliamentary Papers, Exhibition of 1851, COPY of WARRANT under Her Majesty's Sign Manual, authorising the COMMISSIONERS for the EXHIBITION of 1851 to enter upon a Piece of Ground in *Hyde Park,* and to erect Buildings there upon for purposes of the EXHIBITION; and of DEED of COVENANT from the COMMISSIONERS for the EXHIBITION of 1851 to The QUEEN'S most Excellent Majesty, to observe and perform certain Terms and Conditions mentioned in the said WARRANT, and to reinstate and yield up the Site granted for the purposes of such EXHIBITION. Office of Woods, 1851.

[5]Graves, C. L. (1921). 'Mr Punch's History of Modern England, Volume 1 of 4: 1841–1857', p. 40. Available online: https://www.gutenberg.org/files/44267/44267-h/44267-h.htm.

make it so safely, affordably and so quickly, was a result of advances in glass production; the sheet glass process developed by 1838 replaced plate glass and had a faster cooling time and needed less grinding and polishing than plate (Wilson & Mackley, 2000). There had also been changes in taxation which must have helped, window tax (based on number of windows on a building) and also the excise duty on glass (based on weight of glass) being abolished. They were archaic taxes dating from the 17th and 18th centuries, respectively, and would surely have meant that the Crystal Palace would not have been designed. Window tax was abolished in 1845 and then the glass levy removed in 1851, reducing the price of glass by half. Thus, technology and process advancements and a favourable tax system seem to have been conditions favourable to the project (Bryson, 2011).

To celebrate the year, the structure measured 1,851 feet in length. It was 408 in width, and 110 feet at its highest point, the central spine, and enclosed an avenue of elm trees, rather than felling them. This design, based on an agricultural hothouse, replaced the original plan (for an iron roofed brick shed deemed impractical to deliver on time and to cost) and is attributed to Joseph Paxton, head gardener of Chatsworth House, Derbyshire[6] (Bryson, 2011).

Prefabricated from standard parts it comprised a cast-iron truss (just 3-feet wide and a little over 23-feet long) with matching trusses and nearly a million square feet of glass, equal to approximately a third of British annual glass production, and twenty miles of guttering. To construct it in time required the design of new machinery and platforms to increase the productivity so that small teams could erect in a day what hundreds would have previously managed in a week (Bryson, 2011). The guttering was notable for not only draining rainwater but also condensation within that formed on the thousands of glass panels.[7] The building safely and robustly withstood the English weather although prior to its construction cynics had doubts.[8]

Visitors were treated to 14,000 exhibits that pushed the envelope to demonstrate the possibilities of invention, manufacturing, art, and craft from around the world. Examples from the regions and cities of Britain were included, with glass cases designed for the interior to fit with the overall aesthetic of the building.[9] The United States provided many impressive contraptions but underfunded its exhibitors, requiring philanthropist George Peabody to provide emergency funding to get the goods from the docks to Hyde Park. British society still followed a fairly rigid class system at this time, with Chartism and social unrest

---

[6] *The Illustrated London News*, 'Professor Cowper's Illustrations of the Scientific Construction of the Palace of International Industry', Volume 18 Issue 463, 4 January 1851.

[7] *The Illustrated London News*, 'Professor Cowper's Illustrations of the Scientific Construction of the Palace of International Industry', Volume 18 Issue 463, 4 January 1851.

[8] *The Illustrated London News*, 'The Great Industrial Exhibition of 1851', Volume 17 Issue 454, 9 November 1850.

[9] *The Illustrated London News*, 'The Great Industrial Exhibition of 1851', Volume 17 Issue 454, 9 November 1850.

perhaps peeking across on the other side of the Channel just three years earlier and Parliamentary buildings and even the British museum in London fortified in anticipation. The social unrest and the perceived causes, social problems such as poverty and the increasingly overcrowded and dangerous urban environment were captured in the fictional writing of Charles Dickens, whose works provided some commentary on the present and recent past and resonated with the public. Dickens advocated for charity, strong moral principles, and the Protestant faith to bring about progress and major social reforms, of which the Exhibition, which he attended, was perhaps symbolic (Howarth, 1951).

Thousands of people per day of all social classes were able to mingle freely within the Crystal Palace and no riots occurred. This intermingling meant mass attendance and at its peak 92,000 people were in the building. Enabling this was the fact sanitation was of the best standard, with flushing toilets, not yet a common feature. Held over 140 days, it was immensely popular. Six million people attended, including Queen Victoria herself, who visited 30 times (Torkildsen, 2005). Profits of £186,000 were realised, and used to buy thirty acres of land for the building of museums, galleries, and other institutions (Bryson, 2011). Ultimately only £33,038 12s 6d of the loan was drawn upon and very quickly repaid after the exhibition opened, with the Commissioners having taken an extremely cautious approach to protect the liabilities of the guarantors (Walker, 2024). Indeed, Walker (2024) criticises the Commissioners for not acting quickly enough, having waited until financial shortfalls became acute in July 1850 to seek alternative financing solutions. With the limited experience in running such not-for-profit event projects at the time it is clear what the available options were given that the Company Limited by Guarantee form later favoured by many British not-for-profit organisations was not brought into being until the Companies Act 1862 (Cooke, 1950). MacAloon perhaps summarises the Crystal Palace best, and finds traces of Olympic revivalism even in this event, for which sport was not really a component other than perhaps depicted in some form within of the art exhibits:

> [...] the Crystal Palace was indeed a crystal, reflecting and refracting the core values, social categories, ideologies and conditions of Victorian English life. All agreed that nothing quite like it had ever taken place before, and writer after writer struggled to discover some metaphor to express the unique character of this greatest mid-nineteenth-century spectacle. One metaphor is of special interest to us. In the Spectator, an anonymous journalist called the exhibition 'this Olympic game of Industry, this tournament of commerce', and Horace Greeley, too, referred to it as 'the first grand cosmopolitan Olympiad of Industry'. (MacAloon, 2006b, p. 499)

On this note, it is also important to highlight a report sent to The Great Exhibition organisers from the participants representing Greece (JDP Economics, n.d.). Dated February 27, 1852, the report makes explicit comparison to the Olympic

Games. Headed 'The Great Exhibition of 1851 – the mental Olympic games of the united world!' the author continues in glowing terms:

[...] in their efforts to carry into effect the part assigned them in those gloriously conceived and newly revived Olympic games, in which not the physical, but the mental powers of the united world have been called into friendly competition, in order to augment and advance the sources of happiness, and the well-being of mankind.

Greek Revival

By 1859, Greece experienced a notable Olympic revival of its own, known today as the *Zappas Olympics*, but were simply known as *Olympics* at the time. The games were initiated, and funded, by Greek businessman Evangelis Zappas, who was living in Romania. It is worth stating that Zappas wasn't the first Greek national of the 19th century to recognise the ancient Olympic Games as important to that nation's cultural heritage, nor was he the first to propose a revival in the 'modern' era. For one, a poet turned newspaper editor named Panagiotis Soutsos had proposed such a revival and had even lobbied the King of Greece, who in principle had agreed to the event, although nothing came of it. Zappas, who it is thought was at least partly inspired by Soutsos and would later request for Soutsos and his brother to be involved in an Olympic Committee, was however the person with the means to make such a revival a reality (Young, 1996).

Initially, there was resistance from some of the Greek politicians. Modern Greece, as a nation state, had only gained independence from 400 years of rule by the Ottoman Empire in 1830, following a lengthy war (Koliopoulos & Veremis, 2009). In the 1820s, the cause of Greek independence had itself caught the imagination of the Philhellenic Movement, a grouping of scholars and intellectuals who wished to restore the glory of classical Greece, and who interpreted the concept of Greek independence as a victory for Christianity and western civilisation. Such acolytes of the concept included the romantic poets Lord Byron and Percy Bysshe Shelley (Merriman, 1996). By the mid-1850s, when Zappas first proposed his Games, the modern state was still relatively young. An Olympic revival was considered by some to be archaic, primitive, and pagan, rather than the sort of progressive initiative that a new Greece needed in order to shape perceptions among the 'Great Powers' of Europe. Instead, Zappas was countered by these politicians, including the Greek foreign minister Alexander Rangkavis, who proposed an industrial and agricultural exposition, along the lines of Britain's Great Exhibition of a few years earlier. Again, not much happened, but Soutsos published an article publicising Zappas' idea. The idea of an Olympic revival was though also considered as potentially legitimating the status of the Greek royal family (who were in fact ethnically Bavarian and had been installed to the throne by the British, French, and Russians as part of the treaty which guaranteed Greek independence). Thus, King Otto, whose father Ludwig I had been an enthusiast for Greek culture, approved a compromise: Quadrennial Olympic athletic competitions to be sponsored fully by Zappas, who then established a Trust Fund for the events, but as part of simultaneous industrial/agricultural expositions (Young, 1996).

News of the planning for a Greek Olympic event soon spread, including a letter sent to an English local newspaper, *Eddowe's Shrewsbury Journal*. Presumably this newspaper was chosen because the letter's author was aware of the existing event in Much Wenlock. Dr Brookes, who read the letter and pasted a clipping of it to his scrapbook, wrote to the British Ambassador in Athens, Sir Thomas Wyse, to suggest a programme of events for the Greeks to use. Wyse replied to tell Brookes he thought the programme too ambitious for the Greek event, which would mainly feature agricultural and industrial competitions. Undeterred, Brookes, seemingly excited and wanting to contribute to the organisation in some way, wrote back to donate a sum of 10 pounds as prize money for a 'tilting at the ring' competition. This was an equestrian skill involving ring-spearing, which had been introduced by Dr Brookes to the Wenlock Games in 1858 (Young, 1996, p. 10) but thought historically to pre-date even Robert Dover's 'Olympick Games' (Haddon, 2004). This particular event did not actually make the schedule for the Greek Games, but some other athletic events did, including running, jumping, discus, javelin, and pole climbing, with cash prizes. Dr Brookes' money was awarded to 'the best runner of the longest race' in the 1859 Greek Olympics and was in fact the largest cash prize of the tournament. Additionally, non-athletic events including chariot racing were held (Young, 1996).

Zappas' proposal and sponsorship, and the Royal decree for the Games, had provided funds intended for the renovation of the ancient Panathenaic stadium, the home of one of the less important of ancient Greece's ritual games, the Panathenaic games. This would involve restoring the venue in marble, including the seating, and would be the venue for the athletics. Newspaper reports claimed that little more than a 'good cleaning-out' would be required.[10] However, this renovation was not undertaken and the events, which took place in October 1859,[11] were instead held in a flat square in Athens, 'Plateia Loudovikou' (or 'Ludwig Square') it is today known as 'Koumoundourou'.

The Zappas Olympics attracted competitors from the Greek speaking diaspora around the Mediterranean, including the Ottoman territories (Brownwell, 2008), and the square was well attended, including the King and Queen although there were complaints from spectators about poor visibility. It is also not clear if some events descended into tragedy (one runner appears to have collapsed and later died) or into farce. A report of beggars participating alongside more serious athletes may have been a deliberate inaccuracy by some journalists desiring to undermine the games because of the resistance to the idea of Olympianism among some politicians, or perhaps because, unlike strictly amateur sports of the day, Zappas' Games awarded cash prizes and allowed members from outside of the upper class 'gentleman amateur' clique to participate (although this concept of amateurism was far more evident in England than in Greece at that time). However, it is thought that regardless of the quality of the Games or whether

[10] *The Sunday Times*, 'Restoration of the Olympian Games in Greece'. 26 September 1858, p. 2.

[11] 'Varieties'. *Hereford Journal*, 27 April 1859, p. 2.

or not they came close to Soutos and Zappas' poetic vision of Olympic Revival, their significance to the Olympic movement is quite considerable, as a precursor to the eventual international Olympic Games that century. In the short-term, their influence on Dr Brookes of Shopshire, England, and his own Olympic ideas also seems important, as it appears to have spurred him into even more activity and develop an international vision for the Olympic revival (Young, 1996).

Back in Britain: Shropshire, Liverpool, and the NOA

Brookes extended the Wenlock Olympics to include more events, including the javelin throw, which he adopted from the Zappas Games. With new non-athletic events also added (e.g. art and music) Brookes' event now comprised 29 contests. Brookes exchanged more letters with the British ambassador and made the Greek winner of his 10 pound prize, the distance runner Petros Velassariou, the first honorary member of the Wenlock Olympian Class. In 1860, Brookes introduced the Greek influence in the form of mottos and imagery to the Wenlock Games, and also established a peripatetic Olympian Games for the county of Shropshire, held in rotation between the five boroughs of the county, and operating in addition to the local games of Much Wenlock. He also formed the Wenlock Olympian Society as a separate body from the Class to be an autonomous sporting society that could independently organise its own games. In 1861, the Greek Olympic committee and Brookes exchanged letters in which the Greeks refer to the Wenlock committee as a 'sister' organisation (Young, 1996, pp. 28–29). By this time, the games were attracting interest in the media as a possible cleansing and rationalising force in society. One correspondent in the *Shrewsbury Journal* compared the Wenlock Games to the debauchery of the nearby Shrewsbury Show, which they claimed was a 'ridiculous and childish pageant'. While the Olympiad might seem an anachronism born from ancient rather than modern society, a clear benefit was that it provided 'healthy and rational recreation for the bodies and minds of the youth of the neighbourhood' while not neglecting more intellectual pursuits. This was considered favourable as it was claimed to promote temperance and generally recreation in an environment considered acceptable for the attendance of women and children 'without contamination'. Thence to disseminate the concept of Olympism, the Wenlock festival was considered 'well worthy the attention of the philanthropist and the promoters of social science'.[12] Further, the Liberal Chancellor of the Exchequer, William Gladstone, wrote to Brookes in 1862, encouraging him for furthering athleticism among young men as it would improve military readiness, and suggesting that a 'system of gymnastic training' be formally introduced into schools.[13] The twin themes of social progressivism and military readiness would continue to be key drivers in the ethos of British Olympism.

[12]'The Wenlock Olympic Games and Shrewsbury Show', *Morning Post*, 12 April 1860, p. 6.
[13]'GRAND ASSULT AT ARMS'. *Liverpool Mercury*, 4 December 1862, p. 7.

The Olympic term started to be used more broadly away from Wenlock. Another notable event, the Liverpool Olympic Festival, was held in June 1862. The inaugural festival was a one-day event possibly viewed by up to 10,000 spectators, many apparently women. These games were the initiative of two men, Charles Melly (President of the Liverpool Athletic Club) and John Hulley (Honorary Secretary of the club), both of whom participated in the Muscular Christianity movement[14] (Young, 1996). This club took an interest in military preparedness and practised fencing, boxing, wrestling, and gymnastics among other sports.[15] Short-lived, six Olympic Festivals occurred in total, scheduled annually every year for five years mostly in Liverpool, Northwest England, from 1862–1867, albeit the 1865 and 1866 editions were hosted in Llandudno, North Wales. Although without the longevity of the Wenlock movement, the Liverpool movement is notable for being open only to gentlemen amateur competitors[16] a feature typical of its time and important to the Olympic story. Furthermore, for 1863, these were the first British games labelled 'Olympic' that not only restricted participation to the amateur but broadened the invitation to compete 'all nations' and as reflected in the name 'Second International Olympic Festival' although reports suggest that no international athletes took the challenge, thus the event remained a British affair contested between members of regional athletics clubs.

By 1863, participants hailed from throughout the North of England, the midlands, the Southeast, and London, and by the 1864 event, results from the festival were covered in the 'Pedestrianism' (or athletics) section of the *Bell's Life in London and Sporting Chronicle*[17]newspaper suggesting national, and perhaps even betting interest. Despite the amateur nature of the competitors, with strictly no prize money at stake, the organisers created a carnival atmosphere, erecting a grandstand, providing refreshment tents, and providing two military bands playing popular music.[18] As already mentioned, the games were hosted in Wales during 1865 and 1866 and even introduced a 'junior games' for young athletes there, before returning to Liverpool for what would end up being the final edition in 1867. Within a few years, these festivals with international aspirations had run their course, albeit being perhaps the first series to locate in two countries, to restrict entry to amateurs, and the first British 'Olympic' labelled event to at least invite a global participation (Polley, 2011, p. 60). Hulley, an energetic promoter of amateur sports, was made a third honorary member of the Wenlock Olympian Society by Dr Brookes in 1864 (Young, 1996).

Perhaps part of the reason that the series of Liverpool Olympic Festivals stalled was the first attempt at a British National Olympian Games. Establishing an organising body for sport, and then planning the Games busied the founders between November 1865 and July 1866, the month that the first of the Games

[14] *Illustrated London News,* 'Olympic Festival at Liverpool', 12 July 1862, pp. 60–61.
[15] 'GRAND ASSULT AT ARMS'. *Liverpool Mercury*, 4 December 1862, p. 7.
[16] *Illustrated London News,* 'Olympic Festival at Liverpool', 12 July 1862, pp. 60–61
[17] *Bell's Life in London and Sporting Chronicle*. 'Pedestrianism', 2, 204, 16 July 1864, p. 7.
[18] *Illustrated London News,* 'Olympic Festival at Liverpool', 12 July 1862, pp. 60–61

happened. These founders included Dr Brookes, and as chair, John Hulley from the Liverpool Festivals, as well as the German Ernst Ravenstein, the owner of a gymnasium in Kings Cross, London, and president of the German Gymnastic Society, who had corresponded with Liverpool's Melly and Hulley. The purpose of the organising body, the NOA, was to establish a central association that could bring into focus and systematise the myriad Olympian, athletic, cricket, gymnastic, swimming, boating clubs (and similar), and physical education societies that had begun operating around Great Britain. The association would award strictly non-monetary prizes, produce a yearbook, and hold General Meetings in different cities or towns by rotation. A further aspiration was the body would further enthusiasm for physical education by lobbying for the inclusion of sporting or physical elements into existing popular festivals. The title *Olympian* was chosen over *Athletic* because it was considered to have broader applicability than simply encouraging 'excellence in gymnastic exercises', with the allusion to antiquity emphasising the integration of mental and physical culture.[19] The resolution was passed explicitly at the inaugural meeting of 6 November 1865 'That Professional Athletes shall be excluded from competition'. The association would 'pay homage to mental excellence' by appointing honorary members who with notable achievements, for example, in art, literature, or science (Polley, 2011, pp. 66–67). The ethos of the NOA and the growth of amateur athletics, especially away from London, seems to fit into the broader mid-Victorian attempt to rationalise and sanitise leisure time towards the weekend and strictly agreed holidays, reducing archaic practices such as 'Saint Monday' and mass fairs or wakes based around consumption (Reid, 1996; Walton, 1981).

Polley (2011, p. 68) identifies that the NOA and its games combined elements that would come to characterise the modern Olympic movement, namely 'amateurism, masculine sports, medals, a mix of physical and intellectual competition, and a Latin motto to sum up the organization's ideal'. This Latin motto, *Civitum Virtus Civitatis*, translates as 'the power of the state' and is thought to have alluded to the strength of the citizens as being the power of the state, that phrase translated as *Civium Vires Civitatis Vis* was included on a medal created in 1866 to mark Dr Brookes election to President of the NOA. Polley (2011, p. 68) also identifies that although open to 'all-comers' the Games ultimately precluded anyone considered a professional athlete as well as women.

Other 19th-century British Sporting Institutions

The first National Olympian Games held by the NOA occurred in 1866, in London. By far the largest city in England, London was already a sporting capital as well as governmental and administrative capital. We have already mentioned the powerful Marylebone Cricket Club (MCC), founded in 1788, and the FA had also recently founded, in 1863.[20] The FA was at least partly catalysed by

---

[19] 'A National Olympian Association'. *Liverpool Mercury*, 7 November 1865, p. 7.
[20] 'Football', *Bell's Life in London and Sporting Chronicle*, 31 October 1863, p. 2.

inter-city competition, made easier by rail travel, but which presented the challenge of regional rules variations within the same sport. Quite simply, 'rules were needed to ensure that they were playing the same game' (Torkildsen, 2005, p. 40). This was probably true for other emergent sports, but football provides an excellent example, with different rules existing not just between schools but also in regions of the country as the game was popular within other social strata. Rules that emerged from clubs and organisers in Sheffield, where some of the first tournaments were held, became important to the national picture (Westby, 2018). In particular, were those of the upper classes, the school and university 'old boys' network, who established the FA and the first universal Laws of the Game in October 1863, almost 13 years to the day since Dr Brookes first Wenlock Olympics and its own version of a football event. Football would of course become an important part of British culture, and ultimately one of its most significant cultural exports. It was a useful way to socialise workforces and other social groups in the growing towns and cities, fostering local identity and creating identification with institutions such as churches. It also had a temperance dimension, creating a distraction for working-class men from pursuits such as drinking and gambling (Lupson, 2006; Pickford, 1940). It could also be played in the winter, allowing athletic and cricket clubs to maintain their fitness year round (Budd, 2017).

Cricket was also centred on a London based yet more elite governing body, the MCC, which also played games on its own behalf. Associated with aristocratic patronage and matches set up for wagers in the 18th century, in the 19th the game gradually fractured into a more commercially aware approach in the north of England and the Midlands, while becoming more associated with the concept of gentlemanly amateurism in the South of England, though overall remaining committed to an amateurist aesthetic (Stone, 2022). A popular summer sport among all classes, representative sides playing intermittent matches on behalf of counties or the North versus South, or Gentlemen (amateurs) versus Players (professionals) started to emerge, usually played over two innings for each team which took at least three days. The earlier gambling culture persisted into the first half of the century, but was gradually 'cleaned up', and club cricket based on fixed grounds developed around the country, with single innings matches played in fiercely contested regional or local leagues.

An All-England Eleven, or Eleven of England was formed by William Clarke in 1846. Clarke was a Nottingham publican who established the Trent Bridge ground, which often hosted games between teams notionally representing Nottinghamshire and other counties. Clarke developed this into a peripatetic professional team who toured the United Kingdom playing games against representative teams, some of whom were allowed twenty-two players on the field (Major, 2007). Cricket in the first half of the 19th century was largely a professional game, though many players were agricultural, industrial or manual workers who played for modest wages to supplement their income – Clarke was able to lure 'the best' on the promise of a full time wage, although the eleven did include two players who considered themselves amateurs, but their 'expenses' were identical to the full time players (Major, 2007, pp. 179–180). Some of these players joined the first recognised overseas tour to the United States and Canada in 1859, captained by George Parr, an all-England professional (Major, 2007). More significant for the future of the sport, some of these players were among the first English team invited to Australia in the 1861–1862 and 1862–1863 Australian summers (Major, 2007). This inspired further bilateral competitions, and an English touring team lost two 'tests' to the Australians at the Melbourne Cricket Ground in March 1877, inspiring the series known as 'The Ashes'. It took this name after England's loss at home in 1882, prompting a mock obituary notice in the *Sporting Times* (Major, 2007).

Outside of football and cricket, the Oxford versus Cambridge university boat race had also been held annually on the river Thames since 1845. Rowing had emerged firstly as a professional sport among some of the professional oarsmen of the Thames and the Tyne, who had enjoyed a keen rivalry in the mid-19th century, but the university rowers began to eschew the involvement of betting from the end of the 1830s, and started to emphasise rowing as a healthy interest for their students, continuing the ethos of Muscular Christianity from the public schools. Oxbridge at this time delighted in separating itself from profit making business, emphasising the value of a general education, an environment which encouraged the development of an ethos which saw sport to greater fulfilment (Halladay, 1990). Under university dominance amateur rowing developed alongside the professional sport, with the Henley Regatta becoming established as its annual showpiece. Amateurism did not totally replace it for a long time, however, in 1876, both amateur and professional rowing crews headed to the United States to participate in the Centennial Regatta, though the university rowers proudly claimed that Henley medals were prized more than monetary prizes.[21] London provided an ideal meeting ground for the Oxford and Cambridge rowers and the showpiece race between the two became an important part of the sporting calendar.

So, jumping back 10 years, it is not surprising that the NOA chose London as the venue for its Games. However, as London already had an established, and still growing, social and sporting clique, they did not take kindly to the new organisation which it seems to have perceived as entering its territory. Clerks from the City had already formed the Mincing Lane Athletic Club in 1863, which was renamed the London Amateur Athletic Club (LAC) in 1865 (Taylor, 2002). Meanwhile, J. G Chambers, an Old Etonian, hastily formed the Amateur Athletic Club (AAC) in December 1865, with its own 'first annual championship games' then announced quickly in The Sporting Gazette dated 23 December 1965, to be held in March 1866 on a London ground (Beale, 2011, p. 66). The currency for entering these games was the guinea (an archaic unit of account worth £1 1s, or today £1.05), and any athlete who participated in NOA organised events was banned from AAC events then or in future. Beale (2011, p. 67) concludes the AAC 'gazumped' the NOA, and that its hasty formation and announcement of a games was rushed over the Christmas of 1865 solely to thwart the NOA. The AAC and LAC would continue for some years to be the dominant bodies in British athletics, the AAC holdings its meetings at Lillie Bridge Stadium in Putney (ironically also a venue

[21]'English Oarsmen in America', *Pall Mall Gazette*, 16 August 1876.

for professional 'pedestrianism') while the AAC used Stamford Bridge Stadium in Brompton (Taylor, 2002) though, despite their thwarting of the NOA, neither were able to establish a national championship.

National Olympian Games

The NOA meanwhile held its games successfully over three days in three locations within the city. Starting on 31 July 1866 with swimming events in the south-western suburb of Teddington. Day two was held in the vicinity of the Crystal Palace, mentioned previously as the venue of The Great Exhibition during the previous decade. By now, the Crystal Palace had been dismantled from its original location in Hyde Park, in the central/west-end borough of Westminster, and in 1854, was reconstructed in Sydenham, South East London, where it exhibited classical and medieval exhibitions, exotic plants, and musical and dramatic events. The games themselves appear to have taken place in sports and recreation areas of the park, and it was reported to have attracted a crowd of around 10,000 spectators. Contests were similar to those of Liverpool and Wenlock, such as foot races, jumping, and combat sports including boxing, wrestling, events for armed forces personnel and also for civilians dressed up in military garb, including 'sabre versus bayonet' contests. Notably, the hurdles event was won by W. G. Grace, who was simultaneously playing cricket for England five miles away at the Oval, managing an innings of 224 not out, when his captain let him take a short break to attend the Olympian Games. There was also a 'General Competition' which may be considered a forerunner to the modern pentathlon. Day Three was held at the German Gymnasium, a new establishment built a few years earlier and operated by NOA member Ernst Ravenstein. The gymnastic events were of the German variety with emphasis on rope climbing, team-work, vaults, and dumb-bells, in contrast to the Scandinavian gymnastics more popular today which emphasise movement, agility, and stretching (Polley, 2011). This was though a national event, rather than international, the extent of international representation limited to Hulley's appearance dressed in Turkish costume to represent the East (Beale, 2011, p. 67).

The following year, 1867, the NOA held its second Games, this time in Birmingham, hosted by the Birmingham Athletic Club.[22] Again, they were a three-day event, spanning June 25–27, and incorporated ideas from the Wenlock games, such as beginning with an opening ceremony and procession, and there was for the first time in the National Olympics a 'tilting at the ring' tournament (Polley, 2011, pp. 74–76). A stated aim of the Birmingham games was to promote the inclusion of bodily exercise as a regular branch of school education. Brookes was critical of the excessive focus on mental application and school funding relying upon examination results during visits by inspectors. He observed Prussia, where physical exercise had been introduced in the earlier in the century (Beale, 2011).

---

[22] *Birmingham Gazette*, 'National Olympian Association's Visit to Birmingham', 20 April 1867, p. 5.

Events were included for boys under 16 years of age, and there was also indoor swimming, fencing, boxing, broadsword and sabre versus bayonet, athletics including another 'General Competition', gymnastics, and to conclude was an award ceremony and 'Olympian Ball' with speeches about the national importance of physical education and Olympianism (Polley, 2011, pp. 74–76). However, even with the Olympic Games held outside of London, the AAC was still tightening its restrictions on athletic events for all but gentleman amateurs: An athlete could not be considered amateur if he had competed for money, nor whether he had raced knowingly or unknowingly against one who did. There was also introduced in 1867 the infamous 'mechanics clause' barring from participation mechanics, artisans and labourers (MacAloon, 2006d, p. 538; Polley, 2011, pp. 74–75; Taylor, 2002, p. 82). Young (1996) highlights that Brookes refused to introduce such a strict definition of amateurism for the NOA, and thus the AAC which was concerned greatly with social class, continued its stance of barring athletes who had participated in NOA events. Both Young and Polley believe that this was a serious impediment on the development and ultimately the sustainability of the NOA.

The third British National Olympian Games of 1868 were hoped to take place in Manchester, but no club there would agree to host. Thus, the third edition occurred not in a major city, but in the smaller town of Wellington, where the 1861 Shropshire Olympian Games had been held, not far from Much Wenlock. Again, there was an opening ceremony with flags and banners, and crowds reportedly in the thousands. Events included quoits, bowls, a brass band competition, and hurdles, and again speeches about physical education (Polley, 2011). The games do now seem to have retreated to its traditional heartland and taken a more provincial atmosphere in contrast to the London elite of the AAC, and there would be no more British National Olympian Games until 1874.

At this point in our narrative, it is worth reflecting on historical context. This was a time of great social change, particularly for reforming and broadening participation in education as well as other upheavals in the social strata. The attitudes of the AAC were seemingly grounded in strong and deep-rooted social class conservatism. While still the prevailing paradigm, this London clique was also beginning to look archaic. Instruction to abolish slavery in the British colonies had happened with the Slavery Abolition Act of 1833[23] and this had followed earlier movements, such as the ending of engagement with West African slavers in 1807. Despite this, on British soil, the nation's own children were still working in dangerous jobs such as chimney sweeping despite the existence of legislation since 1788, until the Climbing Boys Act was introduced in 1864 to ban the use of boys under the age of 10 for cleaning chimneys[24] (this, a year after the FA was founded and a year before the inauguration of the NOA). Modern professions

[23] Available online: https://www.legislation.gov.uk/ukpga/Will4/3-4/73/1991-02-01/data.pdf.

[24] Available online: https://vlex.co.uk/vid/chimney-sweepers-regulation-act-861267843. For discussion of working practises see Hansard, 29 April 1864. https://api.parliament.uk/historic-hansard/commons/1864/apr/29/chimney-sweepers-question.

with professional entry qualifications were also starting to emerge – for example, Florence Nightingale had founded a nursing school in London in 1860, thereby pioneering modern nursing. The Civil Service also started to move away from the archaic practice of appointment by patronage to open examinations from 1870, and a modern clerical class was emerging (Evans, 1996). The first three editions of British National Olympian Games had taken place just after these innovations but before the Education Act of 1870[25] that made it compulsory for every child to have a school place (Torkildsen, 2005). This is relevant because it places Dr Brookes and colleagues whose work involved helping and providing opportunity to the working classes, and whose Olympian aim involved preaching the gospel of physical education. The NOA was thus likely perceived as part of a progressive movement which the members of the AAC probably perceived as upsetting to the status quo and natural order, of sport but also of society.

Rapid social change was also happening abroad. For example, the United States, independent of Great Britain since 1776, was still a nation in turbulence. Steam engines, an innovation from Northeast England, were soon adopted on the other side of the Atlantic. Much larger than Britain, America presented a huge opportunity for the railways. Beginning in the 1820s, it was really between the 1830s and 1860s that the railroads began to dominate, replacing canals as the main mode of transport for travel and freight (Chandler, 1977). Mid-19th-century America was still very much a collection of states rather than a strongly unified nation. The country was at war with its neighbours Mexico from 1846 to 1848. Slavery was still practised, very much along the lines of race, although a movement to abolish it had begun in the late colonial era. But the matter caused a significant rift particularly between the southern states (and plantation owners therein whose firms were dependent on slavery for their thriving export trade) and the rest of the country, which despite the industrial revolution and expansion of the railroads still included many rural communities and undeveloped regions, where for moral and/or economic reasons, did not want slavery to expand. Without wishing to oversimplify the myriad complicated and contested reasons, suffice to say that by April 1861 tensions about slavery and other issues of state versus federal governance had boiled over into a full-blown civil war between northern and southern states, which lasted until May 1865 (American Battlefield Trust, 2013). In continental Europe, the long struggle continued between liberals who agitated for radical solutions and constitutional government, and conservatives who advocated for the continuation of the *ancient regime* and elements of absolutism, even continuing elements of feudalism in some parts of Eastern Europe (Jones, 2013).

Against this background of economic and social change versus deep rooted social strata, the efforts to create an international Olympic movement, which

[25]See information provided by UK Parliament, available online: https://www.parliament.uk/about/living-heritage/transformingsociety/livinglearning/school/overview/1870educationact/.

included education and challenged the establishment's strict definitions of amateurism, appears to have been very progressive but also challenging.

The Return of Zappas

We have already shown that 1865 was the year that Dr Brookes and colleagues had begun to consolidate the British Olympian movement nationally with the formation of the NOA. It was unfortunately also the year Evangelis Zappas, the sponsor and driving force of the modern Greek Olympian revival, died. Six years after his inaugural games of 1859, there had yet to be a follow-up event, but Zappas was clearly thinking about legacy, and left in his will the instruction that his wealth be used for funding a modern Olympic Games to be held every four years. This was to include financing the excavation and restoration of the ancient Panathenaic stadium, the only stadium in the world built entirely of marble, so that the athletic events would have a permanent venue worthy of such a spectacle, and for the construction of an 'adequate but simple building', which would become known as 'the Zappeion', in which to house the agro-industrial exposition. Zappas' will also left instruction for his body to be buried in Romania, then after four years be dug up and decapitated, the body to be reburied at a school nearby his home in Greek Albania, the head to be reburied at the new Olympic building in Athens and marked by a plaque written in ancient Greek to the effect 'Here lies the head of Evangelis Zappas' (MacAloon, 2006b, pp. 516–517; Young, 1996, pp. 42–52).

The young nation of Greece had experienced more turbulence in 1862, when King Otto was compelled to vacate the throne, and the following year a new monarch was installed, King George I of Greece. A Dane by birth, King George valued the Olympic Games, perhaps as a way to appeal to national pride and signal his Greek-ness, and so in 1869 it was announced the Games would reconvene in October 1870. And so, as a result of Zappas' generous if slightly strange gesture, and a change in monarch, the first modern international Olympic Games to be held in a stadium, took place, albeit a month later than had been announced, in November 1870 (Young, 1996).

The Panathenaic stadium was excavated and prepared, but athletics received only 6% of the total budget, which seems contrary to Zappas' instruction, for comparison it was a sum less than 5% of what Zappas had allocated for the same purpose in 1859 when he had hoped to see the stadium resurrected in his lifetime. Overall, The Olympic Committee for 1870 spent nearly two hundred thousand drachmas, mostly allocated to the agro-industrial exposition, funding another (temporary) building and display cases. In contrast, Zappas' hope for an athletics festival at which spectators would be seated on marble was compromised; yes the stadium was prepared, having been further excavated 1869–1870, but compromises were made and wooden benches were installed instead of bare marble. However, unlike 1859 this time spectators could get a good view of the track and field activity thanks to the tiering and oval shape of the stadium (although open at one end) far more suitable than the flat town square of the previous edition. Athletes were invited three months before the event and asked to report to The Committee six weeks prior to the Games in order they receive supervised training and participate in preliminary events (Young, 1996).

As in the ancient Games, participants swore an Olympic oath to compete fairly, and sang an Olympic hymn. A prize of free seats for life at future Olympic Games was offered to winners, along with an olive wreath presented by King George. Travel expenses could be paid by the Committee, together with uniforms and accommodation expenses, and this generosity attracted athletes from across the Greek diaspora in the Balkans and the Ottoman Empire. An attendance of around 30,000 people flocked to the stadium to spectate. Sports included track and field and gymnastics disciplines, namely 400 metres running, running triple jump, running single long jump, wrestling, discus throw, javelin throw, pole vault, pole climb, rope climb, and individual tug-of-war. Cancelled though were rowing, swimming and equestrian events, although presumably these would have required other venues. Overall, what historians now refer to as the second Zappas Games appear to have been a success (Young, 1996).

The spectre of the class-elitist gentleman amateur concept had become noticeable in Greece by this time though and the Greek 'anti-athletic clique' who had opposed the idea of Olympic revival all along were quick to comment from their own critical perspective, one critic labelling the 1870 Games a 'parody' of the ancient Games (Young, 1996, pp. 42–52). There were several reasons behind this, but one argument against the Olympic revival was that such athletics did not serve a useful purpose in preparing the population for war (or defence) because technology was replacing brawn on the battlefield. As with the AAC in London, this clique, seemingly out of touch with popular opinion, were powerful, and made sure the next edition of Zappas' legacy Games, held in 1875, would be an amateur only affair (Young, 1996).

Once more, Young (1996, pp. 42–52) provides what is probably the deepest scholarly account, and describes them as 'fiasco'. The stadium was hardly prepared and in places obscured by thorn bushes and rocks. Seating arrangements were on crude wooden benches (some of which broke when sat on), and notably this time the Royal Family, perhaps the pinnacle of the social classes, did not even attend, suggesting that the socially elite aspiration was borne only among some members of the political class. The athletes were young men from the universities and private school system. At the previous games a broader range of athletes came from across the social spectrum, but the less diverse games of 1875, far from showcasing the need to focus only on the socially elite, actually resulted in a relatively poor showing in terms of overall athletic spectacle.

The games lasting just two and a half hours were broken by long boring judge's speeches, and the last two events were cancelled. Indeed, the 1875 committee report apparently chose to ignore mentioning the athletics and instead focussed only on the agro-industrial exhibits. Newspaper reports though did report on the games but not favourably, pointing to crowd restlessness, the unreadiness of the stadium, and as mocking ancient antiquity. However, not all of the reports should be taken at face value, Young (1996) questions the motive of at least one reporter, John Mahaffy, whom other academic researchers such as MacAloon (2006b) have turned to, presumably because as an Anglo-Irishman, he wrote in the English language. According to Young, Mahaffy firstly inaccurately wrote that the ancient Olympics had been purely amateur events, an inaccuracy that would plague sport and the Olympic movement for decades to come. He also belittled the Greek Olympic revivalist movement in contrast to that of Britain, which was perhaps unfair: Although scuppered by an anti-athletic clique, the Greek Olympics of 1859 and 1870 had at least stemmed come from good intentions, indicated by the legacy of substantial finance from Zappas' estate (Young, 1996). The exact year that the Zappas series actually ended is debatable, but MacAloon (2006b) suggests 1889, although admits that there is confusion.

It is worth mentioning at this point the excavation and refurbishment of the Panathenaic stadium occurred not long before another archaeology project significant to the Olympic story. Between 1875 and 1881 further excavation work was undertaken on the ancient ruins of Olympia. For Greece this was the first continuous excavation of its scale funded from overseas. The catalyst for these excavations is thought to have been Ernst Curtius, professor at the University of Berlin. In 1852, Curtius gave a lecture on Olympia, witnessed by Friedrich Wilhelm IV and his son, the future Kaiser, for whom Curtius had been a tutor. Twenty-two years later, with the Kaiser's backing, Curtius concluded an agreement with the Greek government; in return for bearing the cost but leaving all finds to Greece, a German team was granted exclusive excavation rights to Olympia (MacAloon, 2006b). Financed by the German government via a Berlin based committee, the project employed German architects and archaeologists, as well as 45 labourers to uncover two square miles, much of it under five or six metres of mud. The dig revealed several temples, treasuries, and other significant structures and over 14,000 artefacts including bronze statues. These finds were temporarily displayed at an on-site museum (Shanks, 2003). The project and its discoveries were news across the world and heightened interest in all things ancient Greek, and Olympian. The final reports were published between 1890 and 1897, but the German government brought out yearly reports from 1875 to 1881 (MacAloon, 2006b).

Meanwhile, in Shropshire

The National Olympic Games had taken place again in 1874, in Much Wenlock, a village setting compared with the stated aims of the NOA to host in principal towns and cities. The Games' connection to the physical education of youth was more clearly the aim than reviving Greek traditions, with contests for essays on physical education in elementary schools rather than for Olympic poetry, and with some events open only to the local school children. Politicians and dignitaries were invited as organisers and officials, one of whom was Thomas Hughes, the author of *Tom Brown's School Days*. By 1877, the Games were beginning to wither on the vine, *The Modern Olympics of the British at Shrewsbury* were now held in conjunction with the local horticultural society's *Shrewsbury Flower Show*. The games were now seeming to be more parochial than national, and only a step above Dr Brookes' Wenlock Games, which continued as an amateur event, although he would not adopt the AAC's strict definition. In 1876, 10,000 spectators enjoyed the Wenlock games, which introduced cycling for the first time at any Olympic event. Brookes, not to be deterred, remained in contact with the Greek embassy in London, his ambition to cooperate with the Greek Olympic movement to help found international Olympic Games, writing frequent correspondence between 1880 and 1893 (Beale, 2011; Polley, 2011; Young, 1996).

This correspondence was helped by John Gennadius, the Greek charge-d'affaire in London, who encouraged Brookes to contact those in Greece who would be positive about Brookes idea for an international Olympic Games. Gennadius became the second Honorary Member of the Wenlock Olympian Society in 1880 (Anthony, 2007). The efforts of Brookes, of the NOA and of the Greek movement were not to bear fruit at this point, although they do not go unnoticed as we shall see in Chapter 4.

British Sport Gathers Pace

Over the same timespan that Olympian sporting events and archaeology were undertaken in Greece, we can observe important moments in the evolution of sport in Britain, beyond the National and Wenlock Games. This included increasingly sophisticated organisation, that increased sporting integrity by creating repeat fixtures, but which also often prioritised an amateur ethos (though professionalism was tolerated in some circumstances). For example, the game of rugby football ('rugger'), which in 1871 splintered from the FA over rules (for the purpose of brevity we may summarise these as to do particularly with handling and 'hacking' between players) holding its first full international fixture (Lupson & Lerwill, 2011). This was followed swiftly by what historians consider as the first full association football (or 'soccer') fixture, both between representative sides from Scotland and England, in 1871 and 1872 respectively (Booth, 2002; Taylor, 2008). It is also worth mentioning that slightly earlier attempts at international soccer had first played since 1870, although these games are considered to have been novelty or pseudo internationals, because the Scottish sides actually comprised London based players with Scottish connections. An annual British 'Home Championship' competition (initially the *British International Competition*, or the *International Competition*) between the British representative sides would emerge from these games through the later 19th century as the first international soccer tournament in the world (Lupson & Lerwill, 2011).

The first ever club football knockout tournament was the FA Cup between English clubs and ran from November 1871 to March 1872 (Lupson & Lerwill, 2011). This idea was soon picked up in Scotland, where a Scottish FA formed in 1873 and held its own challenge cup that same year (Scottish Football Association, n.d.). Wales and Ireland would follow suit in 1877 and 1881, respectively. For association football, these were the first four *national* knockout cup tournaments in the world, although regional and varsity knockout tournaments also existed around the same time (Lupson & Lerwill, 2011). They were also punctuated in 1876 by the start of a series of *World Championships Games* between clubs from different countries (England and Scotland) although it was later in our story, in 1895, that could be considered the first of real significance as the first to feature the champions of respective national leagues (*Sunderland* from England and *Heart of Midlothian* from Scotland) Before then, in 1888, the first ever national Football League (as opposed to a knockout tournament) was formed in England, in September 1888. Similarly it was followed in 1890 by the formation of Irish and Scottish national football leagues (Lupson & Lerwill, 2011).

Urban life thrived, and created demand for sport and recreation. As well as individuals wanting to participate, religious institutions and the temperance movement considered sport as a way in which to draw people away from alcohol and gambling. It was common for churches to establish football clubs, some of which provided the roots of teams still operating today (Budd, 2017; Lupson, 2006). Industry also saw the benefit of sport for employees and football clubs, with industrialists and workers alike backing and organising teams. The team Blackburn Olympic, founded in 1878 following the merger of two prior teams, and is thought to have been named because of the interest surrounding Olympia and the Olympic Games emanating from the aforementioned German-Greek excavation of Olympia at that time. The club experienced some success in the FA Cup, beating more established teams of public-school alumni, such as Old Etonians, to win the tournament. Similarly to the Zappas Olympic Games, Blackburn Olympic's achievements raised the issue of working-class clubs fielding professional players as well as manual workers, versus the gentleman amateur ideal of the more established clubs which had inaugurated the FA and dominated its committees and competitions for the previous twenty years (Sanders, 2010).

We have explained what was happening with football, particularly association football, because of the game's rapid growth and importance to Britain, and eventually to the world. But other significant sports were also evolving. For example, in tennis, a game that in some form had existed for centuries. A major innovation in the game was the variation *lawn tennis*, whereby players could compete on a grass surface. This is thought to have become widespread as a result of a technological innovation (the vulcanisation of rubber) that made it possible to create balls with significant 'bounce'. The formalisation of lawn tennis is dated to 1876, and just one year later, The All England Croquet Club changed its name to 'The All England Croquet and Lawn Tennis Club' and hosted the first major event the 1877 Wimbledon Championship (Country Life, 2005; Wimbledon.com, n.d.).

In cricket, the MCC started to assume *de facto* responsibility for governing the sport as the informal test matches between English and Australian teams gradually turned into fixtures that were considered competitive. It formalised the informal two inning 'first class' matches between counties into a 'County Championship' starting from 1873, started to enforce conduct such as breaches of amateurism, and organised England's representative matches at home, and overseas tours (Schofield, 1982, p. 338). The county system, not always a rational structure of fixtures at first, and often played during the normal working week saw a resurgence of amateurism in the game, uneasily combined with professionals on the same team who were looked down upon and forced to use separate dressing rooms. County cricket was combined with a wish to avoid too overt an ethos of competition on the national scale, though players such as the notoriously entrepreneurial W. G. Grace, who as an amateur scored 50 first-class centuries through the 1870s, brought widespread attention through their exploits (Stone, 2022).

Athletics was also organising. The AAA gave English athletics a single governing body for the first time. It was established in 1880 as a merger between four distinct groupings which subscribed to the amateur ethos – the Northern Counties Athletic Association (NCAA), the Midland Counties Athletic Association and a grouping of clubs in London and the south east including (among others) AAC, the LAC, the Oxford and Cambridge University Athletic Clubs, the Civil Service Athletic Club, and the German Gymnastic Society.[26] The NCAA, which had eschewed the mechanics clause favoured by the AAC, was formed the previous year, on 5 August, in a meeting in Stoke and initially was largely formed of clubs from Lancashire and West Yorkshire (Taylor, 2002). The Midland grouping included nine clubs from the Birmingham and Warwickshire areas.[27] The London clubs lacked an overarching organisation at this time but had pioneered a strict amateur ethos. The fourth main group to join in was the North of Thames Cross Country Union, a grouping of seven clubs including the Railway Clearing House Harriers representing the body which set rates and attributed revenue to the 150 plus railway companies then in operation (Bagwell, 1968). Another workplace club which joined from the start was United Hospitals. It was not initially an exclusively English body, and the Edinburgh University AC was also accepted as a member in December 1880. Scottish and Irish clubs left to form their own AAAs in 1885, though they remained affiliated in terms of rules and sanctions to the English body.[28] According to the minutes of the foundational meetings, the 'National Olympic Association (Wenlock)'[29] were invited to join in 1880 but appear to have not. At the founding meeting it was agreed to frame the common rules based upon the AAC and Oxford and Cambridge rules, and constitutionally a sort of distributed responsibility structure based on a General Committee was adopted.[30]

The organisation developed several foundational principles that enforced amateurism as a principle through organisational efficiency. Three objectives were initially identified – to better manage athletic events through uniform rules, to 'deal repressively with any abuses of Athletic Sports', and to hold an annual championship. Although some founding clubs were given permanent seats on the General Committee, there was a degree of democracy with regional and representative membership added. There was a commitment to avoid monetary prizes, which should instead be Challenge Cups which could not be sold. Winners in Championship Competitions would also receive a gold medal, and a silver was given as a second prize.[31] The General Committee, though composed of volunteers running the

[26]Cadbury Research Library, Special Collections. Records of the Amateur Athletic Association of England, 1872–1997 (hereafter AAA). ATH/AAA/1/2/2/1.

[27]AAA ATH/AAA/1/2/2/1, Amateur Athletic Association Minute Book (AAA Minutes), 1880.

[28]AAA ATH/AAA/1/2/2/1, AAA Minutes, General Committee 13 December 1880; General Committee meeting, 21 February 1885.

[29]As mentioned earlier in this chapter, the NOAs Olympian Games had retrenched to Shropshire and the NOA seems to have lost status and consolidated with Dr Brookes and the Wenlock Olympian Class.

[30]AAA ATH/AAA/1/2/2/1, AAA Minutes, 1880.

[31]AAA ATH/AAA/3/1, Amateur Athletic Association: Constitution, Objects and Lists of Officers and Members: Laws for Athletic Meetings, 1889, p. 10.

organisation in their spare time, was given managerial duties intended to establish the AAA as an institution, such as the control of expenditure, the holding of annual meetings, and the enforcement of discipline among athletes. The two senior executive officials, the Honorary Secretary, and the Honorary Treasurer, were given the title 'Honorary' to demonstrate the voluntary nature of their position, though contemporary accounting standards were adhered to and the accounts audited by committee members. In 1888, a small office was rented in the City of London, at 10 John Street, easily reached from London's financial and civil service offices, and an 'Assistant Secretary' employed at £30 per year to handle the more menial paperwork.[32] Despite its city links, however, the AAA was never a wealthy body and it did not benefit from patronage nor did it enjoy any government funding. It relied mainly on the proceeds of its Annual Championship Sports and other events, together with subscriptions from affiliated clubs and registration fees to sustain itself. Surpluses were run through the 1880s and 1890s, with the book value peaking at £1,967 in 1898, with a £201 0s 2d surplus. Spare money was invested into low-risk investments which allowed for a consistent yield, a strategy typical of the period (Rutterford & Maltby, 2007) valued in 1898 at £273 12s 6d in Great Eastern Railway stock, £557 6s 8d in UK government stock (or Consols) and £254 12s 6d of a Canadian Government Loan.[33] The founding Honorary Treasurer, C. N. Jackson, served from 1880 to 1910; his 'day job' was bursar of Hertford College, Oxford from 1887 to 1914, and he was also treasurer of several sports clubs at Oxford including the University athletics club from 1869.[34]

Discipline was to be enforced by 'prosecuting' any professional who competed as an amateur and suspecting those 'proved guilty of misbehaviour or unfair practices connected with Athletics'. This was supported by a 'Law Expenses Account' into which the association regularly deposited funds.[35] The mechanics clause was not included in the definition of amateur which was fixed as:

> No person shall be considered an amateur who has ever competed with or against a professional for any prize; who has ever taught, pursued, or assisted in the practice of athletic exercises of any kind as a means of obtaining a livelihood.[36]

These principles would guide the AAA for many years in its pursuit of the amateur ideal which was also agreed upon over time with other sporting bodies through reciprocal agreements – in 1883, for example, it was agreed to uphold disqualifications

---

[32]AAA ATH/AAA/1/2/2/3, AAA Gen Committee Minutes, Volume 3, 1887-91, 1887 General Committee Report, p. 2.; ATH/AAA/1/5/2/2 AAA General Statement of Accounts, 1891.
[33]AAA ATH/AAA/1/5-2/2, AAA General Statement of Accounts, 1898.
[34]Bryant, M. (2020, November 12). Jackson, Clement Nugent (1846–1924), sports administrator. *Oxford Dictionary of National Biography*.
[35]AAA ATH/AAA/1/2/2/1, AAA Minutes, founding meeting, Oxford, 24 April 1880.
[36]AAA ATH/AAA/1/2/2/1, AAA Minutes, founding meeting, Oxford, 24 April 1880.

and suspensions passed by the Swimming Association of Great Britain (SAGB).[37] By 1890, this reciprocity was expanded to the National Cyclists Union (NCU) and Amateur Swimming Association (ASA), and by 1902, the Amateur Gymnastics Association (AGA), as well as the Scottish and Irish AAAs.[38] C. N. Jackson, who was a record breaking hurdler as an undergraduate at Oxford, is credited with putting across the case for a looser definition of amateur than the AAC version. This gave the AAA broader legitimacy as the governing body of the sport. Jackson had turned administrator to maintain his involvement in sport after injuring his foot on an oyster shell while competing against W. G. Grace (Bryant, 2020).

Amateur athletics has at times been portrayed as an elitist institution. It is perhaps more carefully considered as a middle-class movement, in essence the spirit of Victorian gentlemanly capitalism at play, which broadened as the clerical class expanded (Heller, 2008a). Industrialisation and urbanisation, as well as improved education brought about an expansion of the clerical and professional classes, and the rationalising tendencies and moral principles of contemporary accountancy, law and finance were applied to level the playing field for the rationalised enjoyment of replicable sport. This meant the keeping of records but also meticulous regulation and licensing of events including a system of handicapping and the creation of a number of roles for officials including judges, starters, stewards, timekeepers, and marksmen to ensure fair play.[39] Many prominent organisations came to form athletics teams or had athletics sections of their sports clubs, including the Great Western Railway, the Teesside steel firm Dorman Long & Co, and the London Private Banks, as well as several police forces, branches of the military, polytechnics and independent schools fitting into the broader expansion of middle-class clerical sport discussed by Heller (2008b).[40] The AAA's Honorary Secretary from 1883 to 1906, Charles Herbert, was drawn from one such workplace club, the Civil Service AC.[41] As early as 1883, 16,000 athletes were registered with the associated clubs, demonstrating a broadening participation base.[42]

---

[37]AAA ATH/AAA/1/2/2/1, AAA Minutes, General Meeting resolutions, March 1883.
[38]AAA ATH/AAA/3/1, Amateur Athletic Association: Constitution, Objects and Lists of Officers and Members: Laws for Athletic Meetings, 1890, p. 10. Amateur Athletic Association: Constitution, Objects and Lists of Officers and Members: Laws for Athletic Meetings and Competitions, 1902, p. 10.
[39]AAA ATH/AAA/3/1, Amateur Athletic Association: Constitution, Objects and Lists of Officers and Members: Laws for Athletic Meetings, 1890, pp. 16–17. Amateur Athletic Association: Constitution, Objects and Lists of Officers and Members: Laws for Athletic Meetings and Competitions, 1902, p. 31.
[40]Amateur Athletic Association: Constitution, Objects and Lists of Officers and Members: Laws for Athletic Meetings and Competitions, 1897, pp. 19–22; Amateur Athletic Association: Constitution, Objects and Lists of Officers and Members: Laws for Athletic Meetings and Competitions, 1902, pp. 20–22.
[41]AAA ATH/AAA/1/2/2/1, AAA Minutes, General Meeting resolutions, March 1883. Amateur Athletic Association: Constitution, Objects and Lists of Officers and Members: Laws for Athletic Meetings, 1897, p. 5.
[42]AAA ATH/AAA/1/2/2/1, AAA Minutes, General Meeting resolutions, March 1883.

While a broad middle- and upper-class membership was fostered typically composed of those who had at least attended grammar schools and polytechnics as well as public schools and elite universities, the AAA was also a broader symptom of Victorian attempts to sanitise society. The concept of amateurism can on one hand be considered a barrier to entry which allowed these office workers to enjoy physical pursuits among themselves, but the adoption of strict rules against betting and the elimination of cash prizes were also attempts to differentiate amateur athletics from the unregulated pedestrianists, by adopting a purist ethical stance. Pedestrianism, or professional athletics, was essentially a type of sports entertainment involving betting on runners who often made no deliberate attempt to win races. The cleansing mission, which may also have been an attempt to make events such as the AAA's Annual Championship meeting 'respectable' and thus open to the attendance of women and children, was evidenced by the affiliation of a team by the North of England Temperance Association,[43] based in Newcastle, in an area where pedestrianism, including the Morpeth Olympics (Chapter 5), was also popular (Taylor, 2002, pp. 79–81). The AAA investigated and took sanctions against promoters who allowed open betting; in 1891, the Willesden Junction Railway Sports Club was told that it must improve its precautionary measures to prevent betting.[44] Thus, amateurism was approaching a sort of religious concept in terms of its belief that athletes could be tainted by association with professionalism. However, as with all attempts to pursue purity the concept did run into contradictions the more stringent attempts to defend it became – runners could be prosecuted for running against professionals, but not for taking part in football or cricket matches containing professionals. Competitions within the military for cash prizes were also not considered to compromise the amateur status of soldiers taking part in AAA matches.[45] Expenses could not be paid for travel to athletics matches within the United Kingdom, but after 1897 were allowable to the AAA Annual Championships (which were an important source of income for the body) or other major championships or if the event was abroad, while to a limited extent the organisation's committee members were allowed to claim expenses to travel to meetings.[46] The AAA played an

[43]Amateur Athletic Association: Constitution, Objects and Lists of Officers and Members: Laws for Athletic Meetings and Competitions, 1897, p. 19.

[44]AAA ATH/AAA/1/2/2/3, Minutes of Monthly Meeting of the Southern Committee, 25 September 1891.

[45]AAA ATH/AAA/3/1, Amateur Athletic Association: Constitution, Objects and Lists of Officers and Members: Laws for Athletic Meetings and Competitions, 1902, p. 9.

[46]AAA ATH/AAA/1/2/2/1, AAA Minutes, General Meeting resolutions, March 1883; AAA ATH/AAA/3/1, Amateur Athletic Association: Constitution Rules, Objects and Lists of Officers and Clubs & c.: Laws for Athletic Meetings and Competitions, 1897, pp. 9, 23–24. AAA ATH/AAA/3/1, Amateur Athletic Association: Constitution, Objects and Lists of Officers and Members: Laws for Athletic Meetings and Competitions, 1902, pp. 9, 12; AAA ATH/AAA/3/1, Amateur Athletic Association: Constitution Laws, Rules for Athletic Meetings and Competitions &c., May 1913, pp. 6–7. AAA ATH/AAA/1/2/2/4, AG Minutes, 24 April 1897.

extremely important role in institutionalising, defending and disseminating the amateur concept within British sport which developed in parallel to international Olympism.

Several other sporting bodies emerged along similar amateurist lines and principles as the AAA, with committee-based structures allowing for distributed responsibility (important for organisational continuity given that administrators were not employed by the associations) based on the strict enforcement of common rules, principles, and record keeping. The NCU was formed as the Bicycle Union in 1876, and by 1883 they had branch committees in Bristol, Liverpool, Manchester, Nottingham, Newcastle-upon-Tyne, Dorchester, and Plymouth to regulate amateur bicycle racing.[47] Races approved by the NCU were increasingly held off-road after 1890 to maintain the respectability of cycling (Carter, 2021), then a new technology, and often in conjunction with athletic meets, which sometimes brought the body into conflict with the AAA despite their broad principles of reciprocity and sometimes overlapping membership.[48] In swimming, there had been attempts as early as the 1820s to create a number of professional bodies for professional swimmers who had operated in a similar manner to pedestrianists, swimming in rivers as well as baths, but these failed to sustain themselves as societal morals shifted to favour amateurism. The first amateur body, the SAGB, was formed in 1869, being renamed as the ASA in 1886, and followed by a Scottish ASA in 1888. These associations were assisted by literal attempts to cleanse the nation – the 1878 Public Baths and Washhouses Act and the 1892 Burgh Police (Scotland) Act which empowered local authorities to build enclosed public baths, providing excellent accommodation for swimming (Parker, 2001). As a demonstration of the collaboration between the bodies, the AAA rented their London office to the ASA for 6s per committee meeting![49] The Amateur Rowing Association (ARA) was formed in 1882 explicitly to consolidate definitions of amateurism in that sport, which had previously been set by the Henley stewards in April 1879, but which were unenforceable outside that regatta. Particularly controversial in rowing was the explicit clause forbidding the involvement of manual labourers which the ARA adopted from the Henley rules, and which led to the establishment of the rival National ARA which did accept manual workers (Crotty, 1998). The formation of governing bodies across a wide range of sports, with the holding of recognised national championships, the keeping of records and common rules for competition, and the use of the voluntary administrative structure to enforce the purity of amateurism was an important aspect of 19th-century British sporting culture which would be influential in shaping the broader ethos of Olympism.

[47] 'The National Cyclists Union and the Tricycle Union', *Daily News*, 27 June 1883, p. 3.
[48] AAA/4/1 News Cuttings re AAA & NCI, 1889–1895.
[49] AAA ATH/AAA/1/2/2/3, AAA Gen Committee Minutes, Volume 3, 1887–1891, 1887 General Committee Report, p. 2.

Chapter Summary

The Great Exhibition of 1851 was a landmark project in the history of nationally endorsed public events of its type, notable for many things, but relevant to us is the fact that it featured international exhibits and had political, technological, economic, and aesthetic motives and outcomes. The approach to finance by subscription and regional fundraising, rather than from the British central public finances, is also noteworthy.

In the history of sport, we note the NOA formed and organised the first English national athletics meeting branded as an Olympian or Olympic-styled games. Doing so involved converging the previously regional Olympian movements, such as those in Liverpool and in particular of Dr Brookes in Shropshire, and building upon their own events to create something on a grander scale, despite the resistance of the AAC. This national movement happened at a time when British sport institutions were forming to administer and codify various sports on a national footing, perhaps catalysed by the connectivity brought about by railways as well as the increasingly urbanised population. These sporting organisations, increasingly designed in distributed responsibility structures with a degree of democracy, are perhaps best understood as an extension of the professional and paternalistic ethos of gentlemanly capitalism (Cain & Hopkins, 1987). The new professional industries of finance, law, the civil service, academia, engineering, and the railways (among others) which were constituted by joint-stock companies led to the formation of bureaucratic organisations requiring a degree of cooperation between professions.[50] Company secretaries, mandated by the 1856 and 1862 Companies Act, for instance, coordinated the activities of company boards which represented diverse shareholder groups. The structure of these bodies and the clerical systems which they employed influenced the development and administration of sporting bodies such as the AAA, NCU, and ASA which aped them to gain legitimacy while using meticulous record keeping and auditing techniques to ensure 'fair play' and the preservation of amateurism. Involvement in sport also allowed for the preservation of masculine identity and healthy recreation for those now working behind desks, while Heller (2008b) also reflects that companies often encouraged white collar employees to play sport to network within and outside of their organisations. Further, enthusiasts for a sport could remain involved after they became too old for active participation by becoming an official or committee member.

But Britain was not alone in its sporting aspirations, particularly when it came to Olympicism. The 'new' Greece was also rediscovering an Olympic heritage, partly driven by political motives and an implanted Royal Family, which saw

[50]For an understanding of the organisational role expected of Victorian and Edwardian company secretaries see Blain, Sir Herbert, E. (Ed.) (1910). *Pitman's secretary's handbook. A practical guide to the work and duties in connection with the position of a secretary to a joint-stock company, public institution, Member of Parliament, etc.* London, Sir I. Pitman & Sons.

Olympic Games as a symbol of Hellenic culture which could galvanise the nation and collective culture, and endear them to their public.

Neither the efforts of Brookes, of the NOA nor of the Greek movement were to bear fruit at this point, although they do not go unnoticed as we shall see. It is the introduction to the Olympic story of a French aristocrat, travelling to research physical education, upon whom the next chapter hangs.

Chapter 4

The French Nobleman, an International Committee and a Global Games

Abstract

This chapter introduces one of the most important characters – Baron de Coubertin, who, inspired by France's 1871 defeat by the Germans sought to both rebuild France's reputation and to find alternatives to war. He took an interest in the British 'muscular Christianity' movement and amateurism, and he came to the United Kingdom to learn about it. He also travelled to the United States where intercollegiate sports were emerging, with competition between the Ivy League colleges in particular providing inspiration. The 1889 Paris Exposition continued the trend of World's Fairs, and followed an ancient Olympia theme as well as featuring some athletic games, further inspiring de Coubertin. By 1894, he was ready to act and convened an 'international athletic congress' at the Sorbonne, a meeting which would lead to the foundation of the International Olympic Committee (IOC) and the allocation of the first games to Athens in 1896 and second to Paris in 1900. We follow the contributions of the British to these events, the Honorary Secretary of the Amateur Athletic Association (AAA), Charles Herbert being involved from the start.

Keywords: de Coubertin; public schools; 1889 Paris Exposition; International Olympic Committee; sport history

Introduction

The previous chapter provided a condensed history of the development of British sport institutions and Olympian or Olympic-styled movements and games in Britain and Greece. We introduced individuals considered to have been important to these revivals, which by the Victorian era of 19th-century England included in particular Dr William Penny Brookes who organised the Wenlock Games in

Foundations of Managing British Olympics: Institutions through Time, 49–63

Published under exclusive licence by Emerald Publishing Limited
doi:10.1108/978-1-80262-095-520251004

Shropshire, but also Charles Melly and John Hulley who had organised similar events beginning in Liverpool (England) and Llandudno (Wales), and Ernst Ravenstein a German born owner of a London gymnasium. With other like-minded men of the time they combined their ambitions, experience, and motivation, forming the first National Olympic Association (NOA) which held the first National Olympian Games in London during 1866. The British context appears complicated by the politics of sport governing bodies and a certain amount of social class rigidity, most clearly emerging in definitions and interpretations of amateurism, and in the resistance to the NOA from the Amateur Athletics Club which appears to have been formed quickly in reaction to the NOA.

We also explained the emergence of modern Olympics in Greece, initiated by newspaper editor (Panagiotis Soutsos) and an entrepreneur (Evangelis Zappas) and held three times between 1859 and 1875, the initiative having been ceased upon by politicians and royalty, and metaphorically wrestled between resistance and patronage by the establishment and social elite.

The United States' example differs mainly because Olympic symbolism and imagery was mostly used in travelling circuses and carnivals. This is similar to some events in Europe, including Britain, but seems to have been used for the first time by a permanent sporting club (rather than entertainment entrepreneurs) by the founding of the San Francisco Olympic Club in 1860, which hosted games in the 1890s. The motive other than spectacle and sport for sports sake apparently was to raise funds for the club. This motivation contrasted with that of Greece (which had also sought to galvanise national identity and support for its new royal family) and Britain (to coordinate sporting opportunity on a national scale and for educational and societal benefit, following Dr Brookes outlook and the earlier idea of 'muscular Christianity', and as a relatively inclusive alternative to the restrictive definition of 'amateur' favoured by the more socially conservative AAA).

The next important development in the story of the Olympic Games, and on British influence and involvement, requires us to turn our attention to France, to a young French aristocrat who had the initiative, ambition, and social standing to galvanise and coordinate the emerging Olympic movements into an international phenomenon.

Introducing Baron de Coubertin

Charles Pierre de Frédy, Baron de Coubertin was born in Paris on 1 January 1863 (Hill, 1996). As a child, he was aware of the siege of Paris and ultimately France's defeat of 1871 in the Franco-Prussian War, which ended French hegemony in continental Europe. He would grow up seeking solutions to his nation's humiliation, and to the damaging effects of conflict, but in terms of strengthening French character, rather than revenge. He had read Thomas Hughes' novel *Tom Brown's Schooldays*. The educational theories of Thomas Arnold, Headmaster of Rugby School, imprinted upon the impressionable young Coubertin. He began to realise the potential of physical education in general education, and it is considered that this reading influenced the future 'Olympian' philosophy as 'a wedding of sport and art ... muscle and mind' (Anthony, 1997, p. 18). Arnold's theories, as presented in the book (a fictional account albeit based on a real school and Headmaster) are of the 'muscular Christianity' school-of-thought, described in Chapter 2 (Anthony (1997, p. 18). MacAloon (2006c) suggests that Coubertin's understanding of Thomas Arnold was distorted, a misinterpretation of a fictionalised account that he believed to be fact, and thus much of the Olympic philosophy which followed is perhaps an accident of history, rather than direct lineage to Arnoldian methods.

As an aristocrat, Coubertin could have joined the upper ranks of the military or opted for a life in politics. Instead, he chose to pursue an intellectual life, studying and writing on topics including education, history, literature, and sociology. His focus turned to physical education and sport in schooling (Hill, 1996). To understand Coubertin's motivation, MacAloon highlights the concept *prouesse* to understand Pierre de Coubertin's life and work in cultural and historic context:

> [...] Actions based on organizational routines and rational expectations bring no credit to an homme de noblesse. The only deeds which bring *honneur* and demonstrate *vertu* are those which belong to a special class of actions called prouesses ('feats of prowess'). (MacAloon, 2006e, p. 355)

> [...] the importance of prouesse in French culture generally and in the classical aristocratic ethos in particular, describes it as the search for spontaneous, irreproducible, unique and conspicuous moral acts, undertaken for honour and not for utility. (MacAloon, 2006e, p. 355)

French aristocrats were expected to make their 'own mark' as an adult rather than rely solely on the honour and kudos of the family name (MacAloon, 2006e, p. 352). This meant that they should seek a vocation, supported by their social standing, but importantly not in a formal profession or occupation, and so would *not* seek positions 'in rationalized, bureaucratic, formal organizations, offering lifelong security, financial reward and regular advancement according to fixed rules' (MacAloon, 2006e, p. 355). When in contact with careerists and professionals it was necessary to establish their amateur status 'to demonstrate that they act disinterestedly for the love of the Faith, the Motherland, Nature, Art, Humanity' (MacAloon, 2006c, p. 394). This might provoke comparison with the British 'dilettante' tradition epitomised by the *grand tour* as a rite of passage (discussed in Chapter 2); the belief that by immersing themselves in the classical arts and culture aristocrats might develop and refine skills and knowledge, a deeper appreciation, and absorb something from what they experienced on their travels. The French had a slightly different approach, as well as seeking to find oneself, travel, and intellectual activity should have public meaning. A young gentleman was expected to research and collect materials for books, so that he might 'profit his nation and to 'find himself an author' back home' (MacAloon, 2006c, p. 394).

The Baron Travels

In 1883, aged 20, Coubertin (who had himself enjoyed a classical education) visited England for the first time, ostensibly to visit public schools and universities in a quest to learn more about the English system of education. He studied the program of physical education at Rugby School, introduced by Thomas Arnold. Coubertin concluded that the muscular Christian approach had driven the expansion of British power during the 19th century. This inspired him towards achieving *prouesse* – his mission would be to make an intellectual case for the inclusion of physical education in the curriculum of French schools. He returned to England in 1886 to carry out more research, and his book *L'Education en Angleterre* ('Education in England') was published in 1888 (Hill, 1996).

A detailed account of de Coubertin's travels and formative experiences around this time is provided by MacAloon (2006c): The first tour of England, in 1883, involved visits to Harrow, Eton, and Rugby schools and to Oxford and Cambridge Universities. Arriving at a school with letters of introduction, he would then meet the masters and invited pupils, take a conducted tour of the grounds, and then wander unchaperoned, observing games and lessons, and joining the boys in conversation, in chapel and at meals. MacAloon (2006c) shows that these fact-finding missions were far from objective, and that de Coubertin's 'ethnography' was merely intended to confirm that Hughes' vision of life in public schools was real.

Coubertin returned to England annually from the summer of 1886, and by 1887, he had visited Charterhouse, Christ's Hospital, Cooper's Hill, Marlborough, Toynbee Hall, Wellington, Westminster, Winchester, and several Catholic schools (MacAloon, 2006c). During the visit of 1886, Coubertin is said to have experienced a vision when visiting the tomb of Thomas Arnold:

> de Coubertin thereafter deified and took as his lifelong hero, prophet and father-substitute. His vocation confirmed by this vision, de Coubertin began in 1887 his '21-year campaign' to bring to France what he took to be Arnold's legacy: la pedagogie sportive, 'athletic education' … The 'Arnoldian system' of school sports, student self-government and postgraduate athletic associations would, he felt assured, be the means by which France would 'rebronze' (rebronzer) after the disasters of 1871, and would create a lasting democratic society as the English had. (MacAloon, 2006c, p. 400)

London Olympia: Commercialising the Entertainment Spectacle

It is interesting to note that at this time, Anglo-French relations were generally positive within Europe, although they competed for colonies further afield, such as in Africa and Asia. Between December 1886 and February 1888, London's new *Olympia* 'Great Agricultural Hall' exhibition building (the name reflecting the fashion at that time for all things Olympic following the Hellenic excavations of the 1870s) hosted its inaugural event, *The Paris Hippodrome*. This event, billed as *The Great Sporting Pantomime* included races and displays involving 300 horses, as well as elephants, deer, musicians, Olympic and classically themed events (Olympian races, Roman charity races, and Roman wrestling matches), and other exotic curiosities such as Arabian horsemen. Billed as the largest hall in the kingdom, it could house 9,000 spectators and was illuminated by electric light (Stokes, 2019). From the perspective of sports governance and institutions, it is worth repeating a point from Chapter 2, that in 1886, the same year as London's Olympia opened (and Coubertin visited) the National Physical Recreation Society (NPRS) was formed in England, out of the ashes of the NOA, which had folded in 1883. Its Executive Committee included Herbert Gladstone (Liberal politician and future Home Secretary), Lord Kinnaird (Treasurer, and later President, of the Football Association), and Dr William Penny Brookes (of the Much Wenlock Olympics and NOA) (Anthony, 1997). The association's emphasis was to promote participation and, as Chapter 3 already explained in detail, organised the 1st National Olympian Games held at London's Crystal Palace in 1866 (Anthony, 1997).[1]

The Olympia event reflects the Victorian trend for organising and commercialising the entertainment spectacle. As society urbanised, and the broader conditions allowed – advances in technology, commerce, and law enabled and resulted from, the industrial revolution. Much has been written about the emergence of limited companies and stadiums paid for by subscriptions and gate receipts in association football (e.g. Arnold, 1988; Dixon et al., 2007; Vamplew, 2004) but to consider only spectator sport and its commercialisation is to understand only one strand of sport and recreation in Victorian society. Authors such as Budd (2017) demonstrate how sports including football but also cycling, rowing, and others, were used for social cohesion and to improve the morals and behaviours of the public. Sports clubs were often established along lines of religion, works, and local areas, sometimes by local churches or clergymen and thought to improve health and sanitation, and to distract people away from the public houses, alcohol and gambling associated with traditional rural pastimes such as cock fighting and badger baiting (Budd, 2017; Holt, 1990; Pickford, 1940).

Following the Hippodrome event, Olympia's next spectacle, was an agricultural show *The First Great Horse* Show, in 1888 (Olympia London, 2025). More importantly to our narrative, that year Coubertin visited the English town of Henley, famed for its Royal Regatta, a boating competition held annually since 1839. Anthony (1997) and Kent (2008) suggest Coubertin was impressed by the event's organisation which he described in terms of three concentric circles, as the nucleus (the deeply committed), the nursery (those who could be educated to the cause), and the façade (those whose position and influence could be useful).

[1]Wellcome Collection. MS.7941/12. (1925). The British Institute of Physical Training. *Brochure of The British Institute of Physical Training (Instituted 1889), and with which is now incorporated The National Physical Recreation Society (Instituted 1885) and Sir James Cantlie's Physical 'Jerks' (Instituted 1921)*. The Rosemount Press.

Another Tour

The young baron had by now refused entry to the army, dropped out of Law studies, and in 1885 enrolled at *the Ecole libre des sciences politiques*. This small school of around 250 students prepared young men for the civil or diplomatic services and was popular with rich and powerful families (MacAloon, 2006c). As a result of his visits to schools and sports, in 1889 Coubertin was asked by the French Government Minister of Public Instruction to investigate the organisation of the schools and universities of the United States and Canada. In France, he organised a congress as part of the Universal Exposition held in Paris that year. More broadly, he undertook a postal survey throughout English-speaking countries. His friend William Brookes sent him a pamphlet containing a copy of Brookes' speech at the 1st National Olympian Games held at London's Crystal Palace in 1866, which articulated the importance of the Olympian idea in education (Anthony, 1997).

Coubertin believed that the US education establishments he corresponded with all favoured the principles of Thomas Arnold, although 'none mentioned Arnold by name' (MacAloon, 2006b, p. 483) and he set sail to New York in July 1889, paying his own expenses. In North America, he travelled for four months from New York to New England, up to Montreal, Toronto, down through Chicago, to the Mississippi on to New Orleans, then Florida, Virginia, Washington, and Baltimore, and back to New York (MacAloon, 2006b). This tour took in many universities and colleges including Amherst, Harvard, Cornell, Montreal, Chicago, Tulane, Virginia, Johns Hopkins, and Princeton, and he was able to learn about others from the people that he met. Although he took some interest in curricula, governance and the role of private philanthropies, his main interests were sports and physical education (MacAloon, 2006b). There was a history of sporting interaction and a transfer of ideas between the East Coast US universities and those in England (Smith, 1988, p. 8).

One of the most important collegiate sports was rowing, with clubs appearing in the United States during the 1830s, and in 1869, Oxford beat Harvard in the first international contest, which took place on the Thames. Then in 1878, the tables were turned when a team from the US University Columbia defeated Cambridge for the Visitor's Challenge Cup, again in England (MacAloon, 2006b). Another area of sport popular with universities was those covered by the umbrella term *track and field*. The New York Athletic Club was founded in 1868, just in time for the evolution of track and field athletics which evolved to their modern form through the 1870s, and by the late 1880s English athletes appeared (MacAloon, 2006b).

North American universities also had their own versions of football, and since 1869 Rugby Union rules had begun to dominate. Soon after, in 1876, Harvard, Princeton, Columbia, and Yale, the 'Ivy League' universities, founded the Intercollegiate Football Association and adopted Rugby rules. By the late 1880s, the intercollegiate games had developed their own version (from which the modern American Football or *gridiron* would emerge) which had begun to spread to other colleges and secondary schools. Games between the prestigious Ivy League colleges drew many spectators and garnered press coverage, all of which apparently impressed Coubertin (MacAloon, 2006b).

Paris Exposition and Games

In France, the Exposition Universelle of 1889 was a world's fair held in Paris, from 5 May to 31 October. Interestingly, this exposition involved athletic games alongside an international festival celebrating progress in science, art, and industry. These Paris Games of 1889 recruited competitors from all social classes, and an ancient Olympia theme permeated the entire event including the exposition; the recent archaeological findings of the German excavators were celebrated as an elaborate reconstruction of the buildings and monuments unearthed (MacAloon, 2006b). This alignment of games with exposition seems to have been noticed by Coubertin (MacAloon, 2006b) although at the time he was perhaps not yet so much concerned with pushing an Olympic movement as he was with his education research mission (Torres, 2005). He did their organise the world's first Congress on Physical Education and began to build his international network of educators, politicians, aristocrats, commerce, culture, and sport that would eventually support him with his international Olympic ambition (IOC, n.d.).

Coubertin was so committed to his educational interest that he rejected an approach to stand for Parliament and would do so at least twice more in the next decade. He would though change the emphasis of his mission from physical education, to simply the organisation of sports, and worked to help popularise and internationalise French sport throughout the next few years (MacAloon, 2006d), for example, establishing the Union of French Societies of Athletic Sports (USFSA; Young, 1996).

Coubertin circulated a notice (inserted in several English newspapers) of the upcoming Paris Congress on Physical Training which he had arranged to coincide with the 1889 Paris exposition and games (MacAloon, 2006b). In response he was also invited by Dr Brookes to visit the Wenlock Olympian Games, publishing on Christmas day 1890 his first article on the Wenlock Olympics *Les Jeux Olympiques a Much Wenlock*. This was Coubertin reporting not leading the Olympic revival, for which he credits Brookes rather than modern Greece, and refers to the tournament as 'olympic games' (Anthony, 1997, p. 19; Torkildsen, 2005, p. 38; Young, 1996, p. 94). Curiously, Coubertin mentioned how other such games had occurred elsewhere in England but claimed that no movement had caught on, perhaps overlooking the efforts of the NOA, although that body had ceased to exist in 1883, its initiative and its motto by now inherited by the NPRS founded in 1885/1886 (Hulley, 2010; John Hulley Memorial Fund, n.d.) so perhaps it appeared at this point in time to have faded like regional pseudo-olympics other than Wenlock, or perhaps he was simply unaware. It is interesting that neither did he acknowledge the revival that had occurred in Greece since around the same time, and MacAloon questions whether or not Coubertin was aware of that (MacAloon, 2006b).

Certainly, the earlier Greek revivals stemming from those instigated by Zappas had ended in 1875, as we reported in the previous chapter. With the dawn of a new decade, in 1890, Crown Prince Constantine of Greece announced the return of the Greek National Olympics (Young, 1996) in a four-year cycle, with *Olympiad v* scheduled for Athens in 1892 (Young, 1996). On 1 May 1891, the Panhellenic Gymnastic Society held the first of its athletic games in Athens, and announces its intention to host Olympics that Constantine announced. The proposed games did not happen, the Greek government claiming lack of funding (Young, 1996). So, at this moment in time when Coubertin was crystallising his ideas about the usefulness of sport and of the Wenlock Olympic Games revival he witnessed in England, there was no coherent Greek movement to catch his attention, despite the connections between the Greek organisers and Dr Brookes.

The Baron and Wenlock: Balancing Progression with Tradition

Regarding his experiences of Wenlock, Coubertin had enjoyed the event 'tilting at the ring' which Young (1996, pp. 81–83) theorises 'probably inspired the medieval portion of Coubertin's subsequent Olympic idea'. This is supported by MacAloon (2006b) who elaborates the games as including '... the inclusion of prizes for literary compositions and artistic works, the Greek banners, slogans, and songs'. MacAloon identifies the inclusion of tilting at the ring as being popular with local young farmers as well as tent pegging, racing, cricket and lawn tennis. Coubertin was taken by the ceremony and theatricality that he witnessed. He identified at Wenlock an amalgamation of traditions, not least the inclusion of females, such as the champion tilter of the ring being crowned with laurels by a lady, before whom he then kneeled to kiss her hand. All in all, Coubertin (1897, cited by MacAloon, 2006b, p. 514) commented on the proceedings as being 'strange' and highlighted:

> three very different forms of civilisation. The dress and the speeches were modern; the use of laurels and the quotations from Greek authors inscribed on the flags and banderoles were antique; the latter part of the ceremony was an homage paid to medieval ideas and theories.

A lasting legacy of the 1890 Wenlock Olympics is an oak tree planted by Coubertin (Anthony, 1997).

Within months of his visit to the Wenlock Olympics and subsequent paper, in 1891, Coubertin was, along with two other people, ordained as fourth, fifth, and sixth Honorary Members of the Much Wenlock Olympian Society (MWOS). One of these people was the Earl of Meath (Lord Brabazon) who had with Brookes petitioned Parliament about physical education in schools, the other was Lord Charles Beresford. Both men were members of the NPRS. Coubertin the same year declined invitation to attend the Wenlock Games but sent a medal to the Wenlock Olympian Society, awarded to the winner of the tilting event (Anthony, 1997; Young, 1996).

Proposing an International Olympic Games

The following year, in September 1892, when the cancelled Athens Olympiad had been due to occur, Dr Brookes made a speech to 6,000 people that was reported in newspapers, proposing an international Olympics (Young, 1996). Soon after, on Friday 25th November, during a jubilee celebration of the USFSA (Union des Société's Françaises de Sports Athlétiques, or in English, the Union of French athletic Sports Societies) held at the Sorbonne, University of Paris, Coubertin also mentioned the possibility of re-establishing an international Olympic revival as being helpful to world peace, as the new free trade of Europe, and asked his audience to help him (Anthony 1997; Young, 1996). Interestingly, Coubertin does not appear to have included Dr Brookes in his plans, and Brookes does not seem to know of de Coubertin's speech until probably 1894 (Young, 1996). In any case, support was not immediately available, Coubertin reflected the audience had interpreted his idea as symbolic rather than literal, although MacAloon suggests that there was a simpler explanation. Many union members had heard the same proposal from other people previously:

> Since nothing had come of these suggestions, they had no reason to believe that de Coubertin was serious .... He had presented no plan, only the magic words, which opened no doors in the souls of his union colleagues. (MacAloon, 2006d, p. 536)

In Greece, around six months later, over two days 14–15 May 1893, the second Panhellenic Gymnastic Society Games were held, with patronage from Prince Constantine, but otherwise unconnected to the planned Olympiad or earlier Zappas Games (Young, 1996). Coubertin was still not involved with the Greek initiatives either and he seems to have little or no awareness of (or interest in) them, meanwhile pursuing his own mission, making his second visit to America that Autumn, where he discussed an Olympic Revival (Young, 1996). MacAloon (2006d, pp. 537–538) reports how he told William Rainey Harper, President of the University of Chicago, about his idea to revive the games thereby doing ground work for the eventual award of the 1904 Olympic Games to the city and the University of Chicago, although history shows the 1904 edition was eventually held in St Louis (Chapter 7). Coubertin also visited San Francisco, New Jersey where he met William M. Sloane, the Princeton Professor of History, and New York.[2] He found tensions between the East and West of the United States, and between its universities and the Amateur Athletic Union there MacAloon (2006d). As explained in Chapter 3, The Olympic Club of San Francisco, founded in 1860, held its own ancient Greco-Roman themed games in April 1893, although there is no evidence to suggest Coubertin as having any involvement, his visit to San Francisco reportedly occurring in the Autumn. Coubertin mentions the visit in

[2]'International Athletic Congress'. *Times*, 18 June 1894, p. 5.

his memoirs,[3] but not that an ancient Greco-Roman themed games had taken place earlier that year, which seems strange; the games had been 'the most important event in the club's history and their fame already throughout California' and so it is unlikely that nobody had mentioned them to the Baron during, or prior to, his visit (Rozmierek et al., 2023, p. 14).

The following year was more fruitful. In January 1894 Coubertin distributed a flyer to sports organisations around the world for a Congress of Amateurs in June, for which Prince Constantine of Greece agreed in April to be honorary member (Young, 1996) as were the King of Belgium, the Prince of Wales, and Crown Prince Carl of Sweden and Norway (Young, 1996). A revised invitation was circulated soon after. The first seven items on de Coubertin's agenda concerned questions about definition and application of amateurism, the eighth with 'The possibility or re-establishing the Olympic Games. Under what conditions would it be feasible?' and relatedly asked whether 'it is possible to believe that these peaceful and refined contests would constitute the best of internationalism?' extending the vision for enabling world peace within his 1892 speech (Young, 1996, p. 88).

An invitation was received by Dr Brookes who wrote to Coubertin to encourage his idea to rotate the hosting of the games, and again with advice about amateur rules (Young, 1996). Although Brookes had initially wanted an international Olympic Games but to be always held in Greece, he suggested that Coubertin's idea to move the hosting around capitals of the associated nations was a better idea (Anthony, 1997). Brookes also wrote to the Prime Minister of Greece (Charilaos Trikoupis) in which he linked his own Olympic efforts in England, the Greek Zappas Olympics, and Coubertin's proposed Olympic revival. Young (1996, p. 93) believes that this suggests Brookes perceived Coubertin's congress and aims as 'the culmination of all previous activity in the Olympic movement'.

On 24 May 1894, the MWOS met to discuss de Coubertin's International Congress, which they welcomed, and suggested the idea for a Greek or Latin motto. This is interesting because Coubertin later adopted 'Citius, Altius, Fortius' (Faster, Higher, Stronger) although that is attributed to his Jesuit mentor Father Didon, and it is unclear as to whether the Wenlock movement had any influence (Anthony, 1997, p. 19).

Less than a month later, on 16 June, de Coubertin's Olympic Congress held its opening banquet, attendees included 78 official delegates, representing 37 sports societies from England, France, the United States, Sweden, Belgium, Greece, Italy, Spain, Russia, Austro-Hungary, and Bohemia (MacAloon, 2006d). Hosted by the Sorbonne and chaired by the former French Ambassador to Germany, Baron de Courcel, with students at the elite university present, geographically the Congress involved representatives from thirteen nations, and others provided written messages of support (Kent, 2008).[4] An ancient Greek hymn, the *Hymm to Apollo*

[3]de Coubertin, P. (1979). *Olympic memoirs* (English language edition reprinted 1989, p. 10). International Olympic Committee.

[4]'International Athletic Congress'. *Times*, 18 June 1894, p. 5; 'Paris Day by Day'. *Daily Telegraph*, 18 June 1894, p. 5.

discovered a few years earlier was adapted and sung by a modern choir, and over the duration of Congress, delegates viewed bicycle races and tennis facilities, athletic presentations, dinners, receptions, and fireworks (Young, 1996). The contemporary response of English commentators about the first day seemed to be that the banquet and performance of the Hymm had been the most successful part of the day. The proceedings were viewed with polite amusement from London where there was a sense of disbelief that an Olympic revival was achievable.[5]

Coubertin appears to have engineered the event to ensure the restoration of the Olympic Games a fait accompli. It had been branded the *Congrès International des Sports*, or 'International Athletic Congress', and was reported as such in the newspapers, Coubertin changed the name on the admission ticket of the opening session to 'The Congress for the Restoration of the Olympic Games' and a telegram was received from the king of Greece thanking Coubertin and the members for having declared the revival, before a vote had even been taken on it![6] The restoration of the Olympic Games was thus a foregone conclusion. Indeed, one day before the congress opened, Coubertin had published an article *Le Rétablissement des Jeux Olympiques* in the *Revue de Paris*, its contents presented the items that delegates were supposedly at Congress to debate, as well as announcing the first games to be held in Paris during 1900 (MacAloon, 2006d).

Thus, the IOC was formally established just one week later, on 23 June 1894 (Torkildsen, 2005). An immediate concern was to find consensus among members as to the meaning of amateur status because the various participating countries all interpreted, defined, and applied the term differently, influenced by different histories, economic, and social conditions (MacAloon, 2006d). Tensions stemming from the class systems at that time emerged regarding this matter, but also to be navigated were nationalism (some French sports administrators were hesitant towards German inclusion) and which activities, such as gymnastics, could be considered as sport (MacAloon, 2006d).

Delegates were divided into two commissions, the first of which took up the concerns of amateurism.[7] By the end of the week, they concluded against the British restriction on manual labourers; distinguished between money for prizes (which they banned) and for expenses (which they left open). They also decided against allowing amateur status to salaried coaches and gymnastics instructors, and settled on what probably seemed the best compromise and the most workable conclusion of a loose consensus, rather than a strict amateur code that could not be agreed upon and imposed internationally (MacAloon, 2006d).[8] The unforeseen consequence of this lack of decisiveness was that the amateur/professional divide would remain a live issue and challenge for sport for years to come.

---

[5]'International Athletic Congress'. *Times*, 18 June 1894, p. 5.

[6]'International Athletic Congress'. *Times*, 18 June 1894, p. 5; Special Wire, and Our Own Correspondent. 'Paris Day by Day'. *Daily Telegraph*, 18 June 1894, p. 5.

[7]'The International Athletic Congress'. *Morning Post*, 19 June 1894, p. 3.

[8]'The International Athletic Congress'. *Times*, 25 June 1894, p. 6.

There were some sports, including shooting, yachting, and horse racing which the committee currently felt unable to extend amateur status.[9]

The second commission was concerned with the Olympic Games and were mostly convinced by de Coubertin's vision for four-year intervals for the games rotating between host cities, comprising exclusively modern sports restricted only to adult participation.[10] There was a proposal for the inclusion of children's or school sports from the Swedish and Greek delegates Bergh and Bikelas, but Coubertin considered this both impractical and risky.[11] It was also agreed for a permanent and stable IOC comprised of a membership tasked with representing Olympism in their countries (MacAloon, 2006d). Coubertin claimed the idea of the games being peripatetic in nature was accepted without great controversy on the strength that Greece, then heavily indebted to its bondholders in Western Europe (Chatziioannou, 2019), would be unable to support the games for more than one edition.[12] He had wanted to hold the first edition in Paris in 1900 to celebrate the new century, but was convinced by the Bikelas to hold the first edition in Athens in 1896, honouring Greece's Olympic heritage.[13] In 1894, Britain's first IOC members were Lord Ampthill and Charles Herbert, Honorary Secretary of the AAA. Bikelas was appointed chair of the organising committee for Athens along with the representatives of other countries, including Ampthill and Herbert.[14] Ampthill resigned soon after, and Reverend de Courcy Laffan, more of whom later, began his involvement Olympism (Barker, 2005). The British press remained less convinced in the principle of an international amateur games than Coubertin narrated in his memoir. One British correspondent argued that sport was already losing its amateur character because athletes had to be dedicated, an international competition would further exacerbate this tendency. They argued that the purity of the original Olympiad, which brought fame to champions, was likely to be more illusory than real, and that its restoration in the industrial era would be likely to create pressure to convert sport from a mere pastime to a business.[15] Not all assessments were gloomy; one correspondent accepted that while professionalism had reduced the achievement of muscular Christianity, they welcomed the spread of football and rowing among other sports on the continent, and hoped that the 'friendly rivalry' of the new games might provoke a truce.[16]

Inspired by his experience at Henly Regatta, Coubertin later wrote that the original IOC was and would remain for many years

> composed of three concentric circles; a small nucleus of active and convinced members; a nursery of members of good will who

[9]'International Athletic Congress'. *Morning Post*, 23 June 1894, p. 5.
[10]'The International Athletic Congress'. *Morning Post*, 19 June 1894, p. 3.
[11]de Coubertin, 1979, p. 12.
[12]de Coubertin, 1979, p. 12. 'The Greek Debt'. *Morning Post*, 23 June 1894, p. 5.
[13]de Coubertin, 1979, p. 12.
[14]'The International Athletic Congress', *Times*, 25 June 1894, p. 6.
[15]'Sports and Pastimes: The Olympic Festival', *Sunday Times*, 24 June 1894, p. 7.
[16]'Modern Olympian Games', *Dover Express*, 6 July 1894, p. 6.

> were capable of being educated; and finally, a facade of more or less useful men whose presence satisfied national pretensions while giving some prestige to the group.[17]

After the 1894 congress he met with Professor Sloane, Demetrios Bikelas, and Ernest Callot at the Paris flat that Bikelas kept. The aim was to decide who would occupy the posts in the governance structure of the nascent commission. Coubertin wanted a structure based on the one he had put in place in the French umbrella body for sport, the USFSA, with an executive Secretary General and a President bringing general oversight to the organisation. Bikelas reluctantly agreed to act as Secretary General for the first four-year cycle and Callot Treasurer, giving Coubertin the 'inner circle' that he required, but also the potential for longer-term continuation of the institution.[18] As we have already mentioned this was a formula the Baron first encountered at Henley Regatta where stewards were self-appointing, but which would allow for a combination of members vetted both by him and outside. This was a suitably flexible but controllable structure which meant he could ensure continuity on a rolling basis beyond one single cycle. This differentiated it from earlier Olympic revivals such as the Zappas attempt which lacked a framework for the continuation of the games. Coubertin's ideas and achievement with the international Olympic movement have been summarised as:

> Established the visionary basis of the Olympic movement. He tried to create a sort of civil religion, a doctrine assembling in an eclectic way ancient Greek philosophical thoughts and occidental humanist ideas for which he coined the neologism 'Olympism' … to prepare an elite of young and virile men for the challenges of the twentieth century. (Schantz, 2018, in Bayle & Chappelet, 2017, p. 104)

Olympism was not a philosophy in the strict academic meaning of the word. In fact, Coubertin made the distinction that he intended a pragmatic attitude to life rather than abstract theory and that 'interpretations and implementations vary with time and cultures'. This vagueness, they claim, is 'certainly a reason for its worldwide success and could be convenient in terms of adaptability to the needs of the future' (Bayle & Chappelet, 2017, p. 106). We extend this line of thought critically to consider that perhaps this vagueness has exposed Olympism to abuse by showcasing or legitimising political regimes that below their surface had little to do with Coubertin's objective of world peace.

The idea of preparing 'man' for modern life links to the educational mission which began Coubertin's journey, and roots Olympism in intellectual, physical, and moral pursuit, the 'classic triad of education' (Bayle & Chappelet, 2017, p. 106). Educational sport, international understanding, and peace activism were closely

---

[17] de Coubertin, 1979, p. 14.
[18] de Coubertin, 1979, pp. 13–14.

aligned from the beginning of the modern international Olympic Games and Olympic movement (MacAloon, 2006f). The list of honorary members at the 1894 Sorbonne Olympic Congress demonstrates ties to the international peace movement; speculation that the organisational design of the new IOC owed at least something to the International Peace Bureau (IPB) thus appears plausible:

> Fully one-third of the Sorbonne patrons list held leadership positions in the International Peace Bureau, the inter-parliamentary International Peace Union and the series of International Peace Congresses. Three eventually were awarded the Nobel Peace Prize. Quanz has discovered an important institutional complement to the analysis of the ideological and educational bases of early Olympism. (Quanz, cited by MacAloon, 2006a, p. 334)

On 25 June 1894, just two days after the formation of the IOC, it was formally announced that an inaugural Olympic Games in Athens during 1896 would precede the Paris 1900 edition (MacAloon, 2006d) the dates consistent with Coubertin's vision for a four-year interval and rotation between major cities.[19] At the same time, there was cynicism in the British press about the viability of the games in both economic and cultural terms, and the impact that they might have on sport, even if amateurism was incorporated within them. As a reminder that Coubertin, Bikelas and Slone's fledgling Olympic revival was just one among many, as the Congress in Paris was wrapping up, the Morpeth Olympic Games committee (Chapter 5), announced they were in a strong financial position and would be holding their games on 11 August 1894.[20] Interestingly for our narrative, delegates had apparently favoured London to host the inaugural games, but Coubertin preferred to allow the Greeks to host the first edition in Athens, and the exact process behind this decision, taken at the Sorbonne, is unknown (Young, 1996). Meanwhile, in October 1894 Courcel, who spoke fluent English, was posted to London as French Ambassador, a move Coubertin may have hoped to exploit.[21] As well as the historic tie to Athens, and the published knowledge and public displays of archaeological excavations, Coubertin may also by now have had knowledge of what was known to have happened at the ancient games. In 1887, Victor Duruy issued an expanded three-volume edition of his *Histoire des Grecs*, which included several pages to the Olympic Games, with reference to archaeologist and historian Ernst Curtius and architect Friedrich Adler's findings and plan of the site (drawn for them by Kaupert and Dörpfeld). It is notable that Duruy was a member, though not an active one, of an organisation called

[19]de Coubertin, P. (1896). Foreword to Part I of the Official Report of the Olympic Games, B.C. 776–A.D. 1896. Published with the sanction and under the patronage of the Central Committee in Athens, presided over by his Royal Highness the Crown Prince Constantine, p. 8.

[20]'Our Own Column', *Morpeth Herald*, 23 June 1894, p. 3.

[21]'The French Ambassador to England', *Times*, 1 October 1894, p. 5.

the *Comité pour la propagation des exercices physiques*, whom Coubertin admired (MacAloon, 2006b).

Chapter Summary

This chapter has introduced Baron de Coubertin, who, inspired by France's 1871 defeat by the Germans sought to both rebuild France's reputation and to find alternatives to war. He took an interest in the British muscular Christianity movement and amateurism, and he came to the United Kingdom to learn about it. He also travelled to the United States, where the emerging intercollegiate sports provided more inspiration. The 1889 Paris Exposition continued the trend of World's Fairs, incorporating an ancient Olympia theme and featured some athletic games. The event further inspired Coubertin, whose involvement was to organise the world's first congress on Physical Education, a useful international networking opportunity. By 1894, he was ready to act and convened an international athletic congress at the Sorbonne, a meeting which would lead to the foundation of the International Olympic Committee and the allocation of the first games to Athens in 1896 and second to Paris in 1900. We follow the contributions of the British to these events, the Honorary Secretary of the AAA, Charles Herbert being involved from the start.

Chapter 5

Athens: The First Modern Olympic Games

Abstract

In this chapter, we consider the first games at Athens, and how they were viewed from a British perspective. The games were a big opportunity for Greece to demonstrate that it was relevant to Europe's present as well as its past. We show that from the start the Olympic Games took on the appearance of a grand project far beyond the status of a mere sports meeting, with considerable construction activity undertaken, not least to restore the ancient stadium in Athens. At the games themselves, international participation was more ad hoc with small groups of individual athletes generally attending out of their own pockets rather than any structured attempt to raise representative teams. But the games took place successfully, and enabled by telegram, the preparations for and the happenings at them were eagerly followed through the British press. We consider the impact of this but highlight that at the same time the success of the professional 'Morpeth Olympic Games' in the North of England demonstrate that de Coubertin's revival remained one among many. From a British perspective, the 1897 Le Havre International Olympic Committee (IOC) Congress would be critical – the Rev. Robert Stuart Courcy de Laffan would attend to represent the public-school sector, but his involvement would be pivotal in formalising Olympism in Britain.

Keywords: Athens 1896; de Coubertin; Le Havre; Morpeth Olympics; sport history

Introduction

The previous chapter introduced Baron Pierre de Coubertin, the process leading to the formation of an IOC and the announcement of the international Olympic Games for Athens 1896 and Paris in 1900. Leading up to the formation of the IOC, Coubertin had busied himself with establishing sport in France and with encouraging international fixtures. Further to the details explained in previous chapters, it is useful to next consider the organising that would prove formative

Foundations of Managing British Olympics: Institutions through Time, 65–89

doi:10.1108/978-1-80262-095-520251005

to the Olympic Games. We then use primary sources and secondary literature to piece together the organisation and experience of Athens 1896, then return to England where another Olympic labelled event was happening.

Structuring Olympic Administration

Coubertin had requested for demonstration games to be held at the Exposition Universelle 1889 World's Fair held in Paris, and was then instrumental in establishing in early 1890, the USFSA. This union, although not the only sporting union in France at that time, seems to have been concerned with intercollegiate sport and represented both the rugby and association codes of football, tennis, rowing, cycling, running (flat and cross-country), enabling the arrangement of meetings, and to lobby for facilities and the cooperation of headmasters. The union had its own weekly publication which alongside Coubertin's *Revue athletique* both of which 'propagandized in favour of Coubertinian notions of sport' (MacAloon, 2006d, p. 531).

In the latter months of 1894 he established the French National Olympic Committee (FNOC), which served as the prototype National Olympic Committee (NOC) (MacAloon, 2006g). It was also the year that France's first indoor bicycle track was built, following similar builds in England that emerged in the 1870s where amateur cycling was a popular sport. The promotion and investment of sport in France contrasts to that of Britain and the United States, where organised sport had emerged from the schools and universities establishing their traditions before authoritative institutions formed to govern them. In France, it appears the converse was true; 'early schoolboy initiatives were almost immediately seized upon, rationalized and promoted by men such as Coubertin, his colleagues and his rivals' (MacAloon, 2006d, p. 529).

So, organising the first ever modern, international Olympic Games under the auspices of the IOC was not the first time that Coubertin had been involved with arranging or governing a sporting fixture or event. All roads had been leading to this point, but the games would be Coubertin's most ambitious project to date, and to do so required the collaboration and teamwork of five main stakeholders, referred to by Chappalet (2018, p. 4) as 'the classic Olympic system':

- IOC.
- (local) Organizing Committees for the Olympic Games (OCOGs).
- NOCs.
- International Sport Federations.
- National Sport Federations.

Of these, the OCOGs were most powerful in terms of the games during Coubertin's lifetime and indeed for around the first 80 years, by which point the negotiation of television broadcasting rights developed in a way that shifted power towards the IOC (Chappalet, 2018). It should also be noted that only a few NOCs existed at the time of the inaugural Olympic Games, the first two, France and United States, having founded in 1894 the same year as the IOC itself, which were followed by Australia, Germany, Greece, Hungary, all of which were established in 1895. In terms of the games, NOCs are responsible for selecting and managing the Olympic team that will represent their territory; however, the first four Olympiads involved many private individuals who entered of their own will, with any 'wins' then being attributed to their nation of origin or residence.

Of course, the Olympic structure does not exist in a vacuum and the national political (and royal) context was also important, particularly in the host nation. In Greece, Prime Minister Tricoupis had returned to office in 1892. The economic situation there was challenging; foreign debt at one third of Greece's income and declining prices for currants (one of the nation's chief exports) were notable problems and in 1893 Greek was bankrupt (Randall, 2011). When the Olympic Games were proposed they must have seemed a further public expense and perhaps not the sort of signal Tricoupis wanted to send to the world, particularly to those to whom Greece owed money.[1] Although it was suggested to Coubertin that Paris might be more suitable and a contingency plan involved Hungary, the Baron insisted it must be Greece (MacAloon, 2006d).

An Opportunity for Greece

The official report of the Athens 1896 Games was published the following year. It contains the same text in two languages, German and English. The first part of the report, approximately one half of its content, is given to a detailed history of the ancient games since 776 BC and discusses also the excavation of archaeology and antiquities in more recent times. Part Two is a far more useful source when studying how the games were planned and delivered, containing an entire chapter dedicated to their organisation, which begins thus:

> The decisions of the International Athletic Congress of 1894 in Paris were received with the greatest satisfaction by all the Hellenes: Athens had been chosen as the place for the inauguration of the Olympic Games! This proposition gratified the patriotic pride of the whole Hellenic race, and the majority of the Greeks perceived at once that substantial advantages for their country might arise from it. This however was not the opinion of the Government, then in power, which afraid, that the outlay for those festivities would fall on the Public Treasury opposed the project most energetically. The Public Treasury was in fact in a state of bankruptcy. How could any ministry dream of spending 500,000 frs for the celebration of International Games whilst the just and legitimate claims of Greek and foreign creditors had to remain unsatisfied! This serious argument seemed irrefutable.[2]

---

[1]de Coubertin (1979, p. 15).

[2]Philemon, T. J. 'Organisation of the Games of 1896', Part II of the Official Report of the Olympic Games, BC 776– AD 1896. Published with the sanction and under the patronage of the Central Committee in Athens, presided over by his Royal Highness the Crown Prince Constantine, p. 10.

While the games might have sounded like a white elephant to Tricoupis, to the Greek royal family it presented a good opportunity to solidify and signal their 'Greekness'. They had already sent congratulatory telegrams to the Paris congress and had patronised the 'Zappas Olympics', so Coubertin's proposals for 1896 must have seemed a logical extension and Crown Prince Constantine apparently 'consented immediately to serve as president of the organizing committee Coubertin was labouring to establish' (MacAloon, 2006d, p. 557). Working internationally did present a communication barrier and Greece turned out to be somewhat different to the Western ideal. Coubertin found that the classical Greek he had been taught at school was useless to him, especially in terms of the pronunciation, but fortunately everyone there spoke French![3]

Coubertin drafted a project plan that estimated a budget of approximately 250,000 Drachma.[4] Athens by now had some facilities already available, not least the Zappeion, the hall built and named after Zappas (Chapter 3) and its archaeology and so it was proposed by Coubertin that hosting the games might cost only around 150,000 francs according to MacAloon (2006d) or 200,000 francs according to Llewellyn Smith (2004, p. 113), but either way a sum of money that could be easily recovered (MacAloon, 2006d). He had also considered that in 1896 the Western and Greek Easters would coincide and scheduled the games to run from 5 to 15 April, meaning that they would be 'resurrected' on Easter Monday (MacAloon, 2006d, p. 560). Coubertin's proposal for the programme was adopted.[5] It was understood that the Athens Games would be an episodic, self-contained project that would have its own budget standing apart from the continuing finances of the IOC. From the United Kingdom, the revival was keenly anticipated but viewed as something of a semi-outlandish scheme or project promoted by Coubertin and the British representative Lord Ampthill, which was broadly welcomed but which had uncertain outcomes. *The Graphic*, for instance, wondered whether athletes would be allowed to wear running shoes or if they would compete barefoot as the ancient competitors had, and why ancient Olympia (which it compared to the London Olympia exhibition venue then run by the impresario Imre Kiralfy) was not chosen over Athens.[6] Sensing the power of the press in shaping perceptions of the project, Coubertin wrote to the London newspaper *The Standard* asking for their support in promoting the enterprise.[7]

Regardless of what facilities already existed, the fact remained that following Coubertin's visit, there remained less than a year-and-a-half in which to prepare, no mean feat considering that the 1896 Games would be the largest public event staged in independent Greece and the largest athletic event ever held in the modern world (Llewellyn Smith, 2004). Additionally, the committee that Coubertin set up in Athens soon realised that the games would cost more like three times his estimate, and that an appeal for funds via subscription or a loan in the

---

[3]de Coubertin (1979, p. 16).
[4]de Coubertin (1979, p. 16).
[5]de Coubertin (1979, p. 16).
[6]'Topics of the Week'. *Graphic*, 3 November 1894, p. 506.
[7]'The Olympic Games'. *Standard*, 2 February 1895, p. 3.

form of lottery were not a practical solution, the government refusing either of these options.[8] Greece was in financial difficulty having become bankrupt, and owed money to other nations. The committee collectively resigned among accusations that as wealthy people they could subscribe the money themselves, and the government's position on hosting the games became parliamentary debate on 6 December when Prime Minister Tricoupis was grilled by his opposition (Llewellyn Smith, 2004). The trade guilds and corporations in Athens attempted to raise their own appeal, but appears not have met with much success apart from a 10,000 franc donation given by a member of the Greek diaspora in England.[9]

A breakthrough occurred in January 1895 when Crown Prince Constantine took charge, as Honorary President of the committee, and by early February a Commission was appointed by Royal Decree.[10] Prime Minister Tricoupis had not yet made terms with his nation's creditors nor found a way forward for taxation that was palatable to the Greek citizens. He resigned in the same month, when his already strained relationship with the Greek Royal Family was pushed over the edge by Constantine's appearance at a demonstration against the government's taxation policy (Llewellyn Smith, 2004).

The Crown Prince swiftly dismissed the organising committee's vice-presidents, in their place appointing as secretary-general Timoleon Philemon (ex-mayor of Athens) as well as two additional secretaries, and his brothers (Prince George and Prince Nicholas) as heads of the working commissions (Llewellyn Smith, 2004). The Crown Prince then established a new organisational structure, headed by the Council of Twelve. This was an inner-circle comprising important political men, partly members of the General Committee, partly of outsiders, which Constantine chaired, offering general supervision and coordinating fundraising.[11] Before the Council of Twelve first sat, the Prince adjoined to the Committee several experts with special knowledge of athletics and gymnastics, or competence and practical value concerning the works to be undertaken. The Prince then divided Committee into different branches or subcommittees, each with a defined responsibility in the preparation for the Olympic Games and preliminary activities.[12] Therefore, we can say simply and specifically that directly below the Circle of Twelve was the General Committee for the Olympic Games, and below that were committees responsible for construction of the stadium, for particular sports, for training Greek athletes, and for the reception accommodation and entertainment of overseas athletes and guests.[13] The stadium committee required archaeologists and included Professor Dörpfeld,[14] who was already involved in the Olympia excavations (Llewellyn Smith, 2004).

The Programme was drawn up according to that proposed by the International Athletic Congress in Paris, with the exception of Equestrian sport, because

---

[8]Philemon (1896, p. 10).

[9]'The Proposed Olympic Games'. *Times*, 26 December 1894, p. 3.

[10]Philemon (1896, p. 11).

[11]Philemon (1896, p. 12).

[12]Philemon (1896, pp. 9, 15).

[13]Philemon (1896, p. 15).

[14]Philemon (1896, p. 15).

Greece had no horse breeds of its own, and Athens no racecourse. Building a racecourse with such limited time and money was deemed impossible and the Prince agreed to the proposal of the Council to exclude horseracing.[15] The full list of nine sub-committees and names of the corresponding members is detailed in the Official Report of the 1896 Games,[16] and may be summarised as:

1. Nautical sports.
2. Shooting.
3. Training Greek athletes.
4. Wrestling and gymnastics.
5. Fencing.
6. Cycling.
7. Outdoor-games.
8. Restoration of the Pan-Athenaic stadion.
9. Reception of guests.

The commission with responsibility for training and selecting Greek athletes held several preliminary events, including in the summer of 1895 and up until 23 March 1896. The latter was reported by British newspaper *The Times* as having been billed as 'The Panhellenic Trial Games' and was held in the stadium and attended by 35,000 people including the King of Greece and Crown Prince (Llewellyn Smith, 2004). Below the surface though, the dynamic between the clubs considered to have been the Greek athletic establishment was tense. These were the centres of preparation, and as late as 1895 a new breakaway club was founded, the Athens Athletic Club (AAC), by the son of one of the Council of Twelve. The AAC was dedicated to amateurism and its founder claimed that members of other leading clubs should be excluded from the Olympic Games because it employed professional trainers. In response, the IOC ruled that amateurism applied only to individuals and not to clubs (Llewellyn Smith, 2004). To find competitors, the Greek committee sent invitations to 2,000 athletic clubs 'in all parts of the world'.[17]

Finance and Construction of the 1896 Olympic Games 'Project'

Coubertin kept his distance from organising, possibly distracted by his recent marriage, but was involved at the international level, encouraging participants from around the world. The new committee was thus left on its own to raise finances and discovered that even the previous committee's estimate was undervalued (Llewellyn Smith, 2004). The Official Report of the 1896 Games explains

[15]Philemon (1896, p. 9).
[16]Philemon (1896, p. 18).
[17]Foreign Office. 1896 Annual Series, no. 1694, Diplomatic and Consular Reports on Trade and Finance: Greece: *Olympic Games*, pp. 20–21.

how, in the name of the Council, signed by its President, an appeal was addressed to 'all the Hellenes'; Each municipality in Greece was asked to contribute its share, each diplomatic or consular agent abroad received orders to do so within their own jurisdiction (it was though 'strictly forbidden' to accept help from subjects of other nations). This appeal was met with a mixed reaction among the Greeks, many of whom, including 'some of the very richest even', refused to contribute anything. Perhaps the whole enterprise appeared unrealistic, particularly at a time when the economy was struggling, and the Olympic Games plan was met with ridicule and contempt from many. Even so, the subscriptions collected in Greece and abroad amounted to twice as much money as had at first been deemed necessary by 'the promoters of the project' to cover 'all expenses for the festivities'. We quote directly here to emphasise two points, firstly that the games and associated entertainments are considered 'festivities' and more significantly for our study of management and organisation, that the Official Report explicitly refers to the planning and delivery of these festivities, the very first modern international Olympic Games, as a 'project'.[18]

Specifically, the contributions of private persons, and the grants from municipalities represented according to the Chief-Register the sum total of 332,756 drachmas,[19] and only 150,000 drachmas had been at first fixed for the expenditure of the inauguration. Naturally some time elapsed before the whole sum was brought together. At the beginning of its labours, the Committee had not at its disposal anything like such an amount. An appeal raised 332,756 drachmas, which was helpful but did not even cover the cost of the stadium (Llewellyn Smith, 2004). The committee made a successful appeal to wealthy Greek expatriates, an established tradition in Greece. As soon as 19 February it was noted this had generated 130,000 drachmas, donations arriving from Alexandria, London, and Marseilles, and by the 22nd 200,000 (MacAloon, 2006g).[20] Eventually the British diplomatic service reported that a subscription of 500,000 drachmas (£12,500) was raised.[21] Additionally, Crown Prince Constantine persuaded Georges Averoff, a wealthy Greek living in Alexandria, Egypt, where he had made his fortune from trade and property.[22] Averoff had previously funded Greek schools – the Polytechnic School, the Military College, and the Reformatory for youthful offenders in Athens, and a Gymnasium and a Young Ladies' College, in Alexandria[23] and a battleship. His support was immediately forthcoming, approving the architect Metaxa's plans to

---

[18]Philemon (1896, p. 20).

[19]Philemon (1896, p. 21).

[20]'Sporting Notes and News'. *Pall Mall Gazette*, 22 February 1895, p. 10; 'Multiple News Items'. *North Eastern Daily Gazette*, 6 March 1895; 'Olympic Games at Athens', *Illustrated London News*, 9 March 1895, p. 291.

[21]Foreign Office. 1896 Annual Series, no 1694, Diplomatic and Consular Reports on Trade and Finance: Greece: *Olympic Games*, pp. 20–21. Pound sterling conversions for Drachmas are given where available.

[22]'The Olympic Games at Athens'. *Derby Daily Telegraph*, 10 April 1895, p. 4.

[23]Philemon (1896, p. 21).

restore the Oanathenaic stadium at a cost of 585,000 drachmas. By 1895, the cost of this had risen to 900,000 (£22,500), and he eventually funded it to the sum of 920,000 drachmas[24] when the stadium cost overran (Llewellyn Smith, 2004).

In April, a new Prime Minister was elected by the opposition party, Theodore Deliyiannis, who was able to give indirect support but could not be seen to divert money from Greece's creditors (Llewellyn Smith, 2004). The government helped how it could, exempting tickets from tax, a gesture that resulted in 200,000 drachmas received from the sale of tickets and commemorative medals,[25] and an issue of commemorative postage stamps for which the games would receive the income of 400,000 drachmas[26] (Llewellyn Smith, 2004). These events all serve to demonstrate to the present-day researcher of global sporting mega-events that project cost underestimates at the time of proposal are not a new phenomenon, nor are economic crises, nor political upheavals in host countries.

The stadium project involved re-opening the quarries of Mount Pentelicon, from which the high-quality Pentelic marble that had been used in the construction of the Acropolis and other ancient Athenian buildings, as well as for Roman sculpture could be found. In addition to quarrying, hundreds of labourers were employed to clear the stadium site and work was supervised by architect Anastas Metaxas (who drew the plans) in consultation with German and French archaeological academies. The site clearing was started as early as February 1895, despite the lack of money, and was perhaps done to increase confidence that the project was progressing.[27] These plans aimed to reflect the heritage of the site as closely as possible, cladding the amphitheatre with marble, although made some concessions to accommodate a wider running track, involving the removal of some seating rows and making the track of cinders (the latter under direction of a Grounds keeper from London).[28] Two statues of Hermes discovered during earlier excavations were included as turning posts and a statue of Averoff was commissioned for the stadium's entrance in tribute to his great gift, which had financed the whole ambitious project (MacAloon, 2006g). The restoration of the 50,000 capacity 'stadion', which had not been excavated until 1869–1870 was in itself considered a worthwhile project which drew favourable responses from British enthusiasts for classical civilisation, who otherwise were unconvinced of the merits of restaging the ancient games with modern sports.[29]

Additionally, the committees oversaw the required construction of a new shooting gallery at Callithea, a velodrome costing 60,000 francs near the tomb of the Greek hero Karaiskakis in New Phaleron,[30] a pier for spectators of the nautical

---

[24]Philemon (1896, p. 22).
[25]Philemon (1896, p. 24).
[26]Philemon (1896, p. 24).
[27]'Multiple News Items'. *North-Eastern Daily Gazette*, 15 February 1895.
[28]'Summary'. *York Herald*, 13 September 1895; Philemon (1896, p. 24).
[29]'The Olympic Games'. *Morning Post*, 16 March 1896, p. 3; Waldstein, C. 'The Olympic Games'. *Times*, 1 April 1896, p. 12.
[30]'The World of Wheels'. *Cycling: An Illustrated Weekly*, vol. X, no. 255, 7 December 1895, pp. 349+.

sports, some contrivances for sheltering boats, as well as several constructions of minor importance concerning nautical or outdoor games, which were begun as soon as was possible.[31] There were public infrastructure works including roads, lighting, greenery, and the bridge over the river Ilissos that connected the stadium with the modern city. But cuts still had to be made; in terms of construction, the equestrian facilities were not built, and so these events were dropped. In terms of scheduling, the games in the stadium were shortened to five instead of six days, while the regatta was cancelled altogether. Other games which there had been aspirations to host including association football, cricket, pentathlon, ice skating, and royal tennis, also failed to materialise. As the work progressed, and the programme was clarified, the English press expressed surprise that discus throwing and Greco-Roman wrestling were the only sports with a classical feel to be included, but this dispelled the misconception that the games were simply going to be a highbrow re-enactment of the ancient games.[32] There was even some highbrow derision of the way modern Greek speakers pronounced 'Phaleron' with a shorter e sound than in classical Greek.[33] For Athens economically, in anticipation of trade, brewers and meat suppliers upscaled their supply, but the price of meat still rose (Llewellyn Smith, 2004) while information for visiting spectators began to be published.[34] By December 1895, there were favourable reports of progress with the arena but there remained a sense that the project might not be completed in time for the sport to begin:

> [...] pessimists predicted that nothing would be ready by the appointed term, they talked of certain failure, and regretted that such a formidable enterprise should ever have been undertaken by so poor a nation, they blamed everything and everybody. The Press made itself the interpreter of these dismal forebodings, and gave vent to most pessimistic opinions.[35]

Facing Resistance

In France, despite having momentum and influence, Coubertin still faced resistance from some individuals and institutions. The French Government reneged on its approval of funding for French representative athletes, and governing bodies for cycling and nautical sport refused to commit to sending any members without assurances of a minimum number of other participating competitors, nations or clubs. Perhaps most dramatically, the president of the Union of Shooting Clubs, resigned from FNOC and vowed to boycott the Olympic Games because shooting was not given as much individual status as he would have liked at Athens, and

[31]Philemon (1896, p. 24).

[32]'Olympic Games at Athens'. *Illustrated London News*, 9 March 1895. p. 291; 'Summary'. *York Herald*, 13 September 1895.

[33]'The Olympic Games'. *Morning Post*, 16 March 1896, p. 3.

[34]'Greece-Olympic Games'. *Morning Post*, 22 April 1895, front page.

[35]Philemon (1896, p. 25); 'The Olympic Games'. *Evening Telegraph*, 17 December 1895, p. 3.

because the Olympic organisers wanted to make his union 'an appendage' of their own committee.[36] Resultantly, France was barely represented at the inaugural Olympic Games, boasting one long-distance runner, two cyclists and 'four or five fencers' (MacAloon, 2006g, p. 574), although Baker (2008) suggests a slightly higher number of nineteen, the difference possibly due to counting individuals as well as those sent officially by France's NOC or clubs, if not an error. Meanwhile, there was also pushback in Germany – following an allegedly fabricated interview with Coubertin published in a French newspaper which upset the German sporting establishment. Coubertin had to distance himself from the article and published a denial in January 1895.[37] The interview was used by the IOC's opponents, one of whom characterised the IOC as 'a temporary organisation which no longer has any reason to exist'.[38] In early 1896, there was a reverse controversy in which it was claimed the Greek Commission had briefed the Germans that they would look more favourably on their participation than that of the French, which was also quickly denied![39] Resistance was fuelled by the popular misunderstanding of the Olympic mission. For Coubertin the emphasis seems more to have been progressive, but in the eyes of the public it was perhaps more romantic. At Athens he encountered a lady from the United States who claimed to have watched the 'Olympic Games' already in San Francisco, attended by the emperor Caesar. Coubertin realised that she was referring to a pageant, or re-enactment as part of an entertainment spectacle:

> Full of good will but no understanding … they were unable to comprehend my idea, to interpret this forgotten thing: Olympism, and to separate the soul, the essence, the principle … from the ancient forms that had enveloped it and which, during the last fifteen hundred years, had fallen into oblivion. (de Coubertin, 1979, p. 6)

The idea of restoring the Olympic Games appeared anachronistic and was not well understood to a public who were perceived romantic re-enactment rather than a progressive international moment based on competitive sport.

Elsewhere, the Hungarian athletic associations were awarded funds to send a team of eight competitors, declaring its intention to compete in June 1895,[40] but other nations such as Austria, Belgium, Holland, Italy, Portugal, Spain, and Switzerland, were represented by individuals, as government was not forthcoming. The Italian athlete, was not even admitted, having 'walked the entire distance between Milan and Athens to get into shape', because 'he had no amateur credentials' (MacAloon, 2006g, p. 575). Claims that 800 German athletic clubs would send entries were not realised.[41] Just 21 Germans eventually participated, and 14

[36]de Coubertin (1979, pp. 22–23).
[37]de Coubertin (1979, p. 23).
[38]de Coubertin (1979, p. 23).
[39]'Greece', *Standard*, 16 January 1896, p. 5.
[40]'The Olympic Games', *Standard*, 28 June 1895, p. 3.
[41]'The Olympic Games'. *Evening Telegraph*, 17 December 1895, p. 3.

Americans (Baker, 2008) – but again some clubs from the United States, such as the Manhattan Athletic Club, seem to have advertised their participation and then not made the journey.[42] Altogether, it was claimed that invitations had been forwarded to over 2,000 athletic clubs around the world, and at one stage claimed that 300 had expressed an interest in sending participants, although not all materialised.[43]

Britain was an interesting case, having pioneered several of the Olympic sports and having its own history of, and influence on, the current Olympic revival. As we have mentioned already, amateur sport had definition and a social-class dimension particularly in England, and without wanting to overstate this, it does seem to have affected the ways in which the British Olympic movements to date had stumbled. British consular staff in Greece watched the developments with interest and even reported on particulars of the stamp issue, which they claimed would be 'of interest to stamp collectors and philhellenes' reflecting the contemporary British enthusiasm for classical Greek culture.[44]

Despite his experience and delight at the relatively inclusive Wenlock Olympic events, Coubertin in his mission had moved mostly in circles of aristocracy, fee-paying schools, and elite universities. Coubertin seems to have left the initiative of British participation to Britain's IOC members, Charles Herbert, Honorary Secretary of the AAA, and Arthur Russell, 2nd Baron Ampthill. Notably, neither attended the Athens Games, and therefore also missed the session of the IOC which took place there. The AAA itself took a laissez-faire approach, not even considering raising a representative team, leaving the decision to participate to clubs and individuals. It did, however, agree to formally recognise the Athens games as falling formally in accordance with AAA laws, giving Coubertin much needed formal legitimacy.[45] Interestingly, the IOC Chairman Vikelis had recommended Coubertin enlist the help of Cambridge University classicist Professor Richard Jebb, but this advice was not acted upon (Llewellyn Smith, 2004). Perhaps because of this there would be no team to represent Britain, only six individual athletes who had British nationality. One of these athletes, G.S. Robertson, an 'Oxford athlete who delighted the Greeks and Coubertin by reciting an original ode in ancient Greek and Pindaric style during the awards ceremony' identified that only French and German language texts of the programme and rules had been posted to Great Britain. It was not until later, near the time that the Athens Games were due to begin that a version translated to the English language was published by a commercial printer (MacAloon, 2006g, p. 575).

Greater barriers to participation from the United Kingdom and Western Europe more generally were perhaps money and time. The *Pall Mall Gazette*,

---

[42]'Multiple Sports Items'. *Sheffield Independent*, 13 January 1896, p. 4.

[43]'The New Olympic Games'. *The Boys' Own Paper*, vol. XVII, no. 868, 31 August 1895, p. 766.

[44]Foreign Office. 1896 Annual Series, no 1694, Diplomatic and Consular Reports on Trade and Finance: Greece: *Olympic Games*, pp. 20–21.

[45]AAA ATH/AAA/1/2/24, Winter Meeting of the General Committee Minutes, 23 November 1895.

despite its conservative orientation, expressed concern that amateurism was a block on participation from Britain or elsewhere – the 'inaccessibility' of Athens meant that only athletes who could afford to travel there, and the time away from work, would be able to participate.[46] This would not be feasible for most British athletes who were drawn from the middle classes. The Oxford and Cambridge Universities (Oxbridge) were prominent in British amateur sport at this time and, despite rumours that British universities might enter a team circulating as early as November 1895,[47] direct contact from the Olympic movement to the university clubs was not made until the month before the games opened. A German language invitation was received by Cambridge Athletic Club, while a notice was posted at Oxford together with a paragraph in a university journal. It was also claimed that if the central Olympic committee was contacted for more information, a reply would explain that 'all information could be attained by subscribing a considerable sum to the journal of the committee' (MacAloon, 2006g, p. 575). Eventually, between six and eight British athletes did go to Athens but as individuals rather than representing any club (MacAloon, 2006g; Baker, 2008). Names included George Robertson, Lawrence Levy and Eugene Sandow, the latter a famous 'strong man' of his time (Anthony, 1997, pp. 19–20).

Perhaps Britain's highest profile involvement was that of travel organiser Thomas Cook, which gained the exclusive franchise for tourism at the games from the Commission (Anthony, 1997, p. 20). The tours were arranged at reduced rates by Baron de Coubertin and his associates including a Paris – Athens round trip priced to travellers at 300 francs for first class, and another from Marseilles by steamship that was made by 200 or more spectators. The trips were advertised alongside Cook's other tours, one leaving London on the 24 March.[48] Hotels and private houses were pressed into service in Athens to provide a range of accommodation.[49] The tourists attracted fell short of the numbers Coubertin had hoped for (MacAloon, 2006g) but is significant as it began an association between Thomas Cook and the Olympic Games and international sport that would sustain into the 20th and 21st centuries (Tennent & Gillett, 2016).

Broadly as the games grew closer belief that they would succeed grew, with one humorous magazine reporting that the fate of 'Olympicuniosity' which had sometimes struck previous attempts at revivals had been avoided.[50]

The First Games

By the end of March 1896, the Panathenaic stadium which was used for athletic events, medical facilities, the shooting range, and the specially built cycling track

---

[46]'Occasional Notes', *Pall Mall Gazette*, 25 October 1895, p. 2.

[47]'English Athletic Notes'. *Edinburgh Evening News*, 7 November 1895, p. 4.

[48]'Multiple Classified ads'. *Standard*, 10 March 1896, front page.

[49]'Olympic Games at Athens'. *Leeds Times*, 1 February 1896, p. 8.

[50]'A series of Olympic games is to be held in Greece next year'. *Moonshine*, 10 August 1895, p. 63.

were ready, the location of the latter at Phalerum having only been agreed since October 1895 (Llewellyn Smith, 2004).[51] Additionally, the Zappaion building was also used, the legacy of Zappas' vast fortune, bequeathed in his Will as his gift to the nation and intended for the Olympic revival he had tried so hard to begin. In 1895, it was used for a meeting of the committee and sub-committees during the preparation phase,[52] and then in 1896, as an indoor arena for the fencing competitions (Zappas.org, n.d.). Outside of the venues, infrastructure was developed: Prime Minister Tricoupis improved ports, built lighthouses on the coast, multiplied railways and high roads on the interior, and better equipped the military, but these investments all required tax rises and the popular opinion soon turned against him.[53]

Despite tax hikes, the appetite of Athenians for the games was evident by the number of spectators attending the opening ceremony on Easter Sunday 5th April, which appears to have been a triumph. Contemporary sources estimated 40,000–70,000 were inside the stadium, a figure difficult to be precise about because attendees were standing, not seated. Even more people filled the surrounding streets and hills, and so the total figure has been estimated between 80,000 and 120,000. To contextualise this Athens had a population of around 130,000 (MacAloon, 2006g). The games were priced inclusively, tiered progressively 'according to proximity of the section to the royal seats'.[54] These festivities were followed by a service on Easter Monday commemorating 75 years of Greek independence. Yet even by the time that the games were opening, the purpose of the games still confused some onlookers, who suggested among other things that the inclusion of cycling, then a new sport based on emerging technology, seemed incongruous with an event that had classical overtures.[55]

The journalist Charalambos Anninos, writing within the official report of the 1896 Games, provides a vivid description events, beginning with the unveiling of the statue to Averoff and then a day-by-day account of each of the ten days of competition. This is a useful source for historians because it describes not only the athletic performances but also captures the experience and anticipation of being there, for example, the sights and sounds of the attendees, ticket-sellers, policing, and security, how full the stadium was for certain events, from the details of what they were wearing to the times of day that things happened. A blow-by-blow account of the arrival of members of the Royal Family is given, including who stood and who remained seated, the speeches given, the sound of the bugle, and arrival of the athletes once the games began. Description of sporting performance

---

[51]Foreign Office. 1896. Annual Series, no. 1694, Diplomatic and Consular Reports on Trade and Finance: Greece: *Olympic Games,* pp. 20–21; Waldstein, C. 'The Olympic Games'. *Times*, 1 April 1896, p. 12.

[52]Philemon (1896, p. 17).

[53]Holmes, B. (1908). *The Olympian games in Athens*. McClure Company (1996 facsimile edition, pp. 37–39).

[54]Holmes (1908, p. 83).

[55]'[ill]NOTES'. *Pall Mall Gazette*, 2 April 1896.

refers to skill, agility, and the reaction of the crowd from amusement at some aspects, to the enthusiastic flag-waving and patriotism of those cheering for the United States. The reader is also treated to details of torchlight processions through the city after dark, and to an account of the Royal Breakfast, to which were invited over 200 people who had in some way contributed including committee and sub-committee organisers, competitors, and representatives. Finally, after the full programme of events, the winners were announced and awarded prizes and another procession took place in the stadium and the King of Greece declared the games closed, before a farewell banquet was given. The full account teaches us the experience of the games and is a helpful document, making it easy to imagine the experience. It is illustrated with various black and white photographs and drawings, which capture athletes and activities from across the programme but with particular emphasis on the ceremonial including prizes, processions, and musicians. All of these are significant, it being the occasion of the first International Olympic Games organised under the IOC, however, the music is especially noteworthy, the Olympic Anthem having been written for these games by Spyridon Samaras, perhaps considered one of the Olympic Games oldest symbols or traditions. The report is accessible easily online for anyone who wishes to read it and so it is enough to provide this summary of its content.[56]

We deem it more useful for our narrative to instead focus on the account of another source; a rich contemporaneous account (perhaps more objective and even from insightful account than that in the Official Report, from the perspective of experiencing the games and the City as a spectator) is provided by the US author, lecturer, traveller, and pioneer of the travelogue, Burton Holmes. His words paint a vivid picture of the spectacle as he experienced it, comparing the modern with the ancient, noting the dark clothing popular in the 19th century:

> The old Athenian spectator whitened or enriched with bright colors the marble sides of the Stadium; we moderns blacken it with our hideous funeral garb ....
>
> [...] But, in spite of it all, the sight is one which thrills us, one the like of which has never before been witnessed in our modern age. The first glimpse of the crowded Stadium is to be numbered among the great sensations of a life time.[57]

Holmes articulates the Games of 1896 as being an exciting spectacle held in a turbulent economy. The Greek currency he described as amusing and annoying, the modern drachma had at one time been worth 20 US cents, but depreciated by the

---

[56]Anninos, C. (1896). 'Description of the Games', Part II of the Official Report of the Olympic Games, BC776–AD1896. Published with the sanction and under the patronage of the Central Committee in Athens, presided over by his Royal Highness the Crown Prince Constantine, pp. 50–116.

[57]Holmes (1908, p. 54).

time of the games. Gold and silver coins had passed out of Greece into the wider continent of Europe, leaving only paper currency, with a drachma by then worth just 12 US cents, and the paper very fragile. A new issue of bank notes was made to correspond with the games, presumably in anticipation of the extra economic activity that the event would bring. These notes were issued in a long-ribbon of coupons, which US athletes would purchase by a yard of drachma. However, the hotels and establishments marketed to foreigners charged on a gold basis (in francs); thus a bill of a hundred francs required 200 paper drachma, while locals would be charged the same number but in drachma not francs, meaning athletes paid double by comparison. If the foreigner would not pay more than a local, the trader would refuse to sell. Travellers tolerated it because these hotels were far more comfortable and hospitable than the Xenodochian Greek-styled hotels used by the indigenous population. Furthermore, there was no five-drachma denomination, thus for goods or services costing that amount but paid with a ten drachma note, the trader would tear it in half in order to give change, with these half-notes more commonplace than intact ten drachma notes once in circulation.[58]

Foreign athletes seem to have enjoyed a good standard of hospitality. Social diversions at Athens included a luncheon held by the King, and there were at least two picnics, one held by the mayor and another given by the American wife of the Russian Secretary of Legation, for the Princes Constantine, George, and Nicholas of Greece and the athletes.[59] There were also, in total, around three hundred competitors from eleven countries, and although we have already discussed the nationalities of some of the athletes who had travelled from abroad, Baker (2008, p. 2) reminds us that two-thirds of them were Greek, meaning that although the Olympic Games were an international event, it was Greek patronage that provided most of the competition as well as the spectators and financing of the project.

Holmes comments on a relaxed approach to record keeping, giving as an example the instance of the 1,500-meter race that was won by an Australian, but was attributed as a US athlete. Someone from the United States tried to explain this but was told by the Greeks 'Oh, well, that is about the same thing; we congratulate you'.[60] US athletes did particularly well at Athens. A party of 14 competitors made it to Athens, mostly students from Harvard or Princeton universities and members of the Boston Athletic Association.[61] At this time competitors, although considered representative of their nations, were there as independents, as no formal national teams existed in the way we think of them today. However, the Boston contingent was the first example of something like an organised team. Despite having travelled a long distance they did particularly well, winning the most first-place (11, compared to host nation athletes from Greece who won 10,

[58]Holmes (1908, pp. 24–27).
[59]Holmes (1908, p. 72).
[60]Holmes (1908, p. 62).
[61]'From Club and Course', *Pall Mall Gazette*, 29 February 1896, p. 9; 'Sporting Notes and News'. *Pall Mall Gazette*, 17 March 1896, p. 8.

but who had far more athletes participating).[62] The Greeks took advantage of their host status and held preliminary trials in the stadium on the days before the games to choose their athletes from the ranks of the leading Greek athletic clubs.[63]

Unsurprisingly, Holmes' account is focussed towards his own nation, which is where the majority of his readership was based. He reports on one remarkable and heroic achievement, claiming how one US athlete threw the discus for the first time in his life at the games, and after only a few tries he then made the winning throw, beating even the Greeks who were more experienced and more practised in technique.[64]

The Greeks, Holmes reports, were very impressed by the US athletes' performances overall. In shooting matches, Americans the Payne brothers arrived on the 'very day of the matches' and to steady their nerves they 'took frequent sips of whisky from pocket-flasks. On the second day not a Greek contestant sighted a gun, without first applying a black bottle to his lips'.[65] Also to reduce glare, the Paynes' used burning matches to smoke the gun metal and the next day, 'although overcast' the Greeks copied this too 'Thus the flattery of imitation was carried to ludicrous extreme'.[66]

Local newspapers also attributed their success to several conjectures and misunderstandings, apparently they had:

> [...] joined to the inherited athletic training of the Anglo-Saxon, the wild impetuosity of the red-skinned Indians! whilst another reported that their athletes had greater endurance because they chewed pitch to strengthen the lungs, a misunderstanding of the athletes enjoying chewing gum! Another misreported the blowing into hands to moisten them before pole vaulting as having bowed heads in prayer.[67]

Great Britain had twenty-three entries in fourteen events, achieving first place in tennis (singles) and weightlifting (one-hand lift), as well as three runners-up (110-m hurdles, cycling 12-hour race, and weightlifting two-hand lift). Tennis player John Pius Boland won a further first-place in tennis doubles, but this has not been attributed to Great Britain due to the duo comprising the German Mr Traun.[68]

The weight-lifting event was notable not only for British success, but for the attendance of Prince George who mingled with contestants, Holmes observed he was large

---

[62]A list of medals awarded using the modern system of national teams and Gold, Silver and Bronze corresponding to First, Second and Third best performance is to be found on the website of the International Olympic Committee. https://olympics.com/en/olympic-games/athens-1896/medals.
[63]'Scraps'. *Graphic*, 28 March 1896.
[64]Holmes (1908, pp. 59–61).
[65]Holmes (1908, pp. 76–78).
[66]Holmes (1908, pp. 76–78).
[67]Holmes (1908, pp. 63–64)
[68]Anninos, C. (1896, p. 99).

and strong; 'during the weight-lifting match he picked up and nonchalantly handed to a contestant a dumb-bell, which the latter could barely lift'.[69] Indeed, throughout the games the Crown Prince was often in the arena 'it was no unusual thing to see him carrying a glass of cognac to a resting athlete, or holding the sweater of another while a contest was in progress'.[70] Royals from other countries also attended at least part of the games – the Crown Prince of Austria-Hungary, Karl Ludwig, and four other Grand Dukes from the Hapsburg Empire took up rooms, while King Alexander of Serbia also visited among rumours that he was seeking to marry a Greek Princess, Princess Marie. He would be unsuccessful in this eventually losing out to the Russian Grand Duke George Mikhailovich who was also trying to win her affections.[71]

On the fifth day of the games was the most anticipated event: the marathon, a special race invented for the 1896 Games and the capstone of the athletic events and perhaps the entire tournament. It was a foot race from the city of Marathon to Athens, a course of 40 kilometres (approximately 25 miles) duration. Holmes reported a huge attendance around the stadium and up the hill overlooking it.[72]

There was a certain amount of drama to the race, a cannon shot was fired to announce when the first marathon runner had reached the outer boulevards of Athens. The winner was Greek Spiridione Louës, in 2 hours and 58 minutes.[73]

In fact, this was a busy day for all involved, because while these spectators enjoyed the marathon outside the stadium, more events such as high jump, hurdles and pole vaulting were held within it, yielding more victories for the United States. Holmes claimed that the Greek Prime Minister, M. Delyannis, turned, to the US Minister and asked 'Why did Columbus ever discover your unconquerable country?'[74]

Prizes for the winners in 1896 were not the gold medals introduced at later Olympic Games, but instead included:

> First, the diplomas contained in large plasterboard rolls, trimmed with gold paper; next, a silver medal, on which is stamped a splendid head of Zeus, and the classic outlines of the Acroplis and of the Panthenon; last and most important, the priceless branch of olive from the sacred groves of far-away Olympia, a prize purposely valueless that it may thereby be invaluable. These are the official prizes, but they are not the only ones, nor even the first, for during the preceding days the people had made their spontaneous offerings. One day a ragged bank-note, worth sixty cents, was thrust into Burke's hands; another day a set of postage-stamps was given him by a small boy, and never could our athletes enter

[69] Holmes (1908, p. 74).
[70] Holmes (1908, p. 74).
[71] 'Greece'. *Times*, 17 March 1896, p. 5; 'Latest Intelligence'. *Times*, 30 March 1896, p. 5; 'The Duke of Saxe-Coburg and Gotha left Charing-cross by the Ostend mail yesterday morning for Mayence." *Standard*, 2 April 1896, p. 5.
[72] Holmes (1908, p. 64).
[73] Holmes (1908, p. 67).
[74] Holmes (1908, pp. 65–66).

> a public cab or carriage without creating a good-natured turmoil among the passers-by, who each and every one claimed the right as Greeks and host to pay the driver of the triumphal chariot.[75]

The games were capped by a victory parade involving all the winners, headed by the marathon victor.[76] Finally, Holmes offers this perspective, reflecting that this had been 'a strictly modern odyssey'[77] but one couched in history. It was the symbolism, spectacle, and aesthetic that were the real winning features of the inaugural modern international Olympic Games:

> It must be confessed that the chief interest of the Olympian Games of 1896 lay in the splendid setting given them, rather than in the games themselves. From the standpoint of modern athletics the contests witnessed by the imposing audience were not remarkable .... No records were broken.[78]

The total cost of the 1896 is approximated as being more 1.5 million drachmas. Of this, the stadium cost 1 million, substantially more than Coubertin's original estimate and the committees revised figure of 600,000. Elsewhere, the shooting hall cost 300,000, velodrome 200,000, and a further 100,000 on miscellaneous other expenses. As well as Averoff's donation which paid for the stadium, a fund-raising campaign raised 300,000 drachmas, and receipts from postage stamps were 400,000. However, the municipality of Athens covered the costs of illuminating and cleaning up the city as well as some of the costs of entertaining the civil list. The case for doing so, the president of the IOC, Greek businessman Demetrius Vikelas, identified three main benefits: Firstly the stimulus to the development of athletic sports in the 'new' Greece; Secondly, the incentive for the development of tourism particularly integration with other European countries with associated financial and moral benefits, and; the contact between the Crown Prince and the people, which had proven his hard work, honesty and decisiveness to them (Llewellyn Smith, 2004).

The British consular service reported on the economic impact of the games with interest, remarking that it was hoped the games would bring an influx of gold to Greece – but, because the visitors to the games chiefly came from Greece and Turkey, and those foreigners that attended 'were not of the wealthy class', an actual fall in the exchange rate of Drachma against gold had happened. Profits were noted to have accumulated to the travel industry including cabmen in Athens, and there was an expectation that if future games were held in Greece they would benefit the country as a tourist destination, perhaps taking interest away from other destinations such as Egypt, Italy, and Switzerland.[79] More questionable was the concept

[75]Holmes (1908, pp. 81–82).
[76]Holmes (1908, p. 82).
[77]Holmes (1908, p. 9)
[78]Holmes (1908, p. 56).
[79]House of Commons Parliamentary Papers, Foreign Office 1897. Annual Series. No. 1782. Diplomatic and Consular Reports on Trade and Finance. Greece, pp. 5–6.

that the Olympiad was useful for the peace movement – there were claims that Greek patriots used the games as cover for planning the 1897–1898 Cretan Revolt.[80]

It is important to understand that in 1896 the IOC and its Olympic Games were still in a form we might today consider prototype. The mission, the will, and the basic structures were there, and a games project was successfully delivered. But a cohesive identity and agreement as to the format and pattern of delivery for the games was not yet settled among members. MacAloon (2006g, p. 590) identifies how the official report notes the presence of 'members of the various commissions' in the reception party. IOC members were being treated as heads of their national delegations or else as technical officials, little more'. Apart from in the marathon race, the sports were not particularly sensational, and no world records were broken. Coubertin claims 'the only great innovation for the time' was that different sports and their administrators cooperated.[81] Furthermore, in Greece it was hoped or perhaps even expected that they might provide a permanent home for the games (MacAloon, 2006g). The Greek Royals especially had hoped that Athens might become their permanent home, but Coubertin deliberately resisted this because he wanted to ensure their international character.[82] The Greek King attempted to use the official banquet to upstage Coubertin and claim that future games would be held in Athens. Coubertin navigated this by pretending not to understand what was going on and then on the last day of the games sending the King an official letter stating that the next games would be in Paris in 1900! While Coubertin standing up to the King was somewhat controversial the Crown Prince of Greece also understood the necessity of moving the games on to a new venue, and the episode blew over without further drama.[83] This was an early challenge to his scheme, from Royalty and indicates that already the games were being seen as an opportunity to stimulate economic and cultural activity, legitimation and for propaganda.

Coubertin proposed to Crown Prince Constantine a series of intercalated competitions within the series of official Olympiads, meaning that the first could be held in 1898, halfway between the Athens 1896 and Paris 1890 Olympiads (MacAloon, 2006g), although opinions varied:

> The London Times too (16 April 1896) made it very clear that the issue was not at all settled, that the idea of intervening Panhellenic festivals was favoured only by the 'members of the International Congress now in Athens', and that without the title 'Olympic Games' and inclusion in the Olympic series, the Athenaea would 'degenerate into a purely local celebration'. Instead the Times proposed making the Olympics fully biennial, with every other celebration in Athens. (MacAloon, 2006g, p. 627)

Ultimately, these-called *intercalated* or *interim games* would be held just once, in Athens in 1906, more of which later (Chapter 9). Despite the formative nature

[80]de Coubertin (1979, p. 24).
[81]de Coubertin (1979, p. 25).
[82]de Coubertin (1979, p. 24).
[83]de Coubertin (1979, p. 25).

of the movement at this time, Coubertin had made his mark, establishing the IOC, catalysing several NOCs, and hosting popular and relatively successful games. He was not shy to write his own place in history; claiming in his essay introducing Part Two of the Official Report of the 1896 Games 'As for myself I hereby assert once more my claims for being sole author of the whole project'. Coubertin of course deserves a lot of credit for establishing an international Olympic movement and these games; however, this singular 'great man' theory is something of a bumptious over-simplification. According to Polley (2011, p. 78), the story of the modern Olympic Games tends to focus on the amateur movement and the alignment of physical recreation with education, the idea of muscular Christianity that Coubertin was enthralled by but had perhaps also misinterpreted or at least over (or even mis-) attributed to the success of British empire. It is only in fairly recent times that the role of Wenlock (and previous British Olympic festivals) and of the Greek revivals have garnered much attention in the Olympic story, something we have tried hard to incorporate into our own narrative of British Olympic history, drawing from literature and from contemporary sources. As such, we follow Polley (2011) in reminding our reader that 1896 was not a 'year zero' marking the end of other 'Olympic' festivals, in the same way that the IOC protects its intellectual property today. Wenlock and others continued, and of particular interest at this point are the Morpeth Olympics, on the basis they are a distinct outlier, completely unrelated to the trajectory of Coubertin's Olympics, but show how the word 'Olympic' still had universal meaning for a multi-sport festival and that it was not always synonymous with the amateur ideal.

Morpeth: A Professional Logic

The Great Games of Morpeth, which in 1882 would begin to use the word 'Olympic' (this was, after all, the fashion following the recent excavations) were a mostly annual event in the mining community of Morpeth, Northumberland in the Northeast of England. It predated the IOC and ran for 88 years between 1870 and 1958 and was bold in its announcement of prize money and attempts to attract professionals. Polley (2011, p. 78) has found 'no links with the National Olympic Association nor with the ancient Olympics', this was a regional and commercial venture:

> Morpeth's Games were run predominantly by local business interests for the benefit of the town, and were largely aimed at working men and working class sportsmen. A decade before the formation of an International Olympic Committee, the Morpeth promoters adopted the title 'Olympic; purely because it added value and status to their endeavours. And because they could. (Polley, 2011, p. 78)

Although Polley (2011, p.11) claims the Morpeth Olympics have been excluded from the official Olympic story because they 'did not conform to the received, purist version of Olympic history' it is possible that his previous observation is actually more accurate, that these were a regional event in a distant corner of England with no attempts to align with existing Olympic movements such as those of Dr Brookes (which in turn fed into Coubertin's mission), nor to deliver social value in the form of education, world peace, nor did they seek to continue or to revive tradition. Rather, the word 'Olympic' was a flag of convenience or piece of branding attached to a money-making venture 'in which gambling played a central role' (Polley, 2011, p. 79) and the games really fit into the tradition of pedestrianism popular in the north-east (Chapter 3). Morpeth, then, as now, was not a major hub in the way that London, Athens, or Paris was, and in 1870 was a much more modest community than its nearest neighbouring cities of Newcastle Upon-Tyne, Durham, and Sunderland (then a town) but was typical of the new industrial towns of the North of England. Morpeth then had 5,000 inhabitants, mainly employed in over 50 collieries, quarries and brickworks, and was served by two railway lines, including the main 'East Coast' route from London to Scotland.

The event does seem to have become something of a big draw, and by using the word 'Olympic' Polley (2011) speculates the promoters were not just jumping on the Olympia bandwagon but signalling that this was to be a major sporting fixture. He reports that The Morpeth Sports Committee invested a large sum of money in 1887 to level the running track, and by 1895 the total attendance was estimated at 15,000, around three times the size of the town's population. As Athens was preparing for the first modern Olympics, in 1896 the Morpeth Sports Committee self-funded a move to a bigger and better site with a dedicated grandstand, running track and wrestling ring.[84] The event reinforced its Olympian character by making classical allusions – for instance, that year spectators were promised 'a display of the five different ways in which the Greeks and Romans of old wrestled', but these bouts would be put on by two professional wrestlers who had given demonstrations in music halls.[85] Thus there was not just what the AAA and their allies would consider professional sport, but also a crossover into the area of what might now be considered sports entertainment. The promoters also advertised that the sports would take place on the appointed day regardless of the weather conditions.[86]

Morpeth was clearly parallel, rather than formative, to the lineage of Coubertin's Olympic Games, an interesting aside or novelty to the way in which the Olympic movement evolved. However, we must realise that to the Northumberland community at that time, the Morpeth Olympics may have been the only modern Olympic Games that they were aware of, or at least that they had a realistic chance of being able to spectate or participate in. At the very least, Morpeth is worthy of our consideration because of its unashamed commerciality and appeal to professionalism, at a time when the Coubertin, and much of the sporting establishment which supported it, at least those in Britain, were concerned with promoting and purifying amateurism. This perhaps shows a class divide, it certainly suggests that the sporting social elites were interested in preserving social order

[84]'Morpeth Olympic Games'. *Morpeth Herald*, 15 August 1896, p. 6. Ordinance Survey, Northumberland Sheet LXIV. SW, Revised 1896, published 1898. NL Smaps Retrieved November 18, 2024, https://maps.nls.uk/view/101027196#zoom=4.2&lat=2367&lon=1940&layers=BT

[85]'Our Own Column'. *Morpeth Herald*, 10 August 1895, p. 3.

[86]'Our Own Column'. *Morpeth Herald*, 10 August 1895, p. 3.

through 'their' sport, and that the IOCs legitimacy was earned from being compatible with the contemporary social order and institutions.

Polley (2011, p. 82) found that prize money at Morpeth for one wrestling contest was over £5, over a month's wages for a working man at that time. Additionally, a special gold medal was awarded to a contestant who allegedly beat the professional pole leaping record of 11′2″, which Polley compares to Athens where only amateurs competed and the gold medal was won with a leap of approximately 10′10″. Whereas Pierre de Coubertin in 1896 described professionalism as a 'threatening evil' requiring eradication, the organisers of Morpeth made great play of the fact that their total pot of £180 was 'The Largest Sum for One Afternoon in England' (Polley, 2011, p. 81).

The amateur/professional divide was also apparent in the Rugby code of football, when in 1895, Rugby League was established in Northern England as a response to rules prohibiting payment to players. There would now be two codes, Rugby Union which was the established and continuing amateur game, and Rugby League, in which professionals were allowed. Following its commercial logic, Rugby League's rules gradually changed to produce a faster spectacle for paying fans (Baker, 1995). The rise of professionalism through most sports, and the different ways in which it was treated and distinguished from amateurism around the world would be a recurring theme throughout the remainder of the 19th century, and for most of the 20th century as well.

Second Olympic Congress: Enter Laffan

In 1897, the IOC held its second congress in Le Havre, France. The agenda for this meeting was on the topic of Hygiene, Education, and History relating to Physical Education and reflected 'Coubertin's desire for sport to be considered equal in value to academic exercise' (IOC, 2021b). The congress allowed itself an open programme to discuss the issues shown in Table 2.

The delegates seem to have focussed on the educational and hygiene elements of the programme, and Coubertin would reflect that sport 'was hardly touched on at all'.[87] This seems to mean that the practical issue of continuing the series of Olympic Games was not prioritised. Attending the session, representing the Headmasters Conference, was the Rev. Robert Stuart Courcy de Laffan (Anthony, 1997, p. 20).[88] Laffan, the Principal of Cheltenham College, arrived late to Le Havre, and apparently not as an Olympic evangelist, but he seems to have left as one. Bailey (1997, pp. 51–52)

[87]de Coubertin (1979, p. 28).

[88]According to Bailey (1997, pp. 58–59) at some point upon finishing university, Robert raised the de Courcy name from being one of his middle names to the status of a surname, to become Robert *de Courcy Laffan*. Although as Headmaster of Cheltenham he was simply Reverend Laffan, in the IOC he was Reverend de Courcy Laffan. This change insinuated an elevated status, perhaps a false nobility to enable a closer association with the founder of the modern Olympic Movement, Pierre de Coubertin. For a detailed discussion and appraisal of Laffan's life and career before and during his involvement with the Olympic movement please see Bailey (1997).

Table 2. The Le Havre Congress Programme.

Education	The psychology of physical exercise: characteristics of each type.
	The distinction between free games and compulsory exercise; advantages and disadvantages of each.
	The moral effect of physical exercise on children, adolescents; influence of effort on the formation of character and the development of personality.
	The organisation of physical training in lycées and colleges; can the pupils organise and run this themselves, and how? Consequences of leaving pupils free to do as they choose.
	The role of authority
Hygiene	The physiology of physical training; rules peculiar to each form of exercise.
	Teaching hygiene in lycées and colleges; programme of such teaching.
	Clothing.
	Hydrotherapy considered as a complement to physical exercise; under what form it should be used
Sport	The question of cash prizes and the definition of an amateur
	The organisation of international competitions; frequency and general conditions.
	The creation of a universal Olympic Union and a 'Universal Olympic Bulletin'.
	The revival and development of physical training during the 19th century; history of this movement in different countries throughout the world

Source: de Coubertin (1978, p. 28).

states that Laffan was presented with a chance opportunity to speak ('in Coubertin's opinion a sort of vacuum had developed in the proceedings, and he considered that the gathering might benefit from hearing the sound of an English voice') but he made a great impression upon Baron Pierre de Coubertin, who was 'convinced that a new collaborator of the most invaluable quality had come down from the heavens to help us' (p. 51). Coubertin gives the impression that Laffan's arrival was a divine or mystical intervention meant to help movement at a challenging time.

Laffan delivered his message confidently and in fluent French, describing his theory of the moral use of the sporting. His ideas were consistent with those of the previous speaker and French youth sport organiser Father Didon but delivered in such a way as to be more inspiring.[89] Following the muscular Christian

[89]de Coubertin (1979, pp. 28–29).

ideal, he made clear the broader value of sport, that through physical exercise a person could know themself better, which in turn would lead to the Brotherhood of Man. This was an overtly philanthropic aim which perhaps reflected his representation of schools rather than sport governing bodies, but a universal message which may have resonated with all and with their memberships. We may also consider that Coubertin might have placed emphasis on Laffan's background and status. Membership of The Headmasters' Conference was strictly by invitation, and institutions could only call themselves Public Schools if their Headmaster was a member. As such, Laffan was the ambassador of the system of education of which Coubertin was so in awe. Laffan was thus inducted into the Olympic movement, he proposed a toast to France at the closing banquet and was co-opted into the IOC before he had departed Le Havre (Bailey, 1997).[90] In 30 years Laffan would miss only two meetings of the IOC, and following the institution's first visit to London in 1904, was central to the founding of the British Olympic Association in 1905 (Bailey, 1997), and we shall explain later in this book (Chapter 8).

Chapter Summary

The first Olympic Games, held in 1896, show that since the very first edition the event had been subject to the motives of politics and diplomacy, was required to find ways to raise finance and to undertake construction projects to upgrade and build facilities, and was organised by nationally administered committees and sub-committees. Royal involvement from the top-down seems to have been a key ingredient to success, as was the attendance of the Greek King and Crown Prince at the Games and ceremonies. The Games of 1896 drew heavily on traditions and a heritage being rediscovered by the 'new' Greece and pomp, circumstance and ceremony was deliberately included in processions and ceremony at the stadium. The Olympic movement was also positioning itself as something of a global institution with its own anthem composed and performed. This led to a conceptual clash – this essentially progressive and modernising project had borrowed from antiquity to legitimate itself, but led to confusion that the project, with the emerging modern rather than classical sports, was somehow not authentic enough. The choice of Athens while symbolically important probably increased this confusion. The economic circumstances of the time and geographic and cultural context were remarkable to the American Burton Holmes who documented his experience, with some aspects seeming shambolic but others spectacular. The United States emerged as a dominant force, with a large and well resourced, well trained 'team' of athletes sent almost as a national representative team at a time when the concept of national teams did not really exist, and contrasts starkly with the British contingent, where awareness of the games had been minimal.

[90]Probably unknown to de Coubertin was a connection between Thomas Arnold, Robert Laffan and George Robertson, speaker of the Greek Ode at the 1896 Olympic Games – they had all been educated at Winchester College in England (Bailey, 1997, p. 54).

Nevertheless, British athletes performed well, winning prizes in some events, most notably in tennis and in weightlifting. The Olympics were really an amateur affair, and in Britain, strict definitions between amateurism and professionalism existed. A version of Olympic Games not endorsed by the IOC already existed in Morpeth, North East England, which was open to professional athletes. In some events, the recorded athletic performance at Morpeth seems to have been better, which suggests that although the IOCs version Olympianism had the support of the establishment and a type of moral purity, it was not the peak of sporting ability. Demand existed, at least regionally, if not among royalty, gentry, or in the pages of *The Times* or *The Telegraph*, for cash-prize sport open to working people.

Chapter 6

Olympic or Not? Paris 1900

Abstract

It was agreed at the foundational congress of the International Olympic Committee (IOC) that Paris should host the second games in 1900, but Coubertin would find his ambitions for a games focussed on the French capital somewhat frustrated. The games were held as part of the *Exposition Universelle Internationale de 1900* which itself dominated the agenda, symbolising the technological and economic achievements of *fin-de-siecle* Europe. We discuss the exhibition as well as Coubertin's attempts to get sporting events included into it, and while these events happened, they were not considered formally Olympic at the time, being only recognised retrospectively. The events were considered important enough however to merit international competition, and the British Amateur Athletic Association (AAA) provided expenses for an athletics team to attend. We narrate the British participation in the events, including the famous cricket match which was the only time cricket appeared in the Olympic Games prior to 2028.

Keywords: Paris 1900; *Exposition Universelle Internationale de 1900*; de Coubertin; tecnhovation; sport history

Introduction

Following the first games, it must have been important for momentum to deliver the second planned Olympiad with, as a minimum, the same prestige and public profile as those in Athens, 1896. The concept had been proven to work in Athens and next Coubertin had promised to bring his concept to his own country, in the city from where he administered the IOC. The Paris Games of 1900 actually took place as part of a World Fair, *Exposition Universelle Internationale de 1900*, between 20 May and 28 October and were 'hardly noticed by visitors' (Baker, 2008, p. 3). In fact, the IOC's official website admits 'The organisers spread the

Foundations of Managing British Olympics: Institutions through Time, 91–126

doi:10.1108/978-1-80262-095-520251006

competitions over five months and under-promoted their Olympic status to such an extent that many athletes never knew they had actually participated in the Olympic Games' (IOC, 2023a). Kent (2008, p. 28) is even more scathing, claiming it 'was relegated to the status of a sideshow'. The athletic events took place in what was little more than a field. There was no cinder running track and no jumping pits. The area was so cramped that a powerful heave of the hammer or javelin would send it right out if the field. In his own memoir, Coubertin vents frustration at the way the games became subservient to the exposition.[1] Regardless of the event's apparent low profile the organisers did consider the Paris games to be a grand undertaking – the official report they produced ran to almost 800 pages, detailing the organisation and results. The production of such an extensive report[2] suggests the organisers felt the need to record the event for posterity and to list the statistics of the games in a way consistent with the other reports produced for the cultural, industrial and agricultural aspects of the Exhibition.[3] It is reasonable to play down the importance of 1900 as an official Olympiad, despite the IOC's modern day claim to it, but we must remember that there had been intent to hold an Olympic Games in Paris during 1900 since the conception of the IOC in 1894. In fact, this had been announced just before the intent to hold the Games in Athens in 1896 (Chapter 5). Coubertin's credited involvement in the successful organisation of (at the very least) the athletics section, a second International Games coinciding with the planned four-year cycle, must have helped the movement to keep going; for example, Norway formed its own National Olympic Committee in 1900 (Chappalet, 2018). A secondary literature or historiography exists to narrate the Exposition and the Official Report of the Games and of the Foreign Office, as well as British (mostly English) newspapers of the time inform us as to how the games were organised, experienced and reported. Again, we were also able to draw upon the writings of US Travelogue writer Burton Holmes, who wrote vividly of the experience of attending the Exposition, if not of the athletic events. We therefore piece together our findings from these various sources to create a narrative from the perspective of Britain but also how the 1900 Games sits in the lineage of Olympic history.

The Second Olympiad: The World Fair Exposition of Paris, 1900

The *Exposition Universelle Internationale de 1900* is remembered in Great Britain more commonly by titles such as the *1900 Paris Exposition*, *Paris Exposition,* or

[1]de Coubertin, 1979, pp. 31–37.

[2]Mérillon. (1901). *Concours Internationaux D'Exercices Physiques et de Sports, Exposition Universalle internationale de 1900 à Paris*. Imprimerie Nationale.

[3]This was reported and catalogued across eight volumes, see for example, the *Liste des récompenses: Exposition universelle de 1900, à Paris/République française, Ministère du commerce, de l'industrie, des postes et des télégraphes*. https://gallica.bnf.fr/ark:/12148/bpt6k9765409t/f1.item.r=diplomes

simply referred to in context as *The World Fair* and we use these (or variations) within this chapter. It is important to know that this was not the first time that Paris had held such an event; the city had also held World's Fairs in 1878 and 1889, and for the 1900 Exposition, the Eiffel Tower (which had been built as the main entrance of the 1889 edition) was repainted, fitted with electric lamps and modified for access, as a central attraction (Vogel, 1961):

> As a tribute to technology and progress, the Paris Exposition was like nothing that had come before it. Visitors marveled at moving sidewalks, wireless telegraphy, the most powerful telescope ever built, and the first escalator ever seen. American innovation and boosterism was evident everywhere. (PBS.org, n.d.)

The proposal for an international or 'universal' exhibition for Paris in 1900 was approved by a Cabinet Council of the French Government at the beginning of July 1892, and immediately reported by British newspapers.[4] The announcement was not without controversy; relations between France and Germany were still tense after the Franco-Prussian war 20 years earlier. France had organised such exhibitions at regular intervals for years, and, following the cycle of events, the next would fall in 1900. The Paris Exposition of 1889 had though stimulated Germany to organise its own event, which it also intended to hold during 1900, in Berlin.[5]

It is a matter of opinion as to whether Germany was rude in its opportunism and 'ought, in common politeness to have inquired … before seizing upon the year'[6] or whether France was stubborn in its subsequent adherence to the cycle. The announcement by the French was though described in *The Telegraph* as 'a new proof of the inveterate hostility of the French people against Germany' and that 'France troubles herself very little about peaceful relations with her neighbours, and is always ready to make any sacrifice for the satisfaction of national pride and national rancour'.[7] Three years later, an English local newspaper suggested the French were growing tired of World's Fairs and that the project was arranged in response to Germany's plan. [8]

The First Great Berlin Industrial Exhibition, was in the end held earlier, in 1896, coincidently the year of the first modern Olympic Games, hosted by Athens in Greece. Although industrial and artistic exhibitions had been held in Berlin since earlier dates, the emphasis in 1896 was to showcase German industry and the importance of Germany and its capital city globally.[9] It was reported in at least

[4]*Daily Telegraph*, 'Paris Day by Day', 1 July 1892; *The Sunday Times*, 'International Exhibition in Paris', 3 July 1892.
[5]*Daily Telegraph*, 'Paris Day by Day', 1 July 1892.
[6]*Daily Telegraph*, 'Paris Day by Day', 1 July 1892.
[7]*Daily Telegraph*, 'Exhibitions in 1900', 5 July 1892.
[8]*Nottingham Evening Post*, Monday 16 September 1895.
[9]https://blackcentraleurope.com/sources/1850-1914/the-first-german-colonial-exhibition-1896/ [accessed 2nd May 2025].

one English newspaper just 13 months before it opened, that upon hearing of Paris 1900, the German organisers had narrowed their scope to just German (and/or sold in Germany) engineering and crafts.[10] However, as we have shown, the controversy over the rival expositions planned for 1900 had existed since 1892 so this was not news. Furthermore, the Berlin Exhibition incorporated The First German Colonial Exhibition, featuring displays of colonial medicine, goods such as ivory and cocoa, recreated administrative buildings and villages populated by 'over 100 individuals from Germany's overseas empire'.[11]

In any case, France seems to have moved quickly to begin its own preparations, it was certainly rumoured that within two years there were said to be one hundred clerks already working on the project.[12] The rumours as to what marvels and attractions might be included seem to have begun entering the local British newspapers in 1894 and 1895; It was speculated there would be a great bridge incorporating theatres and houses constructed over the River Seine,[13] a 'reverse Eiffel Tower' in the form of a 3,000 foot deep hole with underground elevators and a restaurant,[14] a copy of the great Bazaar of Constantinople, and an exact repro of the Alhambra (one of the most famous monuments of Islamic architecture, located in Spain).[15]

An exhibition of the different plans and projects for Paris 1900 ended in February 1895, and the premiums to the successful architects distributed. The decision to host the event within Paris, and close to the Champe da Mars, presented restrictions on space. The 1889 Exhibition had covered around 66 acres, but for 1900 the organisers had expanded the ambition to 99 acres. There could also be potential difficulties of interference with the city's substantial traffic-flow. On the basis Paris was already 'pretty well stocked with dainty remains of the different exhibitions that have been held in the capital since the days of the Third Napoleon', the architects were therefore 'at liberty to pull down any of the existing construction and even to demolish the Eiffel Tower, it they considered it necessary for the general embellishment of their plans and for this Exhibition' so that

---

[10]*Leeds Mercury*, Monday 22 April 1895.

[11]https://blackcentraleurope.com/sources/1850-1914/the-first-german-colonial-exhibition-1896/ [accessed 9th May 2025].

[12]*Cornishman*, Thursday 29 March 1894.

[13]*Cornishman*, Thursday 11 October 1894. The Pont Alexandre III Bridge was built between 1896 and 1900, named after the Tsar of Russia at the time of the construction. Made from a steel base with steel arches and supports, it was decorated with stone pillars, gold-plated bronze statues, and cast-iron lamps, although the theatres and houses do not appear to have been built on it. https://study.com/learn/lesson/pont-alexandre-iii-bridge-facts-history.html#:~:text=The%20Pont%20Alexandre%20III%20is%20a%20bridge%20crossing%20over%20the,river%20in%20a%20single%20span [accessed 2nd May 2025].

[14]*Hull Daily Mail*, Monday 14 January 1895; *The Essex Standard*, which referred to 'the inverted Eiffel', Saturday 9 March 1895; *The Belfast & Newry Standard*, Friday 15 March 1895; *Dover Express*, Friday 15 March 1895.

[15]*Evening Telegraph* (Dundee, Scotland), Thursday 2 May 1895.

Paris 1900 would 'be the essence of the toughest expression of French modern architectural genius applied to exhibitions'.[16]

Much of the preliminary work for 1900 was by 1895 completed, and the work of building the exhibition was planned to commence three and a half years before the opening date, meaning an interim period of 18 months in which to draw-up the final plans and designs of all the gardens and buildings. It was though already decided that any buildings constructed for 1900 would be 'pulled down rapidly, and done away with' once the Exhibition had run its course, The Commissioner-General having:

> resolved that no architect, however beautiful his designs may be, shall be allowed to construct any but extremely light buildings, so that when all is over, nobody will be tempted to clamour for the preservation of all or any of them.[17]

In this sense the organisers of Paris 1900 were following the approach of the The World's Columbian Exposition, also known as the Chicago World's Fair, held two years earlier, which featured nearly 200 new but temporary buildings inspired by neo-classical architecture in their shape and form, and facades painted white, for which it was nicknamed 'The White City' (Britannica, n.d.). Notably, this first Chicago White City would inspire a later amusement park by the same name also in Chicago but opened in 1905 (Chicago Tribune, 2021).

Paris 1900 also promised to avoid anomalies of the past, with better alliance and affinity between industrial exhibits, to articulate a separation of products developed since the 1889 Exhibition, but given the significance of the date 1900 also 'a philosophical and synthetical review' of the 19th century.[18] Regarding current affairs, it was hoped that Europe would be free from Plague by the time of the Paris Exposition[19] and geo-politically there was speculation as to whether or not the German Emperor would attend Paris, the Franco-Prussian War of 1870–1871 still being in living memory of those who had fought and of those who had lost friends and relatives.[20] Germany eventually confirmed its intention to participate in the Exhibition in 1896,[21] the same year that Great Britain announced the appointment if Mr Austin, Secretary of Legation at, the British Embassy, as representative of Her Majesty's Government for the Paris Exhibition of 1900.[22]

---

[16] *The Sunday Times*, M. Alfred Picard, Commissioner-General of the Paris Exhibition of 1900, Sunday 17 February 1895.
[17] *The Sunday Times*, M. Alfred Picard, Commissioner-General of the Paris Exhibition of 1900, Sunday 17 February 1895.
[18] *The Sunday Times*, M. Alfred Picard, Commissioner-General of the Paris Exhibition of 1900, Sunday 17 February 1895.
[19] *Evening Telegraph* (Dundee, Scotland), 6 April 1894.
[20] *The Daily Telegraph*, 'Paris Day by Day', Tuesday 16 October 1894.
[21] *The Daily Telegraph*, 'Paris Day by Day', Wednesday, 8 July 1896.
[22] *The Daily Telegraph*, Friday 11 September 1896.

The German Government proposed to grant 5,000.000 marks, or £250,000, towards the cost of the German exhibit.[23]

Column space of some British newspapers, including *The Daily Mail*, *The Telegraph*, and *The Times* were dedicated to light-heartedly speculating or reporting rumour and plans for imaginative and novel exhibits ('Some of these marvels may he matter of fact, and some may be the vivid offspring of our neighbours' imagination'[24]) particularly bigger, faster, better feats of engineering and science. For example, a 200-feet-long telescope would allow a virtual 'trip to the moon' with an image so clear that it could show 'if there are any big cities, or even a brigade of soldiers marching about' on its surface.[25] Still on a planetary theme, a French geographer proposed a facsimile of the earth 'one hundred-thousandth part of the actual size', but in practical terms, depending on which newspaper reported it, as large as either 418 feet in diameter[26] or 300 feet in circumference.[27]

The Eiffel Tower was central to many proposals, variously; to build a glass underwater restaurant; for two mirrors, one at the top and the other at the bottom, so that people promenading could see a reflection of nearly the whole view; for a spiral railway to run up and down its length; that it could be used as a toboggan chute; that it be encased to resemble the Statue of Liberty at New York,[28] and; that The Eiffel Tower and the Trocadero might be linked by cable bridge from which passengers could travel between the two by suspended cane-bottomed chair.[29] Moving people in mid-air was a popular theme; chosen by the Exhibitions directors from 500 submitted ideas was the idea for a giant telescopic tower seating 20 people would extend to 200 feet, swing and bend, and land its passengers on the other side of the grounds (in contrast, a rejected idea was it was for a 'Temple of Literature', built from bricks 'composed, of the compressed pulp of rejected literary contributions').[30] A year later there was a plan to bring from the Centennial Exhibition in Tennessee, USA, the gigantic see-saw as 'formidable rival' to the Ferris Wheel. The structure held a car at each end of a beam, each holding 25 people, which it lifted up and down, alternatively, up to 150 feet.[31]

The idea for a reverse Eiffel Tower was still mooted, to be connected to other attractions by miniature railway.[32] A structure built from chocolate bricks cemented by nougat and incorporating other sweet products from Parisian confectioners

[23] *The Daily Telegraph*, 'Imperial Parliament', Tuesday 23 March 1897.
[24] *The Daily Mail*, 'Marvels in 1900', Wednesday 2 September 1896.
[25] *The Daily Mail*, 'The Moon Six Miles off', Friday 22 May 1896; *The Daily Mail*, 'Marvels in 1900', Wednesday 2 September 1896.
[26] *The Daily Mail*, 'Round the Earth before Breakfast, Saturday 6 June 1896.
[27] *The Daily Mail*, 'Marvels in 1900', Wednesday 2 September 1896.
[28] *The Sunday Times*, 'The Paris Exhibition of 1900', Sunday 8 August 1897.
[29] *The Daily Mail*, 'Marvels in 1900', Wednesday 2 September 1896.
[30] *The Daily Mail*, 'Marvels in 1900', Wednesday 2 September 1896.
[31] *The Daily Mail*, 'A Giant See-saw', Friday 14 May 1897; *The Daily Telegraph*, 'It is according to legend more than a thousand years', Tuesday 10 August 1897.
[32] *The Daily Mail*, 'Marvels in 1900', Wednesday 2 September 1896.

would also be displayed.[33] There would be castle ramparts and structures to demonstrate progress in the 'arts of war' as well as restaurants serving cuisine from around the world[34] and a restaurant in a rotating tower offering panoramic views of the city with a one-hour rotation time.[35] Similarly, but even more novel, was the suggestion for an enormous vertical screw with a massive revolving nut filled up as a cafe and restaurant continuously travelling up and down.[36]

Later, and in response to a call from the exhibition's promoters for 'an attraction of an extraordinary nature'[37] there were suggestions for yet more curious projects: To erect a memorial temple of present century progress with representations of the eight great nations of Europe, a model town of the future, for example, the year 2000; a miniature hygienic city based on the 'most advanced and perfect hygienic principles, and inhabited by people living in strict accordance with the laws of hygiene'; a house 600 feet high to show how tall a habitable building could be made without danger; a street guarded from end to end by soldiers clad in different historic French uniforms; a wooden reproduction of the horse of Troy capable of holding a thousand people in its internal compartments and a rostrum on its back for a classics Professor to give recitals, and; a huge beauty fair including ladies from every country in the world.[38]

As whimsical as all of this was, it shows the impulse to showcase 19th-century innovation in technology, medicine, culture, and industry through the prism of commercialised public entertainment at the expositions, in a way that today might be termed *technotainment*. In 1896, the reported projected cost of the Exhibition, in British currency, was £1million but that up to £2.5 million would be recouped in gate money alone.[39]

In February 1898, around two years before the Exhibition was due to open, the Royal Commission established for the British involvement with the exhibition held its first meeting at Marlborough House, presided by the Prince of Wales. In his speech, the Prince highlighted the Great Britain had been granted a larger display areas than at any previous exposition and that recognising it would likely have significant influence on British industry and art, necessitated 'the appointment of a Royal Commission larger in numbers and more comprehensive in character than any previous Commission appointed for a similar purpose'. Specific aspects of organising were then identified which would each require individual committees.

---

33 *The Daily Mail*, 'Marvels in 1900', Wednesday 2 September 1896.

34 *The Daily Mail*, 'Marvels in 1900', Wednesday 2 September 1896.

35 *The Daily Mail*, 'Huge Revolving Tower', Wednesday 18 November 1896.

36 *The Sunday Times*, 'The Paris Exhibition of 1900', Sunday 8 August 1897; *The Daily Telegraph*, 'It is according to legend more than a thousand years', Tuesday 10 August 1897.

37 *The Daily Telegraph*, 'It is according to legend more than a thousand years', Tuesday 10 August 1897.

38 *The Sunday Times*, 'The Paris Exhibition of 1900', Sunday 8 August 1897; *The Daily Telegraph*, 'It is according to legend more than a thousand years', Tuesday 10 August 1897.

39 *The Daily Mail*, 'Marvels in 1900', Wednesday 2 September 1896.

Two of these, for executive duties and for finance, would be presided by the Prince of Wales personally, while the other committees would correspond closely with the groups of the classification. A grant of money was placed at the Royal Commission's disposal, of which the Prince remarked 'I fear will prove insufficient. I trust that we may be able to prevail upon the Treasury to considerably augment the grant'.[40] The organisers of the British section thus announced that they would ask Parliament for a grant of £75,000 for its expenses. In contrast, the German Government had reportedly sanctioned a grant-in-aid of 5,000,000 marks/£250,000, the US Government made a Treasury estimate of $350,000, approximately £370,000[41] and smaller nations such as Switzerland had opted to provide from public funds towards its involvement.[42] During May, The Royal Commission moved into offices at St. Stephen's House, Victoria Embankment in Rooms 80–87[43] and the following month made available the classification and rules for exhibitors, together with forms of application for space.[44] The amount of £75,000 was granted and later increased to £125,000 after the Commission asked the Treasury for further funds. Of this, £5,000 was spent on decorating the exhibits, with money also spent on the Commissions overheads and on hiring land and on transporting exhibits to Paris.[45]

The Parisian organisers had, by the Autumn of 1898, divided the area for the Exposition, allocating of the 163,430 square feet of space available, the three most significant amounts of display space were allocated around two-thirds of the land available: machinery and electricity (60,000 square feet), manufactures (25,000 square feet), and agricultural and food products (20,000 square feet).[46] It is worth mentioning at this point that when the Exhibition operated the cumulative space allocated to British and British colonial exhibits, spread over the site by classification, was the largest than at any previous Parisian Exhibition Universalle (see Table 3). The colonial exhibits were however displayed in a separate portion of the exhibition for colonies and dependencies.[47]

Logistically, the movement of people wishing to attend Paris was projected to place much increased demand on railways connecting to the English South Coast from where ferries to France would depart. This was one reason cited behind the amalgamation of the South-Eastern and London, Chatham, and Dover

---

[40] *The Daily Telegraph*, 'The Commission for the Paris Exhibition', Friday 18 February 1898.

[41] *The Daily Telegraph*, 'Imperial Parliament', Tuesday 15 February 1898.

[42] *The Daily Telegraph*, 'The Commission for the Paris Exhibition', Friday 18 February 1898.

[43] *The Daily Telegraph*, 'The offices of the Royal Commission for the Paris Exhibition…', Tuesday 10 May 1898.

[44] *The Daily Telegraph*, Wednesday 15 June 1898.

[45] Royal Commission for the Paris International Exhibition 1900, Volume 1, 1901, HMSO.

[46] *The Times*, Monday 31 October 1898.

[47] Royal Commission for the Paris International Exhibition 1900, Volume 1, 1901, HMSO.

Table 3. Comparison of British Exhibition Space at Paris Exhibition Universalles.

Year	Size of Area (Square Feet)
1855	183,000
1867	280,604
1878	363,018 (plus marine and three other buildings not quantified)
1889	232,845
1900	417,807

Source: Royal Commission for the Paris International Exhibition 1900, Volume 1, 1901, HMSO.

Railway Companies[48] and would be 'good news for people holding investments in the English South Coast and cross-channel travel companies'.[49] Clearly, the Exposition of Paris 1900 was by now a high-profile international event and, as such, vulnerable to politics, protest, and public opinion, in much the same way as global mega-events are in the present. US feminists called for the boycotting of all French goods, and modesties agreed to stop importing Parisian fashions for two years, estimated to cost French shop-keepers $3 million and of potential permanence as once set-up, it would become cheaper to manufacture within the United States and save excise duty. Of relevance to the subject of the Exposition was that a petition began simultaneously to present to Congress asking it to refuse to appropriate the $750,000 proposed for the American exhibit.[50]

A more significant diplomatic problem was that of the Dreyfus affair, a political scandal that lasted from 1894 until resolved in 1906. Thus, it was a 'live' event during the preparations for the Paris Exposition with implications for would-be participants. A Jewish soldier enlisted in the French Army, Captain Dreyfus, was sentenced to a penal colony on the basis of alleged treason, for sharing military secrets with Germany. In 1896, however, new evidence indicated Dreyfus' innocence, which was dismissed. In 1899, Dreyfus was recalled for trial and further punishment but public opinion was divided, with those who supported him blaming his accusers of antisemitism. The issue of antisemitism caused controversy and for some British firms to withdraw from the Exposition. The *Daily Mail* under the headline 'Jew-Hatred in France' speculated an 'underlying motive for the Dreyfus uproar' as being due 'growing hatred of the Jews in France' stemming from the desire for religious preservation, dislike of the commercial success of Jewish capitalists (and this increasing power in society), and relatedly a dislike for capitalism. Finally, as Germany was the 'arch enemy' of France at this time, a German soldier with a Jewish name 'is accused of acting the spy in the French Army it is conceivable that the strongest prejudices of which the

[48] *The Daily Telegraph*, 'Railway Amalgamation', Thursday 30 June 1898.
[49] *The Sunday Times*, 'City Chatter' by A Cornhill Magpie, Sunday 1 January 1899.
[50] *The Daily Telegraph*, 'Fashions and the War', Monday 16 May 1898.

human mind is capable should be arrayed against him'.[51] Jewish merchants in the United States threatened to boycott French manufacturers, especially silks, unless Dreyfus be acquitted.[52] In Britain, a member of the Royal Commission, Alderman Stephens, of Newcastle, declared that 'owing to the dreadful miscarriage of justice, he would not set foot in Paris' and movements to boycott the Exhibition were afoot across Europe, the paper speculated as to the financial impact on the Exposition and wondered whether this constituted reason to delay it until 1901 when the matter might be resolved.[53] British firms mentioned as having intimated their intention to withdraw on the basis of injustice and/or perceived risk from disruption and public disorder include whisky distillers, asbestos manufacturers, transport, and many others from across many regions of England, Wales, and Scotland, demonstrating the scale of the concern.[54] The Dreyfus Affair, although significant, did not stop the Exposition nor cause the extent of diplomatic problems that had been feared. In March 1899, just over a year before the Exposition was due to open, the Prince of Wales informally visited the grounds and was shown the buildings, as well as meeting French President Loubet at the Elsyee.[55] The committees of the Royal Commission over which he presided were meeting in London throughout 1899.[56] By the following month advertisements for hotel accommodation 'specially constructed for the Exhibition year' appeared in *The Daily Telegraph*.[57]

1900 Arrives

In conjunction with the Commissary-General the Exhibition, the French Government announced the programme for the opening of the Great International Fair to be held on Saturday, 14 April 1900, which would involve the President a making speech and then with an entourage sail up the Seine by barge to visit the Pavilions built by some participating nations.[58]

A day earlier, *The Daily Telegraph* dedicated around 4800 words to a lengthy and detailed piece by its own correspondent to describe the scale of the event which had taken over a vast part of the city, reporting a ground surface of 1,080,000 square metres, including constructions extending over 400,000 square metres, compared with the last Universal Paris Exhibition which had covered

---

[51] *The Daily Mail*, 'Jew-Hatred in France' by A. Egmont Hake, Friday 28 January 1898.

[52] *The Daily Telegraph*, 'American Petition to the Kaiser', by Dalziel and Laffan, Friday 8 September 1899.

[53] *The Daily Telegraph*, 'Dreyfus Trial', Tuesday 12 September 1899.

[54] *The Daily Telegraph*, 'Paris Exhibition', Wednesday 13 September 1899.

[55] *Worcestershire Chronicle*, 'Here and There', Saturday 11 March 1899.

[56] *The Daily Telegraph*, 'London Day by Day', Friday 24 February 1899; *The Daily Telegraph*, 'London Day by Day', Wednesday 11 January 1899; *The Daily Telegraph*, 'London Day by Day', Tuesday 19 December 1899.

[57] *The Daily Telegraph*, Classified Advertising, Saturday 22 April 1899.

[58] *The Daily Telegraph*, 'Paris Exhibition', Monday 2 April 1900.

960,000 square metres of land, 290,000 of which were built over. In particular, the article described the various buildings and Palaces housing the exhibits including those representative different countries. The British exhibit deemed was described thus:

> Kingston House, representing Great Britain, is a smaller and, in a way, less ambitious achievement. But, being merely the faithful reproduction of a work not conceived for World's Fairs, it comes up to a higher standard of taste.[59]

The overall effect was a fantastic spectacle. Another article provided more description of buildings and was complimentary of the façade and of the overall effect during the President's barge visit on the Seine, albeit somewhat amused by the reality:

> The foreign pavilions looked as if they were ... enchanted palaces called into being by some mad fantastic magician of the Arabian Nights. It was all stucco plaster of Paris, rococo cardboard, tinselled rubbish and gaudy frippery, if you like, but it was fascinating to look upon. The combined effect as M. Loubet approached the International Quay was irresistible.[60]

Reports of the grand opening appeared in *The Telegraph* as soon as possible, on Monday, 16 April. The Exhibition, it proclaimed, 'was opened with a perfection of pageant and an optimism of eloquence both characteristically French' with speeches by various statesmen focussing on 'solidarity' and 'progress', summarising these pointed to a hope that World's Fairs such as this might 'banish the discord of nations and to realise the dreams of labour'.[61] France's President Loubet us quoted as having ended his speech as follows, which now seems very naïve, knowing how the first half of the 20th century actually developed:

> I am convinced that, owing to the persevering affirmation of certain generous thoughts with which the now-ending century has resounded, the twentieth century will witness the dawn of a little more fraternity, and of less misery, and that soon, perhaps, we shall have passed an important point in the slow evolution of toil towards happiness and of mankind towards humanity. It is under the auspices of this hope that I declare the Exhibition of 1900 open.[62]

---

[59] *The Daily Telegraph*, Paris Exhibition, Friday 13 April 1900.
[60] *The Daily Telegraph*, Opening of the Paris Exhibition, Monday 16 April 1900.
[61] *The Daily Telegraph*, 'Everything Conspired to Enhance the Grandiose Splenders…', Monday 16 April 1900.
[62] *The Daily Telegraph*, 'Opening of the Paris Exhibition', Monday 16 April 1900.

The Telegraph's correspondent was more sceptical or at least objective:

> The world will remain oppressed with problems whose solution will still be embarrassed by practical difficulties to as great an extent as before. Human nature will continue what it was when Thucydides noticed how little it seemed capable of change. World's Fairs increase the gaiety and even the instruction of nations, but they do not regenerate the earth. A sufficiently admirable ideal is achieved by the Exhibition in its own success, but it would be too much, we are afraid, to assert that these ingenious and attractive spectacles are a real factor in the political and moral progress of the world ... English effort, though our national indifference to abstract principles involves certain weaknesses of its own, has always been more deeply concerned with practical methods than with ideal maxims. The real value of the Exposition is in bringing all nations together as the guests of France, and in promoting-the purposes of peace for the halcyon season during which it is open.[63]

The exhibition was not completed on its opening day with many buildings unfinished and empty and horticulture not yet in place.[64] This surprised and disappointed some British visitors, of whom there were broadly two categories at the time of the opening weekend: Firstly, the officials and those on business connected in some way such as exhibitors, experts, mechanics, and other employees. Secondly were 'the usual throng of tourists who cross the silver streak for a few days' stay in the gay city at Easter' many of whom visited the Exhibition. Many of whom:

> expressed the intention of returning at Whitsuntide, by which time order will have been evolved out of semi-chaos .... Thus the ardour of the average British holiday-maker has not been damped by his initial visit to the Exhibition, and he will come back to repeat the experiment.

Regarding other British visitors, who might have been attracted solely by the Exposition, they 'may put in an appearance at a later date, but so far they are conspicuous by their absence'.[65]

The incomplete condition of the Paris Exhibition was blamed for low occupancy levels on the swift Atlantic liners scheduled to sail for Europe during the Spring, although agents hoped for record numbers of passengers in July and August. Whether or not the overall number of tourists were really lower was

---

[63] *The Daily Telegraph*, Everything Conspired to Enhance the Grandiose Splenders..., Monday 16 April 1900.
[64] *The Daily Telegraph*, Opening of the Paris Exhibition, Monday 16 April 1900.
[65] *The Daily Telegraph*, Paris Exhibition, Tuesday 17 April 1900.

a point of debate as larger ten-day boats had been introduced that may have accounted for the swifter ships' lower occupancy, with overall cross-channel carrying capacity having 'increased enormously' since the previous Paris Exhibition of 1889.[66]

By June, *Graphic* reported how much had been completed, the Great British building being the penultimate to be inaugurated, just before that of Mexico. Visitors could experience the moving sidewalk and electric train that were adjacent but ran in opposite directions and both were crowded with people, constantly. Comparatively, the train was quicker than the sidewalk at half the price and offered comfortable carriages and numerous stations. Aside from their *technotainment* novelty appeal, these modes provided an alternative to the Paris horse and carriage cabmen, who threatened strike action corresponding with the exhibition. A standout attraction was *The fêtes de nuit*: At 8o'clock a line of flame ran up the Eiffel Tower, which was instantly outlined by thousands of incandescent lamps, the powerful searchlight slowly revolving, illuminating the city. Simultaneously, the Châteaux d'Eau illuminated and water ejaculated from basins and fountains, buildings aside the Champ des Mars radiated with lines of gas jets, the Trocadero was outlined by thousands of coloured lamps, while large electric lamps on the Alexader III Bridge illuminated the river front. The article also stated The Palace of Electricity was also due to be illuminated by hundreds of thousands of coloured lights, but a fire that had destroyed a switch board 'containing 2400 electric wires' had prevented it from happening thus far.[67]

In addition to the articles cited above, which give some of the most detailed and vivid contemporary English-language accounts of the Exhibition, there is another fascinating source; travelogue writer Burton Holmes, who had previously reported on the first Olympic Games at Athens, was in Paris for the 1900 Exposition although his detailed account relates solely to the World's Fair and includes no description of the associated Olympic Games on this occasion. Nevertheless, it is worth summarising his experiences of the spectacle and operations of the event, to understand the context in which the games occurred, particularly as the early Olympic editions all tended to be adjoined to expositions.

Consistent to the *Daily Telegraph*, Holmes states Paris had not been ready on the opening day 14 April, a situation that remained until part way through June. Although the Palaces of arts were externally complete:

> the interiors were choked with unopened packing-cases and alive with working carpenters. During the first six weeks we scarcely ventured into a big building, and when we did make our rare incursions into Chaos, it was only to retire in confusion, and with torn clothes and dusty boots and hats white with plaster.[68]

---

[66]*The Daily Telegraph*, 'Transatlantic Traffic and The Paris Exhibition', Friday 25 May 1900.

[67]*Graphic*, 'Exhibition Jottings', Saturday 2 June 1900.

[68]Holmes, B. 1908, *Burton Holmes Travelogues: Round about Paris. Paris Exposition* (Vol. 2). McClure, p. 115.

However, Holmes' account demonstrates his keen awareness that the Exposition was a spectacular and symbolic event:

> We stand upon the threshold of the Age of Electricity – the Age of Light .... The Universal Exposition of Paris commemorates the close of the nineteenth century, the Age of Steam.[69]

Holmes, for the benefit of his core readership in the United States compares Paris 1900 to the Chicago Exposition of 1893. He mentions how the buildings at Chicago were in the form of a White City. While Paris is not described as a White City[70] the concept is significant as the same idea would be used eight years later at the Franco-British Exhibition in London. Some architecture, such as the columns of the porches, were inspired by ancient Greek Ionic, Corinthian and Doric design, and a plaster copy of the Greek sculpture the Venus de Milo was placed outside of the Temple of Arts.[71] Other buildings were of French design and decoration.[72]

These extravagant additions to the built environment came at a cost, and Holmes commented on this, reflecting that the cultural value in the form of artistic monuments (naming the Alexander Bridge and the permanent Art Palaces) outweighed the financial cost and four years of disruption during the construction process felt by the citizens of Paris.[73] Paris also benefitted from infrastructure improvements although these may have happened at some point regardless of the Exposition; as well as an Exposition terminal station[74] the Metropolitan 'underground electric road' was the 'only really rapid system of transport' in the city, and was opened in July 1900 which coincided with the Exposition. In this way Paris was catching up with London, England, where an underground train system had operated since 1893.[75] A Plate-Forme Mobile (or Trottoir Roulant) and Moving Sidewalk were amusing features for pedestrians.[76] Holmes' writing gives us insight as to the humour and human interaction of the times as well as a description of the architecture and technology, providing the following anecdote:

> Now the verb *rouler* means 'to roll', and when a punning Frenchman saw a group of English tourists plant themselves upon the rolling walk, he waved his hat and cried, '*Ah, bravo! – Roule Britannia!*' until Britannia's subjects had 'rouled' out of site.[77]

---

[69]Holmes, 1908, p. 336.
[70]Holmes, 1908, p. 115.
[71]Holmes, 1908, pp. 143–144.
[72]Holmes, 1908, p. 144.
[73]Holmes, 1908, p. 151.
[74]Holmes, 1908, p. 312.
[75]Holmes, 1908, p. 166.
[76]Holmes, 1908, p. 231.
[77]Holmes, 1908, p. 240.

The Exposition sought to reflect not only Greek and French architecture but showcased global culture.[78] The 'street of nations' comprised grand and ornamental buildings to represent different countries from every continent[79] and around the Exposition were indigenous people in costume.[80] Great Britain was represented by a replica 17th century manor Kingston House, decorated internally with paintings by Burne-Jones, Reynolds, Gainsborough and Turner.[81] Below the street, there was an international restaurant running along a lower terrace which provided visitors with:

> [...] a gastronomic tour around the world. We breakfast to the music of Hungarian gypsies; at five o'clock we take tea to the tinkling of Neapolitan guitars; we dine to the sound of the Serbian tambouritza or usually amid the clacking of Castillian castanets.[82]

The Paris skyline was marked by *The Big Wheel of Paris*, described by Holmes as 'a brother to the Ferris Wheel that once loomed over Chicago' that enabled visitors spectacular views of Paris.[83] The wheel was located behind specially constructed artificial alps, part of the Swiss exhibit.[84] The skyline was also punctuated by two additions from previous expositions; the Eiffel Tower which Holmes refers to as a 'symbol of modernity'[85] which we have already mentioned as having been built in 1889, and The Palace of the Trocadero. The latter was a remnant of the Exposition of 1878, named after a Spanish fort captured by the French in 55 years earlier. In 1900, it housed the exhibits of Russia, China, Japan, South Africa, and the colonies of France and of other European states. Holmes considered the Japanese buildings inauthentic, and its shops disappointingly sold retail beer and commonplace items from department stores. Elsewhere, the Boer Republic display was more informative, perhaps unsurprisingly showcasing mining methods and samples of gold and diamonds.[86]

Visitors were not only treated to buildings, exhibits, and restaurants. Performances, beyond what could be found in the international restaurant, were also an important feature of the Exposition. Tiny theatres with ballets, cinematographs, tableau vivants, and singers provided a varied programme of entertainment to showcase the arts. Street performers would receive payment from onlookers by, for example, passing around tambourine as a means of collecting money.[87]

---

[78]Holmes, 1908, p. 278.
[79]Holmes, 1908, pp. 184–212.
[80]Holmes, 1908, p. 272.
[81]Holmes, 1908, pp. 194–197.
[82]Holmes, 1908, p. 212.
[83]Holmes, 1908, p. 291.
[84]Holmes, 1908, p. 299.
[85]Holmes, 1908, p. 224.
[86]Holmes, 1908, p. 225.
[87]Holmes, 1908, p. 242.

Elsewhere, Japanese staged fights demonstrated the martial art of Jiujutsu and a reconstruction of Paris in the Middle Ages involved costumed inhabitants, including jokers or minstrels and giants.[88] More statically, greenhouses containing flowers and ferns provided a more peaceful environment.[89] The industrial and technological exhibits were not limited to agriculture, horticulture, mining and transport mechanics, but extended to healthcare; visitors could attend an exhibition of infants confined in patent incubators, and although admission to this was free, a nurse held a tray for donations.[90] With so much to see and do, visitors might require opportunities to rest, for which yellow chairs were available to sit on. Upon doing so, Holmes noticed old women in black appear and charge the sitter two cents. These chairs were owned by a firm *Allez Freres* which translates literally as 'Go, Brothers' to which Holmes quipped 'surely an unfortunate title for a firm whose only desire is that people stop going and sit down'.[91]

Entry to the Exposition was slightly complicated for visitors as money was not paid on the gate, rather tickets had to be purchased from sellers in the neighbouring streets, nominally priced at one Franc, which equated to around 20 Cents in US currency at that time. In practise, the price paid depended upon the day of the week, and when in the duration of the event they were purchased. With ticket in hand, the visitor could now present this at the Exposition entrance, but again this could be a slightly complicated matter; Between opening and 10am the price was two tickets, but from 10 a.m. until dusk just one ticket was required. The rate again doubled in the evening, except on Fridays when nights were reserved for 'the aristocratic public' and the price was four tickets.[92]

The complicated ticketing might have partly resulted from the way in which the Exposition was partly financed. In 1896, 66 million Francs of bonds were issued, with the bearer entitled to 20 admission tickets with a par-value of one Franc per ticket or 20 Francs in total. Bearers also had the right to a 25% reduction in the entrance fee to every sideshow or attraction inside the Exposition gates, reduced railway fares to and from Paris, and a chance of winning half a million francs in an Exposition lottery. Gate receipts were achieved, the bonds being bought by financial institutions, speculators, and private individuals, before the Exposition had opened. With 20 tickets per bond, supply exceeded demand, and when the Exposition did open, the market was already flooded with tickets.[93]

Disruption and Danger in Paris

The construction over-runs and reported chaos around the time of the opening of the Exposition were not the only reported disruption. Such a high-profile

88 Holmes, 1908, pp. 249–250.
89 Holmes, 1908, p. 249.
90 Holmes, 1908, p. 242.
91 Holmes, 1908, p. 294.
92 Holmes, 1908, pp. 123–124.
93 Holmes, 1908, pp. 125–129.

event attended by so many people meant that other incidents happened and were reported in Britain through the national press.

There were many bridges at the Exhibition, connecting thoroughfares intersection the Exhibition Grounds so that visitors could avoid straying onto the roads which would forfeit their tickets. On the afternoon of Sunday 29 April, a 30-foot (approximately 9 metres) high footbridge which connected the Globe Celetese with the rest of the Exhibition, but yet to be opened for public use, collapsed onto the road below. Approximately 50 men, women, and children were rescued and tended to in police stations and chemists' shops, and 10 pronounced dead by that evening. Monsieur Picard, the Commissary-General of the Exhibition, rejected responsibility, saying that the bridge was in the hands of the Municipality.[94] In turn, it was suggested that this particular bridge may have been constructed by private enterprise, rather than government contracts, and that the usual method, wooden beams and plaster supported by masonry, had not been followed; one witness report claimed to have seen only chunks of plaster and wore, but no wooden beams, as might be expected.[95] The plaster in question was referred to disparagingly as 'carton paté (cardboard paste)'[96] but was more likely armé, a reinforced concrete supported by iron mesh, which if badly mixed or too heavy for its iron supporting, can give way, and perhaps with carton paté for decorative features. The veracity of engineering and was even questioned, as well as the scale, overrun and late-stage rush all suggested as contributing factors:

> The great majority are composed of wood and plaster, with adjuncts of iron. Their partitions are of the most, flimsy material, and when it is considered that not a few have upper storeys and staircases, which are bound to be thronged, the outlook cannot be conscientiously described as reassuring. The real truth is that far too much has been attempted, that too little was ready at the appointed date, and that for weeks past there has been a veritable race to get things 'finished' somehow.[97]

Around three months later, the Exhibition was in the news again for a bridge-related problem that occurred on Saturday 18 August, when 'several yards of the balustrade' gave way.[98] Thirty people fell, injuring several, at the distribution of awards ceremony attended by President Loubet and the Ministers.[99] Presumably while on his way to that awards-giving, President Loubet had already experienced drama, an intoxicated man had been detained for breaking through the escort

---

[94]*The Illustrated London News*, 'Accident at the Paris Exhibition', Saturday 5 May 1900.
[95]*The Daily Telegraph*, 'Serious Disaster at the Paris Exhibition', Monday 30 April 1900.
[96]*The Daily Telegraph*, 'Paris Exhibition Disaster', Tuesday 1 May 1900, p. 7.
[97]*The Daily Telegraph*, 'Paris Exhibition Disaster', Tuesday 1 May 1900, p. 7.
[98]*York Herald*, 'Multiple News Items', Tuesday 21 August 1900.
[99]*Sheffield Daily Telegraph*, 'Summary of News', Monday 20 August 1900.

and throwing an envelope into the President's carriage. On the same day, elsewhere at the exhibition, a passenger train ran into an engine, injuring the guard and three passengers and in another incident.[100]

Also in August, British regional newspapers, speculated 'typhoid is increasing in Paris'[101] and perhaps from a news agency circular, reported an attempt on the Shah of Persia's life while visiting Paris, including the exhibition. This was attributed to a French workman who tried to shoot him, motivated by 'passion for notoriety'.[102] It was speculated the Shah did not want to extend his travels to Britain, although the source is not clear about whether that would have happened in any case.[103]

Some newspapers also speculated as to the success or failure of the Paris Exposition, outlining that it was an artistic success but that 'financially speaking' it was 'a distinct failure', which may have been a result of the failure to have everything ready on time or even within two months of opening, the high prices charged by Parisian hotels early in the duration of the exhibition, and 'vile attacks on this nation by the press of France'.[104] The question as to whether or not the Paris Exhibition had failed was mentioned as being 'a constant topic in the Parisian Press' most obviously because attendance had been less than it had been in 1889, although many visitors had travelled from as far away as America and also from rival nation Germany, but that much of the evidence to suggest failure was due to the disappointing nature of the side-shows.[105] These claims are of course subjective and relative but indicate the cynicism towards such events in the news press, even in 1900.

Sport at Paris 1900

According to Coubertin's memoirs 'if there was one place in the world where everyone was completely indifferent to the whole [Olympic] idea, it was Paris ...'.[106] Coubertin had been encouraged by the three directors of the 1889 Universal Exhibition, which included school sports, and assumed that their goodwill would remain forthcoming for 1900. Coubertin proposed the concept of including both an ancient games and a modern games format into the exhibition, which he described as a his 'project' and which would have involved the construction of a reproduction of the *Altis* of Olympia including an exhibition of monuments containing artefacts telling the story of sport from antiquity to the modern era. However, the revival of International Olympism for adults appeared to be a step

[100] *York Herald*, 'Multiple News Items', Friday 3 August 1900.
[101] *Northern Echo*, no title, Friday 1 August 1900.
[102] *Western Daily Press*, Friday 3 August 1900.
[103] *York Herald*, 'Multiple News Items', Friday 3 August 1900.
[104] *Lichfield Mercury*, 'Events of the Week Illustrated', Friday 24 August 1900.
[105] *Manchester Courier and Lancashire General Advertiser*, 'no title', Saturday 1 September 1900.
[106] de Coubertin (1979, p. 25).

too far for the directors. The Commissioner for 1900 was a single individual, Alfred Picard, with his own agenda for the exhibition who, according to Coubertin was not enthusiastic about including games either ancient or modern, and featured ice skating in the section for cutlery, rowing within lifesaving, and sports associations in social welfare. However, what Coubertin does not mention was that the final report for the sport at the exhibition did include all of these of disciplines in a unified way! A multitude of sports and entertainments were planned for inclusion, but Coubertin worried that this would be 'nothing more than a vulgar glorified fair'. On the other hand, de Courbertin talked of his vision being one of elite athletes watched by elite spectators, perhaps to give the event and Olympic movement cache. He had began planning with representatives of the USFSA and the different sport governing bodies in France, forming a committee with a vision of the programme being like the original plan for 1896. Accommodation for athletes would be well-equipped, well-situated camps (the first Olympic village), while the sport federations would provide regulations for the games, form juries, and run the contests. However, the federations did not see Coubertin's vision as the reward for their contribution, and wanted more than involvement itself.

Meanwhile, plans between the French Olympic organisers and the Exhibition committee got confused further by a US Commission who proposed playing fields and competitions 'to teach other countries what real sport was like'. While this plan did not come to fruition it slowed down progress on Coubertin's own plans. In February 1899, Director General, Daniel Mérillon, the President of the French Shooting Federation, was appointed to lead the sports competitions, and Coubertin moved to work with him without formally merging the Olympic organisation into the exhibition. Picard was less keen on this, dismissing the Olympic Games as an anachronism clashing with this festival of *fin-de-siecle* modernity. This led to a power struggle over the status of the athletic games and their Olympic integrity – the Olympic committee reluctantly dissolved, but this created a vacuum for Mérillon who, fearing the games could be relegated to a domestic affair, urged Coubertin to remain onboard to create interest across Europe. Coubertin agreed even though the games would now be called 'The Competitions of the Exhibition' instead of the Olympic Games, something that he considered to be poor and clumsy. Interest elsewhere in Europe was forthcoming though there was concern that German athletes might be made to feel uncomfortable in France, and there was general confusion in several countries about what was happening with the games. Still believing it to be Olympic the sports organisations in the United States, Bohemia, and Denmark contacted the IOC to vent their frustration, while Austria and Canada meanwhile wanted representatives for the Paris games on the IOC, mistakenly thinking that they were still the organisers. This confusion led to the general ad hoc feel of the Paris games – the IOC were still approached to provide juries, while Parisian sports clubs were asked to provide the facilities, rather than new venues being constructed. This led to a sense that the sports were not different from each other, while Olympism as a cause was marginalised. However, the final report tells a more positive and cohesive story of the games and even names Coubertin as one of the organisers of the athletics section, whether ornamental or not, which we will discuss further later. Coubertin did not enjoy the 1900 games which he felt relegated him to 'the role of humiliated vassal'.[107]

There was not a great amount of space given in British newspapers to the sports and games of the Paris Exposition and there does not appear to have been much, if anything, announced about them prior to September 1898. An article in the *Sunday Times* in September referred to the pan-Britanic Games, lamenting lack of momentum in the two years since the inaugural modern Olympics:

> The Olympic Games at Athens in 1896 served for a time to fan the flame of enthusiasm that burned in certain small circles; but the general result after nil did not reach the heights that the would-be promoters of a gigantic international games meeting could have desired.

It was suggested interest would be revived when the preliminary events, presumably British qualifying events, for the Olympic Games of Paris 1900 were held, however readers were also told to expect the Paris event to be vastly different from the inaugural Games. The advance programme that was received by the newspaper included 'almost every branch of sport ... horse-racing, coursing, and shooting seemingly being the only exceptions'. The rules for every sport would be set by the USFSA and open only to amateurs as recognised by them, the AAA of England, and 'other well-known amateur associations'. *The Sunday Times* claimed that prizes would consist 'exclusively of works of art' with no cash value as 'deterrent to the amateur who is so only in name'.[108]

It is reasonable to conclude that in 1900, the second Olympic Games only existed virtually; there were no Olympic ceremonies to herald its opening nor to formally close. Unlike other editions of the Games, the only official report is that of the ***International Competitions of the Physical Exercise and Sports of the Paris Universal Exposition 1900***. Seven hundred and ninety five pages, from cover-to-cover, it is attributed not to the IOC but to the Ministry of Commerce and Industry and under direction of M. Daniel Mérillon, as 'Délegué general aux Concours d'exercises physiques et de sports' (General delegate for physical exercise and sports competitions).[109]

Coubertin is listed as secrétaire général de l'Union française de Sports athlétiques (Secretary General of the USFSA) rather than having an affiliation to the IOC, and he is just one of a long-list of the Heads or representatives of French sporting bodies affiliated to the Exposition.[110] This is a clue about the status of the second Olympic Games in the context of the Exposition to which it was attached,

---

[107]de Coubertin (1979, pp. 31–37).
[108]*The Sunday Times*, 'Sporting Gossip' by Will Scarlet, Sunday 11 September 1989.
[109]Mérillon, 1901. *Concours Internationaux D'Exercices Physiques et de Sports, Exposition Universalle internationale de 1900 à Paris*. Paris: Imprimerie Nationale, p. 5.
[110]Mérillon (1901, p. 8).

Table 4. Proposed Expenditure of Section Committees for the Sport and Games of the Paris 1900 Exposition.

Section	**Cost (Francs, 1900)**
Athletic games	532,614
Gymnastics	511,000
Fencing	59,600
Sport shooting	725,000
Equestrian sport	540,640
Cycling	154,180
Motoring	231,500
Water sport	348,645
Life-saving	76,140
Aerostation	375,000
Preparatory military exercises	103,327
School competitions	56,281
TOTAL	**3,713,927**

Source: Mérillon (1901, p. 413).

or rather nested by the Exposition committee, as part of the broader sport and cultural offering. Indeed, the very existence of a 1900 'second' Olympiad and the list of event winners as having variously won Olympic Gold, silver or bronze is something of a historic revision that might not be remembered at all were it not for the later triumph of the IOC and its games.

The international events were divided into 10 sections: (1) athletic games, (2) gymnastics, (3) fencing, (4) sport shooting, (5) equestrian sport, (6) cycling, (7) motoring, (8) water sport, (9) life-saving, and (10) Aerostation (broadly, air-borne sports, encompassing ballooning and homing pigeons). There were also two more sections reserved only for national competition: (11) preparatory military exercises and (12) school competitions (sub-divided to its own four sections of athletic games, gymnastics, fencing, and sport shooting).[111]

Budgetary and technical interests drove the decision to place supervision and authority with the USFSA but with execution, revenue, and expenditure allocated to the distinct groupings which had autonomy regarding these matters. The proposed expenditure for each grouping is shown in Table 4.

The sum of approximately 3,700,000 Francs was 'very close to that which the first studies of the Preparatory Commission of 1894'. The organisers however wished to reduce the figure while not placing the sections under too much pressure.

[111]Mérillon (1901, pp. 18–21).

Thus, four systems were established, necessitating four types of treaties with the various committees within the sections:

- Six committees (golf, Basque pelota, angling, pigeon racing, school rowing, and school shooting) agreed to take charge of the execution of their respective programmes for a fixed fee and retaining all revenue.
- Three committees (hunting rifle, pigeon shooting, and velocipedy) accepted a package fixed by leaving the public's revenue to the Exhibition.
- Eleven committees (foil, epee, sabre, international gymnastics championship, swimming, water rescue, earth rescue, balloons, school festival, school gymnastics, and school fencing) accepted a fixed package figure and a possible guaranteed figure, leaving it up to the Exhibition revenues from the public.
- Fifteen committees (athletic games, federal gymnastics festival, gymnastics (Seine), shooting at the target, cannon, bow, horse show, polo, automobile, rowing, sailing, motorboats, fire-fighters, military exercises, and school games) accepted a fixed package with a supplement possible guarantee by taking charge on their behalf of all receipts and expenses.

The report of the Paris 1900 Exposition Games is the first in the Olympic archive to contain a systematic breakdown of budget and finance, presumably because the Exposition reporting generally did so. The IOC did not seem to have required it for the report of the 1896 Games and does not seem to have been involved in the 1900 document at all, its inclusion in the Olympic archive being something of a 'land grab' due to Coubertin's involvement and ambition, rather than how it was governed or perceived by its organisers or participants in 1900.

Table 5 provides details of the fixed figure awarded by Grant Organizing Committee, any subsidies as a guarantee, sums taken on the guarantee, profit made on the guarantee, and any deficits on the forecasts. It shows that the lump sum subsidies granted amounted to 967,300 Francs and any grants as a guarantee of 248,120 Francs, that is, a total of 1,215,420 Francs. This was the figure that was to be included in the budgetary forecasts of the Administration about the Committees' execution of their commitments.

Table 5. Committee Expenditure (Francs).

Committee	Fixed Grant	Guarantee Eventual	Call on the Guarantee	Profit on the Guarantee	Unplanned Deficit
Golf	6,000	–	–	–	–
Pelote Basque	6,000	–	–	–	5,000
Angling	14,000	–	–	–	–
Pigeon Fancying	10,000	–	–	–	9
School rowing	1,500	–	–	–	–
School shooting	8,000	–	–	–	–
Shotgun	5,000	–	–	–	–

Table 5. (*Continued*)

Committee	Fixed Grant	Guarantee Eventual	Call on the Guarantee	Profit on the Guarantee	Unplanned Deficit
Pigeon shooting	30,000	–	–	–	–
Velocipedia	100,000	–	–	–	–
Swimming	8,000	2,000	2,000	–	1,500
Water rescue	32,000	2,940	–	2,940	–
Rescue on land	15,000	4,700	2,700	2,000	–
Balloons	90,000	8,000	8,000	–	3,700
School gymnastics	4,000	2,000	–	2,000	–
School festival	12,000	2,100	300	1,800	–
Gymnastics championship	30,000	10,000	6,300	3,700	–
Foil	18,000	6,200	3,400	2,800	–
Epee	15,000	6,000	4,300	1,700	–
Sabre	9,000	1,000	900	100	–
Athletic games	63,200	20,000	–	20,000	–
Gymnastics (Siene)	5,000	7,000	5,900	1,100	–
Target shooting	75,000	20,000	–	20,000	–
Canon	10,000	2,000	–	2,000	–
Arc	25,000	10,000	5,000	5,000	–
Horse show	50,000	30,000	2,400	27,600	–
Polo	20,000	10,000	8,600	1,400	–
Automobile	70,000	30,000	–	30,000	–
Rowing	20,000	10,000	10,000	–	–
Sailing	35,000	5,000	5,000	–	–
Motor boats	30,000	10,000	–	10,000	–
Fire-fighters	10,000	10,000	–	10,000	–
Military Exercises	30,000	10,000	3,000	7,000	–
School games	21,000	3,180	–	3,180	–
School fencing	5,500	1,000	–	1,000	–
Federal gymnastics festival	75,000	25,000	–	25,000	–
Hygiene (medical)	10,000	–	–	–	–
TOTALS	**967,300**	**248,180**	**67,800**	**180,320**	**10,200**

Source: Mérillon (1901, p. 416).

The overall financial outcome was of the 'greatest satisfaction' to the Exposition organisers, identifying only three committees (swimming, Basque pelota and balloons, although the table showed a fourth, pigeon-fancying) had to call for subsidy amounting to 10,200 Francs, but of the 248,220 Francs available as additional guarantee to other committees, only 67,870 Francs was drawn upon. Thus 1,045,300 Francs were spent, meaning that 120,120 Francs were saved against the 1,165,420 Franc budget available to the committees in organising their sports and games.[112]

Other costs borne by the Exposition shown in Table 6 included infrastructure, particularly building stadiums, although these had utility beyond the life of the festival. The official report refers to these as 'approximately 250,000 Francs' (it mentions in text that the City of Paris contributed 150,000 Francs towards the Velodrome, although is not clear if this is separate to the figure given in the table) and thus a total of 1,280,000 Francs expenditure (approximate) however the true figure looks closer to 1,325,950 Francs expenditure when adding up the two totals. The financial explanation in the prose of the report is confusing and inconsistent to the tables and so some caution should be used when considering the approximate let alone the exact expenditure, although it boasts at having been possible through careful management, to award 953,448 Francs value in prizes for 58,731 participants, including 1,587 foreigners.[113]

Considering income from the sporting events (Table 7) is tricky, because the Official Report appears to be an incomplete record with the attendance receipts from only some events listed in tables and calculations, even though it is mentioned elsewhere that other sports, namely Rugby, were profitable and contributed to the income of the Exposition Games. Perhaps these records had not been submitted by the time that the report was written, but it again points to the somewhat

Table 6. Other Costs Associated with Hosting Sport and Games at the Paris 1900 Exposition.

Item	**Approximate Cost (Francs)**
Vincennes municipal Vélodrome	150,000
Balloon Park	80,000
The Vernon Brochure	15,000
Flying stands of the Velodrome	8,500
Fixed stand of the Velodrome	17,000
Install fencing in the village hall	10,000
Total	**280,650**

Source: Mérillon (1901, p. 418).

[112]Mérillon (1901, pp. 412–419).
[113]Mérillon (1901, pp. 412–419).

Table 7. Income from Attendance at Selected Sporting Events at Paris Exposition 1900.

Event	Receipts from Attendance (Francs)
Shotgun	270.00
Pigeon shooting	2,431.00
Vélocipédie	30,597.70
Swimming	1,098.50
Water rescue	1,177.50
Land rescue	509.00
Balloons	15,642.50
School gymnastics	191.00
School festival	934.50
Gymnastics championship	593.00
Foil	3,064.00
Epée	1,644.55
Sabre	936.35
TOTAL	**59,059.60**

Source: Mérillon (1901, p. 419).

ad hoc nature of the games. It is also noticeable that no monies are recorded in the report as being charged to competitors for their participation.

The governance and organising of these sections were undertaken by representatives of relevant French societies. It is in the first of these, the athletic games, where le baron Pierre de Coubertin is listed with the prestigious role of being a Section Vice-President, and his full affiliations are extended to being honorary general secretary of the USFSA and also of being a member of the Higher Commission for Physical; Education of Youth.[114] He was not, however, listed as being involved in the 12th section (Schools Competitions). Table 5 shows that these athletic games received the sixth largest fixed grant and made the joint fourth profit on the guarantee, out of the 36 categories (35 if 'hygiene' which could not generate any profit is removed). We can therefore conclude it was successfully organised, from a financial perspective.

The athletic games section, apart from its assumed importance of being 'Section One' was a broad category encompassing 15 types, some of which would be sub-divided into specific sports or variants, in the order that they are listed in the report. It is noticeable that although this section was part of the international

[114]Mérillon (1901, p. 19).

games, several were particular to France or the Franco-sphere, and several were open to professionals as well as amateurs:[115]

- Races and foot and athletic competitions, including jumps, throwing weights and discs (open to amateurs and professionals)
- Rugby football
- Association football
- Hockey
- Cricket
- Lawn-Tennis (amateurs and professionals)
- Croquet
- Bowling games
- Baseball
- Crosse Canadienne (Canadian Lacrosse)
- Long-paume (an ancestor of lawn-tennis, played in France)
- Balle au tamis (a team sport particular to France)
- Courte-paume (a French ball-and-court game)
- Golf
- Pelote basque (court sports played against a wall, particularly in the Basque region, Spain and France) (amateurs and professionals)
- La boxe et la canne (stick fighting) (amateurs and professionals)
- La Lutte (which appears to refer La Lutte à la corde, or 'tug-of-war') (amateurs and professionals)

The jury for these events comprised twelve French nationals (including Baron de Coubertin) and eleven foreign nationals, among them were Herbert of Great Britain and the Count Brunetta d'Usseaux of Italy, both of whom would have significance to the later Olympic Games of London 1908, as we explain in the next volume.[116]

Races were recorded as being 'Championnats du monde' or World Championships. Prizes for professionals were categorised as first, second, or third, and ranged in value with endurance generally valued more highly (2,500 metres steeple-chase had first prize of 500f, second prize 10f and third prize 50f, whereas the 100 metres race awarded 250f first prize, 80f second, and 40f for third place). Long-jump, high-jump and weight launch awarded prizes only to first and second place. Some events were contested on a handicap basis and the 100, 400, 1,500, and 5,000 metre distance running races also awarded fourth place prizes, although all prizes were typically lower in value and the throwing and jumping handicapped events did not award third or fourth place prizes.[117]

The prizes for amateur events were as *objects d'art*, although a cash value, presumably cost or insurance value, is given in the report. All running distances offered prizes with equivalent value to 400f for first-place, 200f for second and

[115]Mérillon (1901, pp. 41, 58).
[116]Mérillon (1901, p. 59).
[117]Mérillon (1901, pp. 60–61).

50f for third. Throwing and jumping events offered prizes valued at 250f for first and 80f for second place. Amateur handicapped races offered prizes of a lower value. Other events are also listed, such as a relay-race, triple jump, 60 metres and so on, all offering objects d'art ranging in value, some offering prizes only to first and second place, others to fourth or even fifth.[118]

The other sections comprised sports and games some of which will be familiar to modern-day Olympians and others that would not. Among the more interesting and notable are some events considered, or classified at the time of writing, as having been part of the Olympic Games component and some that are not. In any case, events that took place at the Exposition were: cricket (the first time, and until 2024 the only time, it has been classified as having been an Olympic Sport), golf (appearing for the first time in a modern Olympics), gas ballooning, swimming obstacle race, cannon shooting, angling, fire-fighting (within the life-saving category) and, controversially by later moral standards, an event known as 'Tir aux pigeons'. In subsequent Olympiads, this sport was replaced by the variant clay pigeon shooting, skeet or trap, where an insentient and normally inanimate object is projected airborne, providing a moving target for marksmen to shoot at. At the Paris Exposition, societal values were different, and live pigeons provided the target, the first and only time in the history of the modern Olympics that live animals were intentionally killed.[119]

Overall, 58,731 participants were recorded, the majority by far (57,144) were French, with a small proportion (1,587) being from overseas, the majority of foreigners participating in the various athletic games for which Coubertin was a committee Vice-President.[120] The official report draws comparison between the athletic games of Paris 1900 and the first international Olympics of Athens 1896; it is claimed the events were more impressive to watch (although only 2,000–3,000 could fit into the Racing Club Paris stadium which hosted, unlike the 40,000 at Athens) and that many records were equalled or broken. Financially, the American university participants alone had paid an estimated 300,000 Francs to participate, which had been very helpful.[121] Among other American participants was a young management consultant, Frederick Winslow Taylor, later author of the seminal book *Principles of Scientific Management*,[122] who finished fourth in the Olympic golf without handicap and seventh in the competition with handicap. Taylor was a member of the Philadelphia Country Club but how he ended up participating in this event is not known![123]

---

[118]Mérillon (1901, pp. 61–62).

[119]Mérillon (1901, p. 41); Docolympique. 2024. *Untiraupigeonquifaitscandale*. https://www.dicolympique.fr/tirer-est-pas-jouer/.

[120]Mérillon (1901, p. 56).

[121]Mérillon (1901, pp. 60–64).

[122]Taylor, F.W. (1911). *Principles of scientific management*. New York & London. For more details on his legacy see Kelly (2020).

[123]Olympics.com (n.d.). *Frederick Winslow Taylor*. Retrieved November 21, 2024, from https://olympics.com/en/athletes/frederick-winslow-taylor

British involvement and success are recorded in the Official Report, particularly in running events. This was the first time the AAA had provided expenses for a representative team of athletes to visit an Olympic Games following a change in Law 1 and Rule 10 approved in April 1897 that allowed for athletes taking part in international or *bone fide* events to receive expenses as long as they were not paid by the organiser of the event.[124] In March 1900 a sub-committee of the General Committee recommended sending a representative team to the 'Paris Exhibition Sports', and a motion was recommended for the organisation's AGM to vote £100 for the purpose.[125] The AGM duly approved this with the decision also taken that the 1900 AAA Annual Sports, held on the 7th July, should be the selection competition.[126] Edgar Bredin of England won first-prize at the professional races in three distances (100, 400, and 1,500 metres). Amateur runners also won first-prizes in 800 metres (M. Tysoe) and 1,500 metres (M. Bennett), and the English team won the 5,000 metres 'Race of Nations', which appears to have been a relay race comprising teams of five athletes, each team representing a country. British athletes also did well, finishing in first-place in association football, cricket, sailing, swimming, and tennis, as well as second or third places in other athletic events, cycling, golf, rugby union, rowing sailing, swimming, and tennis. British competitors also finished in first, second or third placings when competing for mixed teams in various sports.[127]

The marathon, a defining event for an Olympic Games, was held at the Paris Exposition, which gives the Exposition Sports Olympic credibility, even if they weren't explicitly advertised or reported as being Olympic. The distance was, unsurprisingly, included in Coubertin's section, and listed as an amateur event, the Official Report states that the course was 40 kilometres and won by Théato in 2 hours 59 minutes.[128]

There was some coverage within British newspapers of the sporting events at the Paris Exposition, although most sports were not reported. The coverage

[124]AAA ATH/AAA/1/2/2/4, AGM Minutes. 24 April 1897; AAA ATH/AAA/3/1, Amateur Athletic Association: Constitution Rules, Objects and Lists of Officers and Clubs &c.: Laws for Athletic Meetings and Competitions, 1897, pp. 9, 23–24.

[125]AAA ATH/AAA/1/2/2/4, General Committee Minutes, 17 March 1900.

[126]AAA ATH/AAA/1/2/2/4, AGM Minutes, 24 April 1900. General Statement of Accounts, 1900.

[127]If translated to the present-day Gold, Silver and Bronze system, including only the sports that have been considered by present-day revision is as having been 'Olympic', and aggregating these athletes into national 'teams' (which most events had not been at the time of the Exposition) then Great Britain performed in third place overall and that is how it is currently presented by the IOC. Revisionism continues, as recently as June 2024 the IOC Executive Board approved the change of a second place 'silver medal' (although only silver-gilt medals were awarded to first-place contestants at the 1900 Games) from GB to France. See: https://olympics.com/ioc/news/ioc-executive-board-approves-change-of-lloyd-hildebrand-s-silver-medal-at-paris-1900-from-great-britain-to-france [accessed 25 June 2023].

[128]Mérillon (1901, p. 64).

is ad hoc and perhaps used to fill space, or in regional titles to report on local people who had gone to participate, rather than consistent or extensive coverage in any one paper. Those that were written about all focussed on events in which the British athletes competed, for example, swimming[129] and cycling,[130] or the popular spectator sports of cricket,[131] rugby, and association football, which were already mainstays of the sports pages. As such, readers may have been aware of some of what was happening across the Channel, although the word 'Olympic' (or any variation) are not to be found. Rather, they make reference to, for example, 'the sports held in connection with the Paris Exhibition'[132] or the 'world's championship contests'[133] Another interesting point is that although competitors were not selected by National Olympic Associations they are still referred to as being national representatives or representative teams. For example, there was a cyclist who was 'the English representative',[134] swimmers and water polo players 'representing this country'[135] and 'The Englishmen',[136] 'The English team of swimmers',[137] or '- of champion swimmers',[138] although note the emphasis on *English* rather than British as is the case today, even if the individuals in question were English as opposed to originating from anywhere else in the British Isles. Additionally, two teams were present to compete in water polo but due to the number of other nations represented, only one was allowed to play.[139]

Of the team games reported in British newspapers, all three were under the organisation of the athletic games section that Coubertin was involved with. The first of these to be played was cricket. Cricket was originally scheduled as an Olympic sport in 1896 and was listed in the provisional programme for the Athens Games, published in Paris in January 1895, which would have been the only team sport held. Due to insufficient entries, it was cancelled, but would take place at the Paris Exhibition of 1900. As such, it is claimed to have been the first, and until 2024 the only, time that cricket featured at the Olympics (Buchanan, 1993; Parkar, 2023). The closing date to register participation was 30 June 1900. Originally, teams from Belgium, England, France, and Holland were due to compete across four games between 4 and 20 August, but Belgium and Holland withdrew, 'the Dutch having withdrawn due to not having been able to bring together a complete

[129] *Leeds Mercury Post*, no title, Thursday 9 August 1900; *Pall Mall Gazette*, 'Sporting Notes and News', Wednesday 15 August 1900; *Burnley Express*, 'Notes on Sport', Saturday 18 August 1900.
[130] *Pall Mall Gazette*, 'Sporting Notes and News', Thursday 13 September 1900.
[131] *Sheffield Daily Telegraph*, 'Cricket at the Paris Exhibition', Friday 10 August 1900.
[132] *Leeds Mercury Post*, no title, Thursday 9 August 1900.
[133] *Pall Mall Gazette*, 'Sporting Notes and News', Wednesday 15 August 1900.
[134] *Pall Mall Gazette*, 'Sporting Notes and News', Thursday 13 September 1900.
[135] *Leeds Mercury Post*, no title, Thursday 9 August 1900.
[136] *Burnley Express*, 'Notes on Sport', Saturday 18 August 1900.
[137] *Pall Mall Gazette*, 'Sporting Notes and News', Wednesday 15 August 1900.
[138] Referring to the English team of champion swimmers that competed.
[139] *Pall Mall Gazette*, 'Sporting Notes and News', Wednesday 15 August 1900.

team and the Belgians not having entered a team'.[140] Only the French and English sides remained to contest a two-innings, two-day match at the *Vélodrome de Vincennes*, on the 20th, the date for which was unchanged despite the withdrawls.[141] The velodrome was located in the Vicennes Woods and was built for the Exposition Games, for which it hosted cycling, archery, gymnastics and the team games of association football, Rugby football and cricket (Hammersley, 2016). The surviving poster advertising the fixture does not mention Olympic Games but clearly classifies it as part of 'Exposition Universelle de 1900', under control of Ministère du Commerce, de l'Industrie, des postes et des Télégraphes (McClaughlin, 2024).

The French team was a USFSA representative side, but in reality there were few clubs that played cricket in France. Players were therefore picked from the Union Club and the Standard Athletic Club (which had been formed in 1890 by English workmen imported to construct the Eiffel Tower). Most of the players were thus English, and the organising committee included three surnames which also appear on the French side of the scorecard of the one game played, as well as that of one of the two Umpires.[142] Buchanan (1993, p. 4) identifies one of these names, Philip Tomalin, as not only captain of the French Olympic team but that he was also cricket chairman of the French Sports Federation 'and it is to him that much of the credit must be given for this unique event'.

Although billed as 'France v England' on the poster, the visiting English side was in fact 'Devon & Somerset Wanderers Cricket Club', an established touring side formed six years beforehand, primarily from the Castle Cary Club, supplemented by local men whose job allowed them to leave work for two-week tours. Four of the men who travelled were old-boys of Blundell's, a Devon Public School (Buchanan, 1993, pp. 4–5) and two of their numbers were first-class cricketers (McClaughlin, 2024). Travelling to France was the Wanderers sixth tour and it won all three of its fixtures in Paris during the 1900 tour, including that versus 'France' at the Paris Exposition (Buchanan, 1993, pp. 4–5).

The Wanderers had arrived in Paris the previous day, staying overnight at the Hotel des Trois Princes. It was agreed by the captains that the game would be 12-a-side and each team's extra name was added to the scorecard by hand. The sides were all-amateur, Wanderers leaving their one professional, on the sidelines (Williamson, 2012). The pitch of play 'was in excellent condition'.[143]

The game fielded 24 cricketers in all, instead of the typical 22, and despite its internationally billed advertising, neither side fielded players who really represented their national sides. As such, although the 'Paris Test' in 1900 was the only international cricket match played that year (despite England having played Test matches against Australia since 1877) it does not hold the status of a first-class match, because it was not an 11-a-side encounter, and it was scheduled for just two days.

---

[140]Mérillon (1901, p. 69).
[141]Mérillon (1901, p. 69).
[142]Mérillon (1901, p. 69).
[143]Mérillon (1901, p. 69).

The intended prizes were described as 'In each match, the victorious team will receive an art object; Furthermore, all players who took part in one of the three matches will receive a souvenir'.[144] Both teams received miniature versions of the Eiffel Tower. As winners, the England team were awarded silver medals, while France received bronze (Parkar, 2023).

The cricket fixture was anticipated by the *Sheffield Daily Telegraph*, where cricket was very popular with its Yorkshire readership, but which curiously suggested slightly different dates and details for a duo of two-day matches. The article stated under the headline 'Cricket at the Paris Exhibition' that fixtures would occur on 19–20 and 29–30 August, between a team comprising players from Devon County Wanderers and Notts County Amateurs against a team selected from Standard Athletic and Albion Cricket Cub of Paris. The source for these details is not mentioned in the article but was published a mere ten days before the actual fixture occurred, and no such information can be found elsewhere. It does though reflect the rather ad-hoc and confused nature at the time and perhaps conflated the 'Wanderers other tour fixtures with its Exposition game.[145]

By contrast, association football, received far more attention from the British press. Participating teams were required to register by 15th August and again, four teams were named in the programme, but 'the Germans and the Swiss, for various reasons, were unable to bring a team'. As such, just two games were played, both involving a French side whose opponents were from England and Belgium. The USFSA chose Club Français, which was composed entirely of players with French nationality. The first game, held on Thursday September 20 against the Upton Park Football Club of London, resulted in a 4-0 win to the English side, and was played in front of 500 spectators. Three days later, the French played a Belgian team recruited by M. G. Pelgrims, captain of the Léopold Football Club of Brussels, composed exclusively of students belonging to the Belgian University Athletic Federation (Fédération Athlétique Universitaire Belge). The French won 6-2 'due to the lack of training of the Belgian players and the lack of cohesion of their team where most of the men met for the first time'. This second game was watched by a crowd of 1,500; both games were played at Vélodrome de Vincennes.[146]

Upton Park was a team from the East of London, or Essex County, and as well as its regular fixtures, played regular tours through the West of England and Channel Islands,[147] augmenting its available players with amateurs guesting from other clubs. In 1899, this touring extended to France and the club was asked by the Amateur Status Committee of the Football Association to participate in the 1900 Paris Exposition. Thus, an Autumn tour was arranged to coincide, taking

[144] Mérillon (1901, p. 69).
[145] *Sheffield Daily Telegraph*, 'Cricket at the Paris Exhibition', Friday 10 August 1900.
[146] Mérillon (1901, pp. 68–69).
[147] Upton Park had toured the Channel Islands regularly since 1897 and are credited as a major catalyst in the spread of association football to the island, see: https://www.guernseyfa.com/news/2018/may/04/upton-day [accessed 2 May 2025].

in the Southwest of England and Channel Islands again, as well as France. In the same style as the cricket a few weeks earlier, advertising embellished the occasion, billing 'England versus France'. The game was held on Thursday 20 September, the date for which France versus Switzerland was originally scheduled. This must have meant that Upton Park played its game at short notice, the original Exposition fixture having been allocated to 7 October. Upton Park then had two more tour games in France and two in the Channel Islands, as well as a preliminary round fixture on Saturday 2 September in the prestigious domestic knockout tournament, the FA Cup. Several of the team travelled back to England, ironically playing against a team named Olympic, who knocked them out of the cup 5-0, before returning to France to complete the tour (FA.com, nd; Hammersley, 2016). Upton Park, however, finished the competition not only winners of the first ever Olympic association football match, but also as joint winners of the tournament overall, as the French team beat the Belgian representatives (IOC, 2020). It is noteworthy that in the official Exposition report, the team is referred to as Upton Park F.C. when listing players who featured, but 'équipe anglaise' ('English Team') in the listed fixture dates.[148]

It is interesting to consider the coverage that Upton Park's endeavours received in the British press. As late as 19 September, the day before the opening game, a Reuters circular was published in local newspapers still referring to the original programme, which must have by then been changed; stating that The Upton Park team would play a picked French team that coming Saturday and that the French side would also play games from Belgium, Switzerland, and Germany.[149] In fact, this was still being published as late as Saturday 22nd, two days after the rearranged first fixture had been played.[150] It perhaps came as a surprise then to readers that on Friday 21st, there were reports (and in at least one of the same 'papers) that Upton Park footballers, described as an Essex team, had beaten a team, described variously as a 'Paris eleven',[151] 'Frenchmen' (on the 28th)[152] and 'the Union des Sociétés Françaises de Sports Athlétiques' although Reuters appear confused about the scoring system under association rules referring to 'points' rather than goals.[153] Dalziel news agency provided more accuracy and commented 'The attendance was very small'.[154] The most detailed report was

---

[148]Mérillon (1901, pp. 68–69).

[149]*Manchester Courier and Lancashire General Advertiser*, 'Sporting Intelligence', Wednesday 19 September 1900; *Morning Post*, 'International Football', Wednesday 19 September 1900.

[150]*Sunderland Daily Echo and Shipping Gazette*, 'Football Gossip', Saturday 22 September 1900.

[151]*Chelmsford Chronicle*, 'Essex Footballers at the Paris Exhibition', Friday 21 September 1900;

[152]*Chelmsford Chronicle*, 'Our Sports Column', Friday 28 September 1900.

[153]*Morning Post*, 'Multiple Sports Items', Friday 21 September 1900; *Daily News*, 'International Football', Friday 21 September 1900; *Leeds Mercury*, 'The Morning Express', Friday 21 September 1900.

[154]*Liverpool Mercury*, 'International Football', Friday 21 September 1900.

published, perhaps unsurprisingly, in an Essex newspaper, which emphasised the local nature of the Upton Park Team. Upton Park, it reported, had only arrived at the ground at around 3 p.m. (the advertised kick-off time) and lost the coin-toss, meaning that they began by playing into the sun. They had though scored their first two goals within the opening seven minutes. Injury meant starting the second half with only ten players on the field, and after scoring a third, the French had retaliated with pressure, coming close to scoring, before Upton's fourth.[155] The Chelmsford Chronicle, being local to the team, also referred to the final match of Upton Park's tour in France, mentioning that they beat St. Sevano 5-0.[156]

The third team sport to be played under the athletics section was Rugby football. Participating teams were required to register by 15 September 1900 and the fixtures were scheduled for the consecutive Sundays of 14 October (French team vs German team), 21st (English team vs German team), and 28th (French team vs English team). The English vs German game was cancelled due to the impossibility of either side staying in Paris for so many days. Representing Germany was Fussball Club de Francfort (Frankfurt), unanimously recognised to be the strongest in Germany, which attended with the help of a grant provided by a Committee appointed by the Imperial Government with the aim of ensuring Germany's participation in the Exhibition's physical exercise competitions.[157]

Prizes were an art object for the winning team of each match, and a participation souvenir for all who took part. Materially, these prizes included medals for the First-Place winners that were consistent across the various sports, designed by Frédéric Vernon and minted at Monnaie de Paris. They measured 42 × 60 mm and were made of gilt silver. The obverse was decorated with a winged goddess, arms raised, holding laurel branches in both hands. Below her, a view of the city of Paris and the monuments of the Universal Exhibition. The reverse contained a victorious athlete standing on a podium, holding a laurel branch in his right hand, arm raised, with a stadium and the Acropolis of Athens in the background.[158] It is noteworthy that despite Olympic revisionists awarding Gold, Silver, and Bronze to different nations for the modern-day Olympic record, the medals, although showing Olympic imagery on one side, do not explicitly mention the word 'Olympic' anywhere on them. Nor were they originally won by nations (although athletes and teams nationality were shown in the Official Report, suggesting an inferred representational element to participation). Most interestingly, and as we have already explained, there were no 'Gold', 'Silver' nor 'Bronze' categories at the time that the games took place, although the First-Place finishers were awarded the aforementioned silver gilt medal. There were though categories of 'Gold', 'Silver', 'Bronze' and 'Honourable Mention' awarded to

---

[155] *Essex Newsman*, 'Essex Footballers at the Paris Exhibition', Saturday 22 September 1900.

[156] *Chelmsford Chronicle*, 'Our Sports Column', Friday 28 September 1900.

[157] Mérillon (1901, p. 69).

[158] Olympics.com (n.d.). *The Medals*. https://olympics.com/en/olympic-games/paris-1900/medal-design [accessed 2 May 2025].

entrees of the agricultural categories of the Exposition, and it is perhaps from the agricultural and industrial competitions of the Exposition that the Olympic Games would later adopt the typology.[159]

While 'foot-ball association' gained the most column inches in English newspapers, 'foot-ball rugby' received more space in the Official Report, which included far more detailed reports of the games played, by reproducing the reports first published by the newspaper *Tous les sports*, official organ of the USFSA.[160] Rugby football was the last of the Exposition games competitions organised by the USFSA and also the most popular with the public, although the 'good propaganda' was more effective than immediate success.[161] A wet morning gave way to blue sky for the opening fixture, when Frankfurt played the French Team in front of an estimated 3,500 spectators comprising 2,519 paid entries plus around 1,000 others mostly invited guests and press. This was considered to be a positive outcome, the writer reflected that the Exhibition games fulfilled the USFSA's objective of bringing 'a new audience to our sports' and hinted at prior cynicism, stating the Rugby fixtures had therefore not been 'as useless as people want to say', The German players were more athletic than the French, had abstained from tobacco for 15 days while the French captain enjoyed a cigar before the game. After a successful start, the German team despite its athleticism and smooth play, lost by 27-17. Afterward both teams enjoyed a banquet together.[162]

In the second game, the French Team beat Moseley Wanderers of England 27-8. The report was generous to the Mosley team, identifying they had 'played the day before, Saturday, in Birmingham, then travelled all night. They had a very painful crossing. Landing in Paris at 6 a.m., they were barely able to take three hours of rest before to appear on the ground' and suggesting the team was 'handicapped by 15 points by the circumstances of their travel'. The game, while not as aesthetic in its style of play as the first game, was a success for French Rugby. Apart from the result, it was played in front of over 6,000 spectators, of which 4,389 had paid, generating revenue of around 800 Francs, meaning that the two Rugby games paid approximately 2,400 Francs to the athletic budget of the Exhibition. The report reflected that Rugby was more popular in the West than the East of Paris and that tickets had been priced low to attract East Parisians, but that the large attendances at the games proved Rugby had a clientele in the city.[163]

Back in England, news of Moseley's defeat was reported by several newspapers, at least one of which was drawing upon a Reuter's news release and which reported a crowd of 10,000 spectators,[164] and some articles told of the gruelling

---

[159]Royal Commission for the Paris International Exhibition 1900, Volume 1, 1901, HMSO, pp. 178–179.
[160]Mérillon (1901, p. 69).
[161]Mérillon (1901, p. 69).
[162]Mérillon (1901, p. 69).
[163]Mérillon (1901, p. 69).
[164]*The Morning Post*, 'Multiple Sports Items', Monday 29 October 1900.

fixture schedule and travel.[165] It seems reasonable that fatigue was a contributor to the defeat: At least five of the players are believed to have played for their respective clubs, in England, the day before the game. Clement Deykin, for example, represented the Midland Counties on the 24th October, Moseley Wanderers on 27th October, made the trip to Paris overnight, and then played at the Exposition the next day. How the players in the team were chosen to represent Moseley and play at the Exposition is unclear; four of the players, including the captain, John Henry Birtles, did play regularly for Moseley, with several others also playing for Midlands based clubs (Moseley Society, 2018). We must then speculate this was a similar arrangement to that of Upton Park in association football; a touring side was compiled to include players selected from the Moseley roster and augmented by other men whose commitments, or lack of, outside of Rugby, meant that they were available to travel. Newspaper readers in London were reminded the popularity of Rugby in Paris again the following month, a few days after the closure of the Exposition,[166] when the Catford team from London faced Racing Club de France at the velodrome of the Parc des Princes, watched by 4,000 spectators.[167] An overall impact and legacy of the 1900 Games was the overarching objective: The Exposition Report concludes that the broader aim of the Sports of the Exposition had been achieved with reference to bringing together humanity internationally, and for the educational value of sport, and that despite the overall high financial cost to host them, a greater good had been achieved.[168]

Chapter Summary

The games of the 1900 Paris Exposition were clearly not the Olympic Games that Pierre de Coubertin had in mind when, in 1894, he announced a 1900 Games for Paris. The inaugural games held in Athens during 1896 illustrate the political and financial requirement to host such an international amateur multi-sport event, even compressed within two weeks. So, the timing and location of the Paris Exposition presumably seemed like the perfect opportunity to saddle to an existing large-scale public event that would draw an international audience. The practical reality was quite different, and the power dynamic of the Exposition Committee and that of the fledgling IOC appear such that there is no mention of the word *Olympic* in the Official Report, not the medals, although running races were referred to as World Championships. Unlike in Athens, the events, of which there were many, were spread across several months rather than days and it is not clear which events Coubertin would himself have considered part of any Olympic Games, although presumably his diverse athletics section would be the minimum at the time. The IOC and Olympic historians have retrospectively selected a

[165] *The Morning Post*, 'Multiple Sports Items', Monday 29 October 1900; *Cornishman*, 'Football', Thursday 1 November 1900.
[166] *The Morning Post*, Tuesday 13 November 1900.
[167] *Pall Mall Gazette*, 'Sporting Notes and News', Monday 19 November 1900.
[168] Mérillon (1901, p. 420).

breadth of events, studied the records of performance, and awarded gold, silver, and bronze places, but this is a revisionist approach not reflecting the prizes nor the awareness, or indeed existence, of the IOC in any official capacity at the time. Indeed, the medal categories now used by the IOC seem to have only been used outside of the sport events, evidence shows that they were categories for the agricultural prizes. It is telling that in the Official Report, Coubertin's involvement is recorded as having been via the UFSA rather than of the IOC. Nevertheless, we have given a significant treatment to the games and the Exposition that we consider having been its parent. The scale and ambition of the Exposition is significant, being the most notable such event since London's Great Exhibition of 1851. It is thus of relevance to understand its planning and delivery. Being located in France, across the Channel from England, makes this an important event that the British were aware of, as the coverage in newspapers shows us, reporting as they did on its announcement, anticipating the spectacle, and reporting the experience and some of the sport results in events for which it was thought there would be British interest, due to success or involvement. The decision to associate Olympic Games to World Fairs would continue after 1900, the reality of holding the games necessitating it rather than any great benefit to Olympicism garnered from the experience of 1900. As we shall see, these were important times in the establishment of the IOC and of the games, the World's Fair connection helping but also hindering their development.

Chapter 7

St Louis 1904

Abstract

The British continued to contribute to the International Olympic Committee (IOC) as a movement despite their lack of formal participation in the 1904 games, which while originally intended for Chicago, were held in St Louis. The 1904 IOC Congress was held in London, and made the decision that Rome would host the 1908 games. We narrate this event and how it was a precursor to the founding of the British Olympic Association. We also discuss the St Louis Games themselves including the move from Chicago and the lack of British involvement which we posit as being a financial reality, as well as considering how they appeared from a British perspective. The British Government did however involve itself in exhibiting at the Louisiana Purchase Exposition to which the games were somewhat porously attached. Thanks to Reuters telegrams the games still received coverage in British newspapers, providing continuity, while perceptions that St Louis was a dangerous place on the American frontier persisted.

Keywords: St Louis 1904; Louisiana Purchase Exposition; anthropology days; Amateur Athletic Union; sport history

Introduction

The Paris Exhibition of 1900 was a celebration of modernity, marking the end of the 19th century and optimistic about the 20th. The Games of the 1900 Paris Exposition were not the Olympic Games that Pierre de Coubertin had in mind, and lessons had been learned. The international Olympic movement was still not as established as Coubertin wanted it to be and already he was facing resistance and opposition to the games and their ownership. In this chapter we show how Coubertin persevered but how, once again, politics and rivalries would encroach upon his vision. The Olympic Games would again be tethered to a World Fair, this time in the United States, and again Coubertin would distance himself from the event.

Foundations of Managing British Olympics: Institutions through Time, 127–145

Published under exclusive licence by Emerald Publishing Limited
doi:10.1108/978-1-80262-095-520251007

In Britain, the death of Queen Victoria in 1901 represented the end of an era, while more directly for British participation in the Olympic movement Sir Howard Vincent, the Conservative MP (Member of Parliament) for Sheffield Central and both a soldier and senior policeman joined the IOC as British representative (Anthony, 1997, p. 20). Queen Victoria was succeeded by her son, Edward VII who was crowned on 9 August 1902, and who would later become important to the story of Great Britain and the Olympics.

We draw upon the existing historiography as well as reports of the games and newspaper articles, to narrate how the Olympic Games of 1904 happened to be held in St Louis, and how the games and wider Exhibition to which it was associated were reported in the British Press. By doing so, we continue our story of the development of the international Olympic revival and the perceptions and interest in Olympic Games in Great Britain. We start in London, at the sixth session of the IOC.

Sixth IOC Session in London

1904 was a very important year for the Olympic movement in two ways. Most famously was the third Olympiad, held in St Louis, United States, which we shall discuss in due course. Secondly, at the sixth session of the IOC separate to its congress, the Italian city of Rome was selected to host the games of the fourth Olympiad, scheduled for 1908. Rome, which had worked on its bid since at least 1903 was chosen ahead of three other candidate cities: Berlin, Milan, and London.[1] Although events would conspire against this choice, as we shall explain later (Chapter 9).

The session where that decision was made was held in London, England on 22 June. It was arranged by the Rev. Laffan who 'attracted much favourable attention with its faultless organisation and his ability to arrange meetings for the representatives with such luminaries as the Prince of Wales and King Edward VII' (Kent, 2008, p. 37). The location would later prove ironic. Laffan worked with an organising committee and welcoming party, which involved Charles Herbert (Secretary of the Amateur Athletic Association since 1883 and a member of the IOC), politicians Sir Howard Vincent, Sir Lees Knowles, and Herbert Gladstone (who the following year became Home Secretary), Lord Kinnaird (a famous sportsman who at that time was President of the Football Association and Director of Barclays Bank), and the famous English international cricketers The Earl of Darnley (Previously the Hon Ivo Bligh, and by now retired from the game), CB (Charles Burgess) Fry and WG (William Gilbert) Grace, the latter two of whom were regarded as all-round sportsmen (Anthony, 1997; Barker, 2005).[2]

---

[1]IOC Study Centre (hereafter IOC), CIO-JO-19085-RONE-CORR. 'ROME 1908' article de presse 1904.

[2]Present at the Congress for England were Sir C.E. Howard Vincent, Lord Kinnaird, Earl of Darnley, Hon. Herbert Gladstone, Rev. De Courcy Laffan, Sir Lees Knowles, Sir W.H. Grenfell, see Minutes of the Meeting of The Committee of International Olympic Games, Held at London, June 20–26 included in Sullivan, J. E. (1905). *Spaldings Athletic Library Official Athletic Almanac for 1905*, 'Review of the Olympic Games of 1904'. American Sports Publishing Company, p. 277.

This was the first the IOC had held an event in London and Laffan and the committee made sure to create a great impression. As well as being greeted by some of the most prominent individuals from sporting society, delegates attended dinners at Mansion House and Fishmongers Hall, and visited Windsor and the Society of Arts, where Coubertin gave a speech about reviving the games and Victor Balck presented on Scandinavia's winter sports, supported by illustrative magic lantern slides (Barker, 2012). They were greeted also by the Mayor of London, met the Prince of Wales for drinks at Marlborough House, and attended a reception with King Edward VII at Windsor Castle, and witnessed the Trooping the Colour at Horse Guards Parade, the official birthday parade of the Monarch (Barker, 2012).

Sport was also on the agenda and on Tuesday 21 June the delegation visited the cricket ground Lord's where a touring South Africa national team took on the County side Middlesex on the second of a two-day test (Anthony, 1997; Bailey, 1997; Barker, 2005). Missing the end of the cricket match, which ended in a draw, the delegation visited Regent's Park and the Royal Taxophilite (archery) Society, at the invitation of Colonel Henry Walrond, a keen archer who would himself later become formally involved with British Olympic administration (Barker, 2012). Other notable visits included on Sunday the 26th a luncheon at Taplow Court, the home of Mr W. H. Grenfell and a row on the Thames Grenfell was a keen rower having been President of the Oxford University Rowing Club and Captained The Maidenhead Rowing Club (Grenfell History, n.d.) and would become significant in the British Olympic story.[3]

The decision to award the fourth Olympiad to Rome was made at the event held at the Society of Arts. Prospero Collona, the mayor of Rome had sent 'an impassioned plea to the IOC, which had the desired effect' (Barker, 2012, p. 4). Until this point, Rome and Berlin had remained the only cities to be considered, but Doctor Gebhaedt, for Germany withdrew his request and assured his vote for the Italian capital. Thus, Rome was chosen unanimously.[4] The Italian bid was headed by Count Brunetta d'Usseau, the Italian delegate attending the London Congress, and a sport enthusiast credited with the introduction of physical exercises into modern education. He was supported by a large number of representatives of the Italian Sports Federations, and had impressed them with his explanation of the benefits of the games including its educational dimension. Furthermore, he had calculated the sums necessary for Rome to host, proposing the appointment of a commission to study the means of carrying out the work by bringing together the support of all of these societies.[5]

---

[3]Minutes of the Meeting of The Committee of International Olympic Games, Held at London, June 20–26 included in Sullivan, J. E., 1905, *Spaldings Athletic Library Official Athletic Almanac for 1905*, 'Review of the Olympic Games of 1904'. American Sports Publishing Company, New York, p. 283.

[4]Minutes of the Meeting of The Committee of International Olympic Games, Held at London, June 20–26 included in Sullivan, J. E., 1905, *Spaldings Athletic Library Official Athletic Almanac for 1905*, 'Review of the Olympic Games of 1904'. American Sports Publishing Company, New York, p. 281.

[5]IOC, CIO-JO-19085-RONE-CORR. 'La IVe Olympiade Aura Lieu A Rome En 1908', *L'Italie*, 24 June 1904.

It was decided in London that the 1908 edition of the Olympic Games would take place in an Olympic week falling in the Easter holidays, within a wider programme of games and sport events occurring from the month of February to the month of July.[6] This programme would occur in three phases: The first period, from the month of February to Easter (April 19) would be concerned with national and international shooting matches, fencing, various equestrian events, tennis, balloon, longue paume, basketball, association and rugby football, cricket, and firemans' competition. The second period (Easter holidays) would host an International Olympic Games Congress, automobile races and an aerostatic competition exhibition.

The third period would be held outside of Rome, at either Civitavecchia or Naples for regattas, for rowing boats (Royal Italian Rowing Club), regattas for sailing and steam boats (Royal Italian Yacht Club), propellers, life-saving Competition on land and sea, etc. The cycle was to be crowned by fêtes and by an Exhibition of Sports and Industries and by meetings and possibly also an Art Exhibition.[7] It was reported elsewhere the Olympic programme would also include international competitions in mountaineering, athletics, gymnastics, hockey, golf, lawn tennis, swimming, Basque pelota, podiatry polo, cycling, and water-polo. There would also be congresses on physical education and sport.[8] Upon awarding the Games to Rome, Coubertin, with Count Brunetta D'Usseaux, sent a telegram from the Italian Embassy in London to King Vittorio Emmanuel III (Barker, 2012).

The members representing Sweden, Norway, Holland, and Denmark requested the Committee should be the arbiter of the Programme of the Olympiads, although Count Brunetta d'Usseaux countered, referring to the preceding Olympiads, for which the host committees had a great degree of freedom to develop their programme, and asked that this approach could apply also to Rome. The Committee also decided that Berlin, which had so generously renounced its candidature for the fourth Olympiad and voted in favour of the Rome bid, should be granted the Annual Congress of the IOC,[9] although this idea does not seem to have materialised, Berlin would not host congress until 1930.

It is thought that the London Congress not only impressed the visiting delegates from overseas, but also 'galvanised Britain's three IOC members (Charles

---

[6]Minutes of the Meeting of The Committee of International Olympic Games, Held at London, June 20–26 included in Sullivan, J. E., 1905, *Spaldings Athletic Library Official Athletic Almanac for 1905*, 'Review of the Olympic Games of 1904'. American Sports Publishing Company, New York, p. 277.

[7]Minutes of the Meeting of The Committee of International Olympic Games, Held at London, June 20–26 included in Sullivan, J. E., 1905, *Spaldings Athletic Library Official Athletic Almanac for 1905*, 'Review of the Olympic Games of 1904'. American Sports Publishing Company, New York, p. 281.

[8]IOC, CIO-JO-19085-RONE-CORR. 'La IVe Olympiade Aura Lieu A Rome En 1908', *L'Italie*, 24 June 1904.

[9]Minutes of the Meeting of The Committee of International Olympic Games, Held at London, June 20–26 included in Sullivan, J. E., 1905, *Spaldings Athletic Library Official Athletic Almanac for 1905*, 'Review of the Olympic Games of 1904'. American Sports Publishing Company, New York, p. 281.

Herbert, Reverend Laffan, and Colonel Sir Howard Vincent)' to circulate a letter proposing the 'formation of a British Olympic Association' (Barker, 2005, p. 70) an idea that would bear fruit the following year and as we explain in Chapter 8.

The Third Olympiad: St Louis, USA

The first two of Coubertin's modern Olympic Games had been hosted only by European cities; Athens and Paris. Coubertin had visited the United States in Autumn 1893 but had found little support for his ideas among American sports enthusiasts and academics except for William Slone, a Professor of European History at Princeton. As well as visiting the Olympic Club of San Francisco, he visited the Chicago Exhibition and the Chicago Athletics Club, which made a lasting impression on him.[10] As a result, at the First Congress of the IOC in 1894 it had been tacitly agreed that the United States would follow Greece and France in hosting the games, and Chicago duly stepped forward.[11] Chicago was accepted, chosen over Berlin, Copenhagen, and Stockholm as host at an IOC meeting in Paris on the 31 May 1901 and this was considered such a big success for the city that a crowd of 6,000 students at the University of Chicago organised a 'mammoth bonfire' to celebrate (Matthews, 2005, p. 17). An ambitious programme was designed including sport, literary, and artistic events, published in three languages – English, French, and German.

The games were promoted in France by the Chicago industrialist Charles R. Crane, who enlisted a Parisian lawyer to push for the cause. The event was further promoted by a Chicago lawyer, Henry J. Furber, who proposed running it along commercial lines, forming a corporation which would issue 2,000 shares of stock at $100 per share. Furber had early hopes that the Chicago Games would be the most successful yet and had estimated that the $200,000 that this raised would easily be repaid as the games would raise $375,000 of income. This plan was put into action in February 1901 when the International Olympian Games Association was formed and issued a prospectus to raise $250,000. There was no shortage of interest to invest in the project – street merchants, hospitality, and transportation companies, having an interest in attracting visitors, pledged to invest $85,000, while four other investors with links to Crane pledged $50,000 each. Grand plans were made for the event including an 11 acre, 800 feet by 130 feet, stadium seating 75,000 spectators which would be 60 feet high and have a mechanical retractable roof. Intended to be a temporary structure, this spectacular construction would be dismantled once the Olympic Games were over. However, the proposed site of the stadium on the Chicago Waterfront facing onto Lake Michigan proved controversial with local residents and merchants who claimed the structure would violate local building rules, which triggered a planning dispute that went all the way to the Illinois Supreme Court. The Court ruled that the stadium could not be built east of the Illinois Central Railroad tracks, meaning that the stadium would have to be in the north of the city. This dampened hopes of a naval display encouraged by President Roosevelt taking

[10] de Coubertin, p. 10.
[11] de Coubertin, p. 39.

place in conjunction with the games and seems to have terminally damaged the project (Findling, 2004, pp. 25–28). By April 1902, six sections of Games Planning were identified by the Chicago committee, and a 'midway' feature as also being considered (Findling, 2004, p. 57):

(1) World's championships in all international sports;
(2) Competitions in games peculiar to certain nations;
(3) Demonstrations of other athletic events, including a revival of the ancient games;
(4) A military display, perhaps held in conjunction with the formation of the newly authorised National Guard;
(5) An exposition of sporting goods; and
(6) An Olympic Congress after the games to analyse the 'lessons' of the event.

The plan was well worked out by the time of its effective cancellation in May 1903, when the International Olympian Games Association formally dissolved the corporation. Tables 8 and 9 show some of the business plan for the Chicago event which were well worked out, down to the tenure of individual staff.

Plans for Chicago had been ambitious – in addition to the naval display would be forty separate competitions. This would include some 'novelty sports' such as a potato race and a pole vault over distance instead of height, and a boy's schedule containing sixteen track and field events (Findling, 2004, p. 27). James E. Sullivan, the Secretary-Treasurer of the Amateur Athletics Union, appears to have lost patience with the Chicago organisers and threatened to run his own rival games in St Louis, Missouri. Sullivan had been frustrated with the IOC since it had refused to give him a seat in 1900, and had threatened to set up an alternative series of games in the United States (Findling, 2004, p. 24). Sullivan was extremely powerful in the American sporting landscape – as well as co-founding Chicago Athletic Club, he was a sports equipment entrepreneur through his company Sullivan Sporting Goods, and he had also been in charge of American athletes in Paris (Matthews, 2005, p. 9). There was a broader rivalry between St Louis and Chicago based on regional economic geography. In 1893, St Louis, then the fourth largest city with a population of 575,000 (Matthews, 2005, p. 93), was passed over in favour of Chicago to host the celebrations of the 400th anniversary of Columbus discovering the Americas.[12] In 1901–1902, there was a dispute over a drainage canal, which started in Illinois but which flowed into the Mississippi River near St Louis (Findling, 2004, p. 29). St Louis did however secure the celebration of the 100th anniversary of the Louisiana Purchase in 1803, when the United States had bought the lands of French Louisiana from Napoleon Boneparte, which ended up happening in 1904 because of project overruns.[13]

---

[12]de Coubertin, p. 40.
[13]de Coubertin, p. 40.

Table 8. Chicago Projected Administration.

Item	Cost (dollars)
Director (1 year)	5,000
Secretary (3 years at 2,000 dollars pa)	6,000
European Agent (3 years at 600 dollars)	18,000
Stenographer clerks (1 year)	2,000
Head janitor (3 weeks)	150
275 janitors (12 days)	3,300
20 ticket sellers (4 weeks)	1,200
Keeper	170
12 day labourers (15 days)	270
2 carpenters (15 days)	120
Electricity	2,500
Water	90
Furniture	300
Rented office space (12 months)	600
Advertising, including the press office, circulars	10,000
Prizes (not including those offered by the International Olympic Committee	5,000
Reception of representatives	20,000
Music (100 musicians, 12 days)	7,500
Shows – Fun	25,000
Sundry	4,000
Total (given in report)	175,000
Total (authors calculation)	191,800

Source: IOC CIO-JO 19085-ROME-CORR, Divers doc concernant les you a rolle en 1908, 1903. Dalla 'Revue Olympique' Del Gennaio 1901: L'Opera Del Comitato Internazionale Olimpico.

The Move to St Louis

The plan, projected to cost \$575,000[14] was moved to St Louis because the organisers of the Louisiana Purchase Exposition began to plan sports activities to eclipse the Olympic Games, which they used as leverage in attempting to get the Olympics moved. The St Louis organisers had begun campaigning for this as early as October 1902, when they requested the games be moved at an evening banquet

[14]IOCCIO-JO19085-ROME-CORR, Divers doc concernant les you a rolle en 1908, 1903. Dalla 'Revue Olympique' Del Gennaio 1901: L'Opera Del Comitato Internazionale Olimpico, pp. 24–28.

Table 9. Chicago Projected Income.

Item	Dollars
Standing room	360,000
Concessions	10,000
Sundry	5,000
Total income dollars	375,000
Capital of the shareholder company	200,000
Dollars	575,000

Source: IOC CIO-JO 19085-ROME-CORR, Divers doc concernant les you a rolle en 1908, 1903. Dalla 'Revue Olympique' Del Gennaio 1901: L'Opera Del Comitato Internazionale Olimpico.

(Matthews, 2005, pp. 26–27). The political case for this grew through the autumn, though the IOC were split as to whether this should happen. Coubertin, in his memoir claims that the games were moved to St Louis following the loss of the lakeside venue in Chicago. On 23 December 1902, he claims to have contacted President Roosevelt about moving the games to St Louis, who 'opted in favour of the transfer'.[15] What is less clear is how credible Sullivan's threat to move the games was, and it is possible Coubertin still feared a breakaway Olympic movement in America. One credible weapon that Sullivan did have was the site of the Amateur Athletic Union (AAU) 1904 Track and Field Championships, which he wanted to incorporate in the Department for Physical Culture at the Louisiana Purchase Exhibition, and could be run at a time inconvenient to the Chicago organisers and take US athletes away from the games (Matthews, 2005, pp. 20–23). Coubertin thus appears to have reluctantly acquiesced, despite concerns about the limited sports facilities available in St Louis, and on 10 February sent a telegram to the Chicago organisers simply saying 'Transfer accepted' (Matthews, 2005, pp. 32, 38).

With the benefit of hindsight Coubertin must have regretted the whole episode. Held from 1 July until 23 November 1904, the third games were, like the Paris Games, an adjunct to a World Fair, despite claims that it would be a separate event (Matthews, 2005, pp. 26–27). Further, Coubertin gave way to Sullivan and the AAU, allowing them to organise the games without his involvement or that of the IOC more generally, without himself communicating with them or even visiting, although there was an assertation that the Olympic, or *Olympian* brand was to be used to avoid a repeat of the Parisian experience. Sullivan, meanwhile, had been announced chief of the Physical Culture Department and director of the Olympic Games in July 1903 (Matthews, 2005, pp. 98–104). However, the term *Olympian* ended up being used as a broad catch all for the physical activities of the Exhibition, whether inside the allotted days of 29 August–3 September period (Matthews, 2005, p. 106). The project of the Exhibition and the games was still

[15]de Coubertin (1979, p. 41).

vast, despite the lack of IOC involvement – 19.5 million people came to the Exhibition, and there were considerable civil engineering projects in connection with it – 70 miles of streets were rebuilt, thirty miles of new streets added, while 450 new streetcars purchased for the transit system. These ran to the site at the Forest Park fairground every 15 minutes. Further, the site itself was so massive that it required a railroad to transport attendees around it (Matthews, 2005, pp. 108–109). As with previous World's Fairs, there was attempt to represent aspects of the whole world in a single site, with the intention of demonstrating the progress of culture and technology. There were displays of indigenous peoples from Africa, Asia, and South America who lived on site, as well as displays of scientific achievement and engineering – airships and Ferris wheels were included, and scholars and educators from around the world gave talks and debated (Matthews, 2005, p. 109).

The Olympian Games happened at the end of the summer, as the culmination of a series of events. Earlier in August there was a series of Anthropology days at the stadium in which the indigenous peoples from around the world took part in athletic events including track and field events. It is not clear, but this may have been carried over or adapted from the Chicago idea or competitions in games peculiar to certain nations (see above). The events were organised by Dr Simms, of the Field Museum in Chicago and Dr Luther Halsey Gullick, and were presented as an experiment in understanding the athletic abilities of the various peoples who took part in a range of contests over two days based on the perception that they would be natural athletes. The various peoples did not perform very well, not because they were strangers to physical activity, but because they were doing it outside of their normal context. Compared to American athletes who were used to engaging in competitive track and field sports and training regularly, the peoples were given one day's previous instruction by Martin Delaney, the athletics and football coach of St Louis University,[16] but this was clearly inadequate, particularly as the instruction was done through the medium of interpreters. Not having seen or participated in the sports before, the peoples misunderstood what was expected – for instance, in the one hundred yards race, either stopping at the finishing tape or running under it. Generally the peoples were unable to perform in a way approaching existing records. They lacked cultural reference to the sports, and the games were not universally familiar – people were from around the world – including the Ainus from Japan, Native Americans including people from the Cocopa and Sioux tribes, and Pygmies from Africa.[17] A finding was claimed on the basis that 'savages' lacked 'natural athletic ability', and future lecturers and authors told to omit this claim but it is perhaps not surprising that this exercise in what we refer to as *anthrotainment* did not have the expected findings.[18] Some authors (e.g. Brownell, 2008; Gøksyr, 1990; Parezo & Fowler, 2007) have claimed

[16] 'Yes, We have no Delaney'. *St Louis Post-Dispatch*, 24 October 1934, p. 16.
[17] Sullivan, J.E., 1905, *Spaldings Athletic Library Official Athletic Almanac for 1905*, 'Review of the Olympic Games of 1904'. American Sports Publishing Company, New York, pp. 249–259.
[18] Sullivan (1905, p. 259).

these events were overall intended to demonstrate white cultural supremacy and American imperialism, and certainly within the sporting evidence there was an assumption of the inherent supremacy of the American approach to track and field events.

Unlike the Exposition of Paris, 1900, the organisers of St. Louis did not publish an official report of the games – neither the IOC nor the AAU who effectively organised the games and prepared the American athletes are known for taking responsibility for producing a report. The historical record hinges on two documents – the report by Sullivan which is incorporated within *Spalding's Official Athletic Almanac for 1905* – an existing series of sporting almanacs,[19] and a second report apparently privately published by Charles J. P. Lucas via a printer called E. B. Woodward.[20] This on its own demonstrates the extent to which the 1904 games were a private enterprise. Over the summer alongside the *anthrotainment* sports several other contests which were branded 'Olympic' – there was a lecture course, but also a series of age group sports from elementary school to collegiate, as well as loosely aligned events such as 'Turners' Games', a hybrid of track and field and gymnastic disciplines. These were branded the 'International Olympic Turners' Championship'; there were also 'Olympic Irish Sports' involving track and field events as well as Gaelic sports such as football and hurling. These were existing championships rebranded Olympic with no official recognition, other than the agreement between Coubertin and the Exposition organisers. There was also Olympic Basketball, and an attempt at Olympic College Football which proved impossible to organise as no teams apart from St Louis University would appear for free.[21] In both reports the actual Olympic sports are shown as consisting only of track and field events, and individual sports clubs (such as New York AC or Chicago AA) or university teams such as Cornell or Princeton are shown as competing alongside countries such as Germany, Hungary, Ireland, and Cuba.[22] Nonetheless, Olympic and World Records were claimed, with the connection back to Paris as the 'second Olympic renewal' also made, comparing the performance of American athletes across both competitions.[23]

Prizes included Gold, Silver, and Bronze medals for those placed first, second, and third respectively, as well as laurel wreaths of victory for the winners.[24] Prizes aside from Olympic medals were of the highest value allowed under AAU rules and more ornate than any previous US amateur prizes, in the form of silver cups to the winners (Mathews, 2005). These 'handsome special Olympic souvenir cups'

---

[19]Sullivan, J. E. (1905). *Spaldings Athletic Library Official Athletic Almanac for 1905*, 'Review of the Olympic Games of 1904'. American Sports Publishing Company, New York.

[20]Lucas, J. P. (1905). *The Olympic Games 1904*. St Louis, MO. Woodward & Tiernan Printing Co.

[21]Sullivan (1905, pp. 171–247).

[22]Sullivan (1905, pp. 265–275); Lucas (1905, p. 143).

[23]Lucas (1905, p. 97); Sullivan (1905, pp. 265–275).

[24]Lucas (1905, p. 13).

were sponsored on a basis that might be considered philanthropic but could also be viewed as early Olympic sponsorship. Trophies were awarded to winners of the Marathon, 100-, 200-, 400-, 800-, 1500-metre runs, 200- and 400-metre hurdle, running broad-jump, running high jump, running hop-step-and-jump, three standing jumps, lifting the bar-bell, throwing the discus, the 56-lb weight for distance, and the 16-lb hammer, and for putting the 16-lb shot. Notable is the Cup donated by Mr F.J.V. Skiff, as a prize awarded to the winner of the '100-meter dash' in the Olympic Championships, because he was Director of Exhibits of the Louisiana Purchase Exposition. A photograph of this trophy was included in the report published in the Spalding almanac authored by Sullivan.[25] Also included is a photograph of what was perhaps most significant of all, the Spalding cup, presented by sport entrepreneur A.G. Spalding and awarded to the club scoring the greatest number of points at the International Olympic Games element of the Exposition sports.[26]

Albert G. Spalding, of Spalding Sporting Goods and co-founder of Chicago Athletic Club, was American Director, in charge of US athletes, at the Paris Exposition (Olympic) Games of 1900. That 1900 team had contained two University of Chicago students and was coached by Alonzo Stagg, coach and former player of the Chicago American Football team. This had been instrumental in the Chicago Tribune newspaper giving extensive coverage to the 1900 campaign, creating awareness of the Olympic Games in the city which must have laid foundations for the city's initially successful bid (Mathews, 2005). When Chicago and St Louis had begun to tussle for the games, Spalding, despite being such an important figure in Chicago sporting society, in October and November of 1902 'urged the Chicago and St Louis partisans to meet and work out the conflict' (Findling, 2004, p. 27). This was a shrewd move as the games, which may have died with the planning rejection in Chicago, were successfully resuscitated to the benefit of Spalding's business: A.G. Spalding & Bros installed gymnastic appliances in the 'complete gymnasium' exhibit at the World's Fair eventually hosted in St Louis. The exhibit was awarded the Grand Prize and Gold Medal, an advertorial within Spalding's own sporting almanac was self-congratulatory in its tone, commending the firm as being 'alive to the imperative need of the times' and 'to be congratulated on their enterprise'. It was carefully stipulated every Spalding article used in the Olympic Games of 1904 was purchased at 'full retail prices'. These articles extended beyond those in the gymnasium exhibit to include the following used in competitions: Goal posts and nets, tennis poles and nets, archery targets and stands, roque sets, golf balls and clubs, boxing gloves, 16-1b. hammer, 16-1b. shot, 56-1b. weight, discus, vaulting poles, vaulting standards. Readers were invited to purchase a replica discuss 'sealed in box and guaranteed absolutely correct' priced at $5.00 each.[27]

---

[25]Sullivan (1905, p. 202).
[26]Sullivan (1905, pp. 163, 202).
[27]Spalding (1905, p. 264).

Why No British Involvement?

In something of a backward step from 1900 there was no British official athletics team at St Louis, despite the AAA rules potentially allowing for one. This was not an act of resistance or an expression of indifference but a practical response. The Reverend Laffan expressed his disapproval of St Louis hosting to Coubertin, but he had little formal power over the sporting bodies at this time (Llewellyn, 2011, p. 636). The AAA decided in December 1903 not to send a representative team based on the expenses that would be incurred, though Herbert was told to communicate to the organisers of the games that the AAA would do all in its powers to support them.[28] This decision was reviewed but reinforced in May 1904. It was similarly decided not to send a touring team to New Zealand and Australia in December 1904.[29] Historians such as Llewellyn have put this down to conservatism on the part of the AAA, but in financial terms it was a small organisation which did not have wealthy benefactors, relying mostly on the subscriptions of its affiliates and the profits (often in excess of £100) from its Championship Sports meetings to survive. Its December 1903 accounts show a small deficit for the year of £44 9s 11d, while the Balance Sheet showed total assets of £1559 14s 9d.[30] The 1903 Championship, held in Northampton, attracted a crowd of 6,000 but turned a profit of only £34 18s.[31] To put this into context, the cost of a single athlete travelling to St Louis can be loosely estimated. Keeling (2008, p. 26) shows that a steerage passage on a Liverpool–New York liner operated by Cunard, then aimed at migrants to the United States, would at the time of the games in the third quarter of 1904 be available for a historic low of as little as £3 19s return. This low fare was as the result of a price war which unfolded in 1904, and when the decision was taken at the end of 1903 the fare was still at £9 4s. A rail fare from New York to St. Louis, however, would cost almost as much again – based on a then average fare per passenger mile of $0.0203 over a distance of 950 miles, this comes to $19.28, or almost £4 2s for a single ticket.[32] A December 1903 projection puts the return cost for an athlete at around £17 6s before considering the costs of accommodation, sustenance or travel to Liverpool to start the voyage to St Louis. Sending a team of 10 athletes, equivalent to that sent to Paris for £100, at the price known in December 1903 would have cost £173 for just the Liverpool–St Louis journey alone.

---

[28]AAA ATH/AAA/1/2/2/4 Minutes of the General Committee, 12 December 1903.

[29]AAA ATH/AAA/1/2/2/4 Minutes of the General Committee, 28 May 1904.

[30]AAA ATH/AAA/1/5-2/2 AAA Accounts for the Year Ending, 31 December 1903.

[31]'The AAA Championships'. *Edinburgh Evening News*, 6 July 1903, p. 4; AAA ATH/AAA/1/5-2/2 AAA Accounts for the Year Ending, 31 December 1903.

[32]Rail fare per mile taken from Federal Coordinator of Transportation, 1935, *Passenger Traffic Report,* Washington, DC, p. 146. Distance is by road as rail distances are unavailable, but can be assumed to be similar. Conversion: Lawrence H. Officer and Samuel H. Williamson, 'Computing 'Real Value' Over Time With a Conversion Between U.K. Pounds and U.S. Dollars, 1791 to Present', Measuring Worth, 2024.

To fund this, the AAA would have to dip into its reserves, held in railway shares and government debt, amounting to £857 2s 7d with no obvious financial return and no knowledge of its likely financial performance in 1904. St Louis would clearly be an unacceptable stretch on the AAA's resources in a period when self-reliance was considered a virtue in voluntary organisations, and financial difficulties would be embarrassing for the professional reputations of its committee members. Furthermore, the AAA was not registered as a limited liability company, meaning that the committee could be responsible for paying creditors if it collapsed. We may also assume the St Louis Games similarly fell beyond the resources of other British amateur sport bodies such as the NCU and ASA, as well as their equivalents in France including the USFSA. This illustrates the geographical restrictions on the viability of international sport in this early era, and it should be remembered that the achievement of these events at all was quite remarkable. Lucas did however claim 'neither France nor England was missed' but that American entries had made Paris successful, and that this tendency continued at St Louis![33]

The only representation from Europe came from a small band of athletes who travelled from Ireland, Germany, Hungary and Greece, but the registration of athletes was somewhat ad hoc. Three athletes were attributed to Ireland – two, John Daly and Thomas Kiely, travelled from Ireland under self-raised funding. It is even claimed Daly sold prizes to raise the money to travel, a move which would have risked censure from the athletics authorities (Irish Independent, 2012). Retrospectively, Daly and Kiely as well as John Holloway, an Irishman who already lived in America, have been attributed to the Great Britain team by the IOC because Ireland was not a sovereign state at the time, but contemporaneous sources show them as Irish.[34] Two Kaffir tribesmen, Lentauw and Yamasani, from Zululand, South Africa, participated in the marathon.[35] These men had served as messengers for the Boers during the Boer War and had been brought to St Louis as exhibits in a show recreating the conflict. They also took part in the attempted anthropological sports events (Cleophas, 2024). The organisation was somewhat ad hoc – Lucas suggests that a group of ten Greek marathon runners either registered late for the marathon or simply turned up on the day.[36] The two Kaffir tribesmen finished 9th and 12th, even though one of the two, Lentauw, was chased by a dog for almost a mile off the course, losing six or seven minutes.[37]

The race had a grand finale, being won by Fred Lorz of the Mohawk Athletic Club, New York, but Lucas had himself caught him riding in an automobile some of the distance![38] Lorz completed the race on foot and entered the stadium to the cheers of the crowds, but the title was given to Thomas J. Hicks who represented

---

[33]Lucas (1905, p. 15).
[34]Lucas (1905, p. 143).
[35]Lucas (1905, p. 48).
[36]Lucas (1905, p. 47).
[37]Lucas (1905, p. 57).
[38]Lucas (1905, p. 46).

the Cambridge, Mass, YMCA team, who, though English, had chosen to represent his adopted country. He, however, was 'kept in mechanical action by use of drugs'[39] and his trainers resorted to experimental methods to keep him going:

> As Hicks passed the twenty-mile post, his color began to become ashen pale, and then another tablet of one-sixtieth grain strychnine was administered him, and two more eggs, besides a sip of brandy. His entire body was bathed in warm water, including his head, the water having been kept warm along the road by being placed on the boiler of a steam automobile.[40]

Another contestant, William R. Garcia, ended up with a severe haemorrhage of the stomach, and there were general reports of the runners suffering ill effects. Certainly there is evidence cars passed on the roads and throwing up dust, although it is less clear whether this was traffic supporting the race or general traffic. Another runner, Carvajal, was said to have taken the run less seriously, and stopped frequently to talk to the crowds by the side of the road and even stole two peaches along the way.[41]

Unfortunately, Coubertin's grand vision of a truly international tournament was not entirely realised at the 1904 games, as athletes attributed to just nine nations were present, although national teams as such did not yet exist, and the majority of competitors were from the United States (Baker, 2008, p. 4). The event therefore amounted to a 'glorified American National Championships' (Kent, 2008, p. 29) with US athletes winning twenty-two out of the twenty three track and field events (Baker, 2008, p. 4). The overall spectacle seems quite disorganised. Baker (2008, pp. 3–4) damningly summarises the St Louis Games were 'generally regarded as the worst in the history of the Olympic movement' and McAloon (2006e, pg. 331) claims 'the failures of the 1900 Paris and 1904 St Louis Games, which could have ended this series of modern Olympic Games'.

British Perspective

British perceptions at the time were likely shaped by the resources they had access to, in a period when cinema was very new, and live theatre and shows were the main entertainment media. St Louis is not in the Wild West, but the popular perception of America was based on the imagery and excitement of the Wild West. From at least 1857 onwards circuses and shows with an American theme had been touring Britain, displaying Native Americans and an image of their way of life. Perhaps foremost in this was Buffalo Bill's Wild West show which periodically toured England, Wales and Scotland from 1887 to 1904 operating on the promise that it was not just fiction, but a chance to see the people who had experienced the American frontier (Meethan, 2010). Displays at the shows

[39]Lucas (1905, pp. 46, 58).
[40]Lucas (1905, p. 53).
[41]Lucas, pp. 46–52.

typically included demonstrations of Pony Express riding, emigrants crossing the plains, a display of justice in the early days of the frontier, recreations of Custer's last stand including Native American war dances, and cowboys staging rodeos, lassoing cattle and riding bucking broncos. There were even US Cavalry displays, re-enactments of ambushes by Native Americans and bareback horse riding. This played into perceptions that North America was a perilous frontier land (British National Buffalo Bill Archive, n.d.). Only 40 years previously the American Civil War had also captured the news agenda with dramatic accounts of combat and danger.[42] Decades later, British journalists were still claiming the only food available was buffalo meat (Guttman, 2002, p. 25) although the veracity of these journalists' claim is unverified.

The Louisiana Purchase Exposition was reported by the British newspapers, including regional as well as national titles, which printed articles often relying on news agencies rather than by staff writers, probably due to the distance and expense of reporting from so far away. The Exhibition, which reportedly cost $50,000,000, benefitted from good weather on its opening day, 30 April 1904, on which 50 foreign Governments provided elaborate displays.[43] There was interest in Britain among the establishment, as two weeks later, on Saturday 14th May, a 'large party of well-known municipal representatives' from Britain, organised by Lord Lyvedon, left the port of Southampton on the fittingly titled American line owned/operated S.S. St Louis,[44] a vessel measuring 535.5 × 63 feet, built in Philadelphia and had served the Southampton to New York route since launch in 1894 (Solem, n.d.). The timing of their visit appears to have coincided with the opening of the British Pavilion, which formally opened on the evening of Thursday 26th May with a reception by the management.[45] The Exposition proved popular, and by 21 July, 5,100,000 had attended.[46] British success at the Exhibition totalled 695 awards, including 142 Grand Prizes, and medals comprising 250 gold, 170 silver, and 134 bronze,[47] a medal hierarchy that Lucas claims had also been in place at every modern Olympic Games, although historical evidence reported in previous chapters contradicts this assertion.[48] Its possible that he conflated the Olympic events with those of the expositions which had such a hierarchy for their industrial and agricultural competitions. The success included a Grand Prize for King Edward for the Victoria Jubilee souvenirs displayed in the historical Department.[49]

---

[42]See for instance 'The Truth About the Battle of Gettysburg'. *Nottinghamshire Guardian*, 21 August 1863, p. 5.
[43]*The Financial Times*, 'St Louis Exposition', 2 May 1904, p. 3.
[44]*The Citizen*, 'For the St Louis Exhibition', 14 May 1904, p. 4.
[45]*Sunderland Daily Echo*, 'The British Pavilion at St Louis', 27 May, p. 5; *Sheffield Daily Telegraph*, 'The St Louis Exposition', 28 May, p. 8.
[46]*Portsmouth Evening News*, 'The crows at St Louis', 31 August 1904, p. 2.
[47]*Daily Mail*, 'British Awards at St Louis', 25 November 1904, p. 3.
[48]Lucas, 1905, p. 13.
[49]*Sheffield Daily Telegraph*, 'King Edward a Prize Winner at St Louis', 27 October 1904, p. 6.

The Olympic Games element was to be held in an arena built to hold 25,000 spectators.[50] An article credited to the news agency *Reuters* published by *Sheffield Daily Telegraph* emphasises the international catchment of athletes, who were from 'all over the world' and refers to St Louis 1904 as 'the third renewal of the Olympic Games'. The article compares results to world records, referring to the winning time in the 400-metres race as being one fifth under that of the world record 'established at the Olympic Games in Paris in 1900'.[51] This is interesting to read because as we have shown (Chapter 6) the Official Report of the Paris Exhibition Games of 1900 did not use the word 'Olympic' to describe them. *Portsmouth Evening News* reported the winning time of the 400 metres hurdles race but that it was not accepted as a record as the victor, Hillman, had knocked down a hurdle. The same article did mention a new record had been set for shot-put, in 'Bar-bell' lifting, and 200 metres race, the latter described as being an 'Olympic Games record'.[52]

Results were also reported for the mile handicap and running high-jump. Elsewhere the article referred to 'the Olympian Games contest at St. Louis', rather than Olympic, but it does refer to the competitors by nationality, attributing the mile-handicap win to Daly of 'Ireland'. The reporting is interesting as the title of the games is indecisive between Olympian or Olympic, although it shows how the games offered news worthiness, as world records were broken.[53] A similar finding, again in *Sheffield Daily Telegraph,* reports on running broad-jump, shot-put, 500 metres race and discus. Once more, world and Olympic records are mentioned, and the 1900 Paris Games are again referenced in relation to the 500 metres race for which the winning time was slightly over the 'record' (although this time it does not stipulate World or Olympic). The headline to the article again shows inconsistency, using the word 'Olympian'.[54] *The Times*, crediting *Reuters*, referred to 'the Olympian swimming tournament' as a headline but 'Olympic' in its text, perhaps the headline being a decision by the newspaper, and referring to an 'Olympic record' in the 220 yards event and referring to each winner by their name and by the country to which they affiliated, with the exception of the US competitor who is attributed to New York state.[55]

Contrastingly, another article credited to *Reuters*, did use the word *Olympic* consistently, in headline and in test, and again referred to a 'new Olympic record' being created by the winning time of the 1,500 metres race. The games had concluded, with the United States having won 34 of the 38 Olympic events, the only other winning countries being Canada, Ireland, Germany, and Greece. Again, it is noticeable that the total first-placing of the United States is calculated, the

---

[50] *The Financial Times*, 'St Louis Exposition', 2 May 1904, p. 3.
[51] *Sheffield Daily Telegraph*, 'St Louis Balooning Competition – one competitor gives up', 30 August 1904, p. 7.
[52] *Portsmouth Evening News*, 'The crows at St Louis', 31 August 1904, p. 2.
[53] *Portsmouth Evening News*, 'World of Sport', 1 September 1904, p. 3.
[54] *Sheffield Daily Telegraph*, 'St Louis Olympian Games', 2 September 1904, p. 5.
[55] *The Times*, 'The Olympian Swimming Tournament at St Louis', 7 September 1904, p. 4.

tendency to remark on the United States' success perhaps offering a first glimpse at what would develop into a formal approach of country-rankings at later Olympic Games.[56] These Olympic events at the Exposition, or at least those considered Olympic in 1904, are referred to in one news source as those that began in the Stadium on Monday 29th August and continued until Thursday 1st September, held 'under the auspices of the Athletic Union of the United States'.[57] although Lucas' report records the 'official' International Olympic Games element as having included contests up to and including 3rd September.[58]

It is interestingly how the aforementioned articles refer to Olympic records, at such as early stage in Olympic history, and that two refer to Paris, despite the 1900 games not having been reported or officially recorded as being Olympic. Perhaps these pieces were from news released by the IOC itself, keen to boost its own standing? Throughout the articles we also observed state affiliations for US competitors but national for those who had travelled from abroad, reflecting the method used by the organisers and included in the Official Report.[59] Other Olympian events and other Exhibition sports not under the Olympic banner reported in British newspapers included the one-mile and 100 hundred yards swimming events,[60] 50 yards, 220 yards, 100 yards back-swimming and 440 yards handicap swimming,[61] ballooning,[62] half-mile handicap running, 400 and 60 metres running races, broad jump, 16 pounds hammer,[63] Marathon race of 40 kilometres,[64] 200 metres and one-mile handicap running, 400 metre hurdles, shot-putting, barbell lifting, running high-jump,[65] running broad-jump, putting the weight, 800 metres race, throwing the discus,[66] and the 1,500 metre race.[67] Although ballooning was an Exposition-only event, and not part of the Olympic Games, The *Sheffield Daily Telegraph* wrote that the Exposition did offer a prize, but that Mr Meyers, one of just two competitors, gave up after landing 21 miles to the north-west, unable to find an eastward current. His rival, Mr Tomlinson, was more successful, having been last seen 200 miles to the north of St Louis, and travelling East.[68]

---

[56]*Sheffield Daily Telegraph*, 'Olympic Sports at St. Louis', 5 September 1904, p. 9.
[57]*Sheffield Daily Telegraph*, 'Olympic Games at St Louis', 30 August 1904, p. 7.
[58]Lucas (1905, p. 9).
[59]Lucas (1905).
[60]*Edinburgh Evening News*, 'General News', 6 September 1904, p. 6.
[61]*Sheffield Daily Telegraph*, 'Olympic Games at St Louis', 7 September 1904, p. 5; *The Times*, 'The Olympian Swimming Tournament at St Louis', 7 September 1904, p. 4
[62]*Sheffield Daily Telegraph*, 'St Louis Balooning Competition – one competitor gives up', 30 August 1904, p. 7.
[63]*Sheffield Daily Telegraph*, 'Olympic Games at St Louis', 30 August 1904.
[64]*Sheffield Daily Telegraph*, 'Olympic Games at St Louis', 31 August 1904, p. 9.
[65]*Manchester Courier & Lancashire General Advertiser*, 'Olympian Games at St Louis', 1 September 1904, p. 7.
[66]*Sheffield Daily Telegraph*, 'St Louis Olympian Games', 2 September 1904, p. 5.
[67]*Sheffield Daily Telegraph*, 'Olympic Sports at St Louis', 5 September 1904, p. 9.
[68]*Sheffield Daily Telegraph*, 'St Louis Balooning Competition – one competitor gives up', 30 August 1904, p. 7.

This small article is not insignificant, as it demonstrates how the news media were interested in the sport competitions of the Exposition Games generally, rather than limiting their space to the Olympics.

Crime, Theft, and Peril

The 1904 Exposition was marked by reports of violent crime and theft[69] and in June a fire completely destroyed Hoo-Hoo House, the lumberman's building resulting in damage of $60,000 and there was a separate, smaller fire in the elephants' barn causing panic among the animals which all escaped to safety.[70] A cyclone hit the Grounds on Saturday 20 August in which three people died and 150 people were 'more or less injured' and 200 blocks of buildings were ruined, damages estimated at $100,000.[71] Even royalty was not immune; several portraits of the Russian Tzar Nicholas were mutilated[72] and Prince Fushimi, the Emperor of Japan's representative, was robbed of $5000 worth of jewels left at his hotel.[73]

According to Royal Commission

As with Britain's previous involvement with such international expositions or 'world's fairs' the Crown and British ministers were interested to know what had been achieved by participating. Funding of £150,000 from the Treasury was paid over instalments spanning two financial years (£80,000 in 1903–1904 and £70,000 in 1904–1905). The largest expenditure was £48,000 on exhibits. Other areas of expenditure included items including a payment for the expenses of the London Metropolitan Police to guard the British exhibits at St Louis, freight, insurance, decoration, entertaining. By contrast, exhibit sales totalled just £7,995 10s 1p and presumably it was hoped that more return on the investment would be generated longer term through exports along with prestige and soft power.[74]

Chapter Summary

The British sat out the St. Louis Olympiad, although as we have illustrated this was as much of a financial decision based on the expense of reaching St. Louis as a sporting decision. The British Government did choose to participate in the Louisiana Purchase Exposition itself, but as the Royal Commission's funding did not extend to athletics, the AAA as a small volunteer and unincorporated body felt unable to take the financial risk of participating. This decision came even as

---

[69]*Sunderland Daily Echo & Shipping Gazette*, 'Terrible St Louis', 22 June 1904, p. 4.
[70]*Edinburgh Evening News*, 'Fire at St Louis Exhibition', 25 June 1904, p. 6.
[71]*Sheffield Daily Telegraph*, 'Cyclone at St Louis', 22 August 1904, p. 7.
[72]*Western Times*, 'Mutilating the Tsar's Portraits', 30 September 1904, p. 16.
[73]*Aberdeen Journal*, 'Japanese Prince Robbed at St Louis', 25 November 1904.
[74]Royal Commission for the St Louis International Exhibition for 1904, the Report of His Majesty's Commissioners for the International Exhibition, St Louis 1904, London, HMSO.

Herbert was one of Britain's IOC representatives, though Coubertin had been less than happy with the relocation of the event from Chicago and appeared to leave its organisation to Sullivan. This lack of official sanction is likely to have further dissuaded Herbert and the AAA from investing in the event, but the absence of the British and French from the competition seems to have been considered a diplomatic slight. Archival evidence is lacking but we can assume that other British sports took a similar view to athletics, although it appears that only athletics were officially included in the Olympic competition, with other events such as swimming being considered sideshows. The United States was not formally represented either, with individual athletic clubs appearing as teams in the results alongside the names of other countries. The 1896 and 1900 events had been somewhat ad hoc, but it could not really be said that 1904 was much of an advance towards sporting integrity. The boundary with the Exposition and its broader anthropological exhibits and entertainments was also somewhat porous, with the series of games claimed to be 'experiments' in getting peoples from around the world to participate in 'American' sports. The events of the games themselves were however reported in British newspapers, and there was a sense of continuation with 'Olympic' records gaining attention alongside the broader events of the Exposition. The perception that St Louis was on the cusp of the Wild West and as such newly tamed place of danger perhaps even increased interest in the games. The Exposition, with its streetcar expansions and building projects, remained a large-scale project capable of capturing the popular imagination in a period when most entertainment had to consist of live experience in some form. Just because the British did not participate directly, did not mean they were not interested, and the concept of the spectacle happening thousands of miles away contributed in a small way to perpetuate interest in the movement in Britain.

Chapter 8

Developing British Sporting Institutions

Abstract

In this chapter, we look at the actual formation of the British Olympic Association (BOA) in 1905 led by Britain's three IOC members – Charles Herbert, Reverend Stuart de Courcy Laffan, and Colonel Sir Howard Vincent, together with the Conservative MP William Grenfell (later Lord Desborough). The BOA was a voluntaristic and amateurist organisation built on top of the network of existing sporting associations which aimed to further a knowledge of Olympism in Britain as well as formalise Britain's representation at the IOC and provide a framework for British sporting representation. We more formally introduce some of the members of the BOA and attempt to place them within their wider context. We also consider the parallel development of international football at this time which the British also played a key role in; this would be important to our story as the Olympics attempted to include international football from the start, in a period where the prevalence of professionalism was tightly regulated.

Keywords: British Olympic Association; amateurism; international football; FIFA; sports history

Introduction

The IOC, having formed in June of 1894, was a decade into its existence at the time of St Louis. While holding the games outside of Europe for the first time seemed a step forward they also held up a mirror to Coubertin who must have realised they had yet to become a truly international phenomenon in the way he envisaged. Part of the challenge seems to have been due to the lack of National Organising Committees. France and the United States formed National Organising Committees in 1894, while Australia, Germany, Greece and Hungary established committees in 1895. Norway followed suit in 1900. This total of seven National Olympic Committees, five of which were in Europe, meant that the

Foundations of Managing British Olympics: Institutions through Time, 147–164

Published under exclusive licence by Emerald Publishing Limited
doi:10.1108/978-1-80262-095-520251008

Olympic cause was growing but only slowly. The following year, 1905, was particularly important for our narrative of Britain's role in Olympic development. A direct result of Laffan's involvement and friendship with Coubertin was the formalisation of British involvement by establishing the BOA.

Forming the BOA

We have already mentioned that prior to the existence of the IOC, a national Olympic body had already existed in England, the National Olympic Association (NOA), the formation of which is often attributed to the efforts of John Hulley (of the Liverpool Olympic movement), Dr William Penny Brookes (of Much Wenlock), and E. G. Ravenstein (President of the German Gymnastic Society of London). That institution was never affiliated with Coubertin's IOC and had in fact closed in 1883, 11 years before the IOC was founded. But there is an organisational link, beyond Coubertin's interest in Dr Brookes and Much Wenlock.

The NOA's ethos and motto ('Civium virtus civitatis tutamen' meaning 'the power of the citizens is the defence of the state') was inherited by the National Physical Recreation Society (NPRS) an organisation founded in 1886, and both the President and Treasurer of the NPRS were members of the IOC's 'Comité Britannique' from 1902 (Hulley, 2010; John Hulley Memorial Association, n.d.). The NPRS was a philanthropic and voluntarist organisation closely affiliated with the YMCA and YWCA which aimed to promote physical health and fitness among the working classes. It had an especial focus on the winter months, when outdoor physical exercise was difficult, and as well as advocating for the provision of suitable indoor spaces it aimed to act by itself hiring suitable halls, provide small grants towards apparatus, and encourage the government to introduce 'systematic physical recreation' in the relatively new boarding schools. Among its council members were the cricketer and government minister Lord Harris as well as the FA Secretary Charles Alcock and its Treasurer Lord Kinnaird, who offered his services as NPRS Treasurer for some years, with its banking provided by his family bank, Ranson, Bouverie & Co which in 1888 merged into the powerful Barclay partnership (Acrkill & Hannah, 2001).[1] Herbert Gladstone, the son of the Liberal Prime Minister William Ewart Gladstone, served as the NPRS President, and along with Kinnaird appears to have taken an active interest, presenting its annual shield on at least one occasion.[2] The body worked closely with the YMCA to promote and finance new gymnasia for public use, and the Prince of Wales lent his support by opening these establishments. On one occasion in Liverpool the Prince was accompanied by the King of Sweden, perhaps significant given the role played by the Swedes in the development of the Ling gymnastics tradition (Lundvall, 2015) which the NPRS hoped to emulate.[3] Perhaps best considered the

[1]'National Physical Recreation Society'. *Morning Post*, 14 June 1886, p. 3; 'National Physical Recreation Society'. *Evening Telegraph*, 11 May 1891, p. 3.
[2]'National Physical Recreation Society'. *Evening Telegraph*, 11 May 1891, p. 3.
[3]'Opening of a Gymnasium by the Prince of Wales'. *Manchester Courier and Lancashire General Advertiser*, 9 June 1888, p. 8.

social responsibility wing of British sport the body claimed to have 20,000 affiliated members by 1890, even if it had had to go into a 'certain amount of debt' to fulfil some of its aims, and its Secretary, Colonel Onslow, did not have Honorary before his title, suggesting a professional position.[4] Emphasising a range of drills, athletic, and gymnastic activities, the NPRS was egalitarian, organising competitions for children as well as adults, and girls and women as well as boys and men.[5] Unlike the sporting associations its activities covered the whole United Kingdom, including Scotland and Ireland in its competitions,[6] although in 1897 this brought it into conflict with the Irish Amateur Gymnastic Association which threatened to exclude clubs taking part in the NPRS's annual shield competition.[7] The Scottish AGA had also attempted to sanction clubs from taking part in 1894, although this stance was undermined by the giving of 'free permits' for the body's competitions, which included a high jump, from the Amateur Athletic Association (AAA) and the (English) AGA.[8] Ultimately, because of the distinct nature of its mission the blue collar oriented NPRS appears to have been broadly tolerated by the more white collar amateur bodies, probably because it occupied a slightly different domain to them.

To truly champion and foster the Olympic cause in Britain would require a dedicated Olympic association with members representing as many sports as possible. The BOA was formed in 1905, and inaugural affiliated bodies included the NPRS. Direct lineage can be thus traced from the earlier British Olympic organisations (Hulley, 2010; John Hulley Memorial Association, n.d.).

The 1904 IOC Congress held in England had been an important occasion in the momentum behind Britain's three IOC members (Charles Herbert, Reverend Laffan, and Colonel Sir Howard Vincent) to propose forming a fully-fledged British Association. Actions from that meeting involved circulating a letter to propose it as well as holding a meeting to form the organisation (Barker, 2005). The letter was sent to numerous sporting organisations around Britain and aroused some supportive discussion. For instance, mention of it appears in the gymnastics column of the Dundee *Evening Telegraph* where the local columnist gave it their support.[9] The foundational meeting occurred on 24 May 1905 at The House of Commons in London. It was presided over by the Conservative MP and former Metropolitan Police administrator Sir Howard Vincent (Lucas & Emsley, 2010). William Grenfell, also a Conservative MP, was elected inaugural Chairman of the BOA, with Reverend Robert Laffan named as Honorary Secretary (Anthony, 1997; Bailey, 1997). According to Barker (2005), Laffan's position was at first temporary, and little else is known as to what else happened at the meeting

[4] 'National Physical Recreation Society', *Standard*, 26 May 1890, p. 2.
[5] 'St.Winifred's Club'. *Sunday Times*, 26 July 1903, p. 8.
[6] 'Gymnastics'. *Evening Telegraph*, 29 January 1890, p. 3.
[7] 'Gymnastic Crisis'. *Evening Telegraph*, 6 December 1897, p. 4.
[8] 'Gymnastics', *Evening Telegraph*, 24 November 1894, p. 3. AAA ATH/1/2/2/4, General Committee Minutes, 8 December 1894.
[9] 'Gymnastic Notes'. *Evening Telegraph*, 24 November 1904, p. 3.

although the members of the new body were listed in the *Olympic Review*. We do know that three objectives were identified:

(1) To spread in Great Britain a knowledge of the Olympic movement.
(2) To secure that the views of the British Associations shall have their due weight and influence in the organisation of the Olympic Games.
(3) To ensure the participation, both in Olympic Games and in International Athletic Congresses, of representatives properly accredited by the great Athletic and Sporting Associations of Great Britain and by Educational Authorities interested in Physical Education; and to facilitate the attendance of such representatives.[10]

Importantly, from the start it was expected that the body would build on the existing network of associations, rather than seek to replace them. This approach would give British Olympism a core purpose of furthering the amateurism of these bodies on the international stage. Importance was also given to the educational value of sport, reflecting the origins in muscular Christianity and broad social progressivism (although despite the involvement of the NPRS relatively little weight was placed on this in the early years). Perhaps the choice of venue for the opening meeting was more for legitimacy than convenience though the reasoning for the choice is not documented.

The new BOA established a provisional council of members who mostly represented the various national sporting associations that comprised the Association's membership. By the time a provisional constitution was agreed in April 1906, it was proposed that two-thirds of the council would be directly nominated by the sporting associations, with the remainder elected by an unspecified constituency. There was also an expectation that the BOA should act as the IOC's representative in Great Britain, and that there should be a recognition of the international significance of the Olympic movement with the principle that Britain 'should assist in guiding its development and in promoting its success'.[11] This body appears to have been an attempt at creating an umbrella organisation based on, and extending upwards, the principle of distributed responsibility and consensual decision-making. It represented the various administrating institutions of British sport, in order to represent the United Kingdom's interests at the IOC. The BOA Council (hereafter the BOAC) was essentially a new top layer of the hierarchy. Pickford (1940) describes early football regulation as being the development of a series of democratic structures which allowed overall cooperation while allowing for local control and representation, and many of the sport administration bodies formed in the wake of the Football Association (FA) in 1863 followed a similar ethos.

The FA was probably the largest of these administrating bodies by 1905, having a book value of more than £18,000, turning over in excess of £25,000 in 1906

[10]University of East London Library Archive, BOA/M/1/1, BOA Council (BOAC), 1906–1912, BOAC Minutes, Provisional Council Meeting April 1906.
[11]BOA/M/1/1, BOAC Minutes, Provisional Council Meeting April 1906.

and having adopted its own parliament like structure in 1887, with an FA Council elected by ten electoral divisions representing member clubs, County FAs and bodies such as the Army, Navy, and Oxford and Cambridge Universities.[12] The AAA was much smaller, having a book value of just over £1,797 and a turnover of just over £635 in 1906. But despite enjoying the financial stewardship of C. N. Jackson, it had stagnated financially, running small losses from 1901 to 1905.[13] It also had a distributed responsibility structure; Alongside 18 members who represented the founder clubs, members were elected onto a General Committee intended to proportionally represent three regions who were themselves sub-associations – the North (11 members), Midlands (10 members), and South (10 members). Two of these, the North and Midlands, formed notionally independent athletics associations of their own. There was further provision for one member from the West of England and one to represent the Midland and Northern Counties Associations. These geographical regions were exactly defined under rule 1 in the organisation's rulebook as the Southern region laying south of the line of latitude 52 degrees north with the addition of Norfolk, Suffolk, Essex, and Hertfordshire, except for the Welsh counties of Brecknock, Carmarthen, and Pembroke, which were placed in the Midlands region along with anywhere 50 miles south of Birmingham. The Midlands extended north until the 53rd parallel, from where the Northern region would extend to the Scottish border.[14] Each region had a certain amount of autonomy over the 'prosecution' of athletes for disciplinary offences and ensuring the registration and regulation of competition, rigorously enforced by voluntary 'honorary local officers' but the principle was that all activity should fit within the framework of the 24 AAA constitution rules, its 28 laws, and 14 further guidelines (as specified in the 1902 handbook).[15] The structure, systems, and culture of these organisations, attempted to be highly rationalised and regularised to protect the underlying amateur ethos, with the object of allowing the results of an event in, say Darlington, to be compared with one in Dover.

The sporting association organisational form, essentially a confederation, echoed the committee or board structures of local government, parliament, and British business around this time, which allowed for the distribution of responsibility while allowing the constituent bodies (themselves usually constructed of committees) to retain their independence. A number of founding members of the BOAC had experience of representative government outside of sport – including as members of the London County Council (LCC), a new local authority formed for the London region in 1889. The LCC was one of the new breed of English local authorities formed in 1889 which based themselves on collective

[12]'Sports and Recreations', *Blackburn Standard*, 17 September 1887, p. 7.

[13]AAA ATH/AAA/1/5/2/2 General Statements of Accounts and Balance Sheets, 1900–1906.

[14]AAA, 'Amateur Athletics Association: Constitution Rules, Objects and Lists of Officers and Clubs &c.: Laws for Athletic Meetings and Competitions, 1902, p. 6.

[15]AAA, 'Amateur Athletics Association: Constitution Rules, Objects and Lists of Officers and Clubs&c.: Laws for Athletic Meetings and Competitions, 1902.

responsibility and committee structures (Finer, 1934; Shaw, 1904), often avoiding pooling executive responsibility which was left to salaried managers in professionalised directorates such as Highways or Tramways (Kellett, 1978; Morrell & Watson, 1928; Turner & Tennent, 2021). Further, the involvement of figures from the civil service, academia, education, and religion in sport, such as Charles Herbert, a civil servant, C. N. Jackson, an experienced college bursar, and Reverend Laffan, allowed for the transfer of not-for-profit organisational experience and expertise from those fields, as well as of accounting practice. Profit making business in the United Kingdom had also incorporated board and committee structures into its logic by the second half of the 19th century, particularly at stock market listed firms in sectors such as home and overseas railways (Boughey, 2009; Turner, 2013), utilities (Platt, 1977), overseas resource exploitation (Harvey & Press, 1990; Mollan, 2018; Tennent, 2013; Wilkins, 1988), banking (Acrkill & Hannah, 2001), and some industrial firms (Popp, 2006) where ownership was highly dispersed. Boards were typically composed of a combination of large shareholders and senior managers together with professional men including accountants, bankers, financiers, engineers, and lawyers, as well as non-executive directors from other industries, or politicians or peers. These boards, often dominated by outsiders, advised and supervised lower-level management hierarchies often based on functional or divisional responsibility on behalf of the shareholders (Acheson et al., 2015; Foreman-Peck & Hannah, 2012; Hannah, 2007).

The men who founded the BOAC were men of society, from the upper or middle social classes, who had experience of or were influenced by these organisational norms. Many had notable public school and/or a background of sporting achievements with the ancient universities of either Cambridge or Oxford. Some of these individuals even had experience of competing in prior Olympic Games, or in the cases of Laffan and Herbert, were members of the IOC by the time that the BOA was formed. Some had experience as Members of Parliament, and there were at least five members who were active in the Conservative party and its related faction on the LCC, the Moderates. All would have had technical skills and knowledge of sport, education, administration, and organisation, and some had first-hand experience of working in the law and politics. As far as we can verify, the following names were members of the first BOA from its inception, or first few months:[16]

R' Hon. Lord Desborough of Taplow, Born William Grenfell

Chairman Grenfell was an accomplished sportsman and mountain climber and at some point in 1905 was awarded by Coubertin with an Olympic Diploma of

[16]BOA/M/1/1, BOAC Minutes, Provisional Council Meeting April 1906. Cook, T. A. 1908. *The Cruise of the Branwen*. Privately Published, pp. 4–7 gives a full listing of how its membership expanded to organise the 1908 Games (see Volume Two, forthcoming).

Merit, to encourage him in his passion for sporting achievement and in its development (Kent, 2008). He was raised to the peerage on 30th December 1905 as Baron Desborough of Taplow, and he is named as Lord Desborough hereafter. He played cricket for Harrow and was a keen rower and fencer, helping to found the Amateur Fencing Association (AFA) in 1902. He was a Liberal MP for Salisbury in 1880–1882, 1885–1886, then in Hereford 1892–1893. Conservative/Unionist MP for Wycombe 1900–1905.

President of five national governing bodies: Marylebone Cricket Club (MCC), Lawn Tennis Association, AFA, National Amateur Wrestling Association, and AAA. He was also President of the Bath Club from 1894 to 1942, and a member of the Carlton Club (then the national Conservative club) (Beckett, 2012; Who Was Who, 2007).

Hon. Secretary. R' Rev. Robert Stuart de Courcy Laffan M. A.

A Church of England clergyman, Laffan, had previously been a very successful headmaster of King Edward VI School, Stratford-upon-Avon where he introduced physical education – having built classrooms and a gymnasium largely out of his own pocket. He moved to be Principal of Cheltenham College in 1895 but resigned in 1899. He became rector of St. Stephen's Wallbrook with St. Benet Sharehog in 1899, a Church adjacent to the Mansion House in the City of London – and very close to the Bank of England, as well as serving as Chaplain to 12th Battalion London Regiment (the Rangers) 1904–1912.

Joined the IOC in 1899, and also served on the LCC Technical Education Board, 1900–1904 (Bailey, 2012).

R' Hon. Lord Montagu of Beaulieu

A keen rower, shooter, and cyclist – as well as a fully trained railway locomotive driver and fitter, and later an enthusiast for motor cars, he is also Vice President of the RAC, and the founder and editor of *The Car*. He also raced motorboats – where Lionel de Rothschild was his partner and was a director of several South African mining firms. Conservative MP for the New Forest 1892–1905. He was a member of a number of clubs – Carlton, Beefsteak, Royal Automobile, Royal Aero; Royal Yacht Squadron, Cowes; Royal Motor Yacht (Storey, 2004; Who Was Who, 2007).

Colonel Sir Howard Vincent, K. C. M. G.; C. B.; M. P.

A member of the IOC since 1901. Soldier, Newspaper reporter and politician. In 1878, he was given the job of developing Scotland Yard as its Director of Criminal Investigations, then became the Conservative MP for Central Sheffield in 1885, serving until his death in 1908. A member of the LCC 1889–1896 (Lucas & Emsley, 2010; Who Was Who, 2007).

Sir Lees Knowles, C. V. A. C.

A former president of the Cambridge University Athletics Club and champion amateur athlete, he studied law, and in 1882 was called to the bar at Lincoln's Inn. A politician and writer on military matters, he was a member of two City livery companies – the Merchant Taylors and the Plumbers, and was on the board of several charities. He was created Baronet in 1903 and helped host the IOC on their visit to London in 1904. He was a member of several clubs – Carlton, Junior Carlton; Union, Constitutional, Manchester (Who Was Who, 2007).

H. Benjamin, Esq

Past President, Amateur Swimming Association – represented swimming on the BOAC.[17]

T. W. J. Britten

Honorary Treasurer of National Cycling Union (NCU),[18] he had attended the 1894 meeting which founded the IOC.

William Hayes Fisher MP (Later Lord Downham)

He is the President of the National Skating Association (NSA) since 1894. A lawyer, called to the bar in 1879, he was Conservative Member of Parliament for Fulham from 1885 to 1906. He became the Chairman of the Royal Patriotic Commission in 1904. As a Conservative MP he was in the Carlton Club (Pugh, 2008; Who Was Who, 2007).

Reginald Claude Moor Gillett Gridley

Amateur Rowing Association and Leander Honorary Secretary, he was also elected to the Committee at Henley Royal Regatta in 1903.[19]

Charles Herbert

Hon Secretary of the AAA since 1883 and Civil Servant (Chapter 3), also an IOC Member since the Sorbonne Congress in 1894 (Chapter 4), Coubertin described him as part of the immovable trinity at its head.[20]

George Rowland Hill

First elected to the Rugby Football Union (RFU) committee in 1879 he was a referee and also a member of the International Rugby Board since 1890. Hill

---

[17]BOA/M/1/1, BOAC Minutes, Provisional Council Meeting April 1906.
[18]BOA/M/1/1, BOAC Minutes, Provisional Council Meeting April 1906.
[19]BOA/M/1/1, BOAC Minutes, Provisional Council Meeting April 1906.
[20]de Coubertin, 1979, p. 9.

had been Honorary Secretary of the RFU from 1881 to 1904 before becoming its 18th President, and as a staunch defender of amateurism opposed the breakaway of the northern clubs to form Rugby League in 1883. He had worked on Brunel's Great Eastern steamship laying a transatlantic cable. A Civil Servant – record keeper in the Principal Probate office at Somerset House, he was also a Moderate (Conservative) member of LCC – as was his sister. He also served as Chairman of the Borough of Greenwich Conservative Association from 1887, and was in the Junior Carlton and Sports clubs (Sheard, 2004; Who Was Who, 2007).

Alfred Hutton

The first president of the AFA (originally the fencing division of the AGA) from 1895 until his death in 1910, a keen historian of the sport he wrote extensively on the subject. Outside of sport he pursued a career in the military, serving in the 79th (Cameron) Highlanders from 1859 to 1873, and was also a founder and Chairman of the Central London Throat and Ear Hospital 1874–1904 (Sieveking & Lock, 2004; Who Was Who, 2007).

Edward Lawrence Levy

Honorary Secretary of the Amateur Gymnastic Federation of Great Britain and Ireland since 1900 and Honorary Secretary of the AGA of England since 1901.[21] A member of Birmingham Athletics Club and the Birmingham Institute of Athletics, he had travelled to the 1896 Olympic Games in Athens, where he judged events after his own discipline was not included. He also wrote extensive articles about the games for the *Birmingham Daily Post*.

E. Edgar Syers

President of the *Ski Club of Great Britain* in 1906,[22] it was in Figure Skating that he had competed at the World Championships in 1899. His partnered his wife, Madge, with whom he won unofficial world pairs championships in 1902 and 1904 (IOC, 2023b).

Frederick J. Wall

Served the London FA from 1881 where he sat on the Rules Revision and Emergency Committees before advancing to Vice President, then Honorary Secretary and Treasurer. Then he represented Middlesex FA on the FA Council from 1891. When Charles Alcock retired in 1895, Wall was encouraged to apply for the position of Secretary to the FA because of his experience in sport and in law. He was then employed professionally as Secretary to the FA, a rare professional

[21]BOA/M/1/1, BOAC Minutes, Provisional Council Meeting April 1906.
[22]BOA/M/1/1, BOAC Minutes, Provisional Council Meeting April 1906.

executive in British sport, and he became a Fellow of the Chartered Institute of Secretaries.[23]

Colonel Sir Henry Walrond

He is the Honorary Secretary of the Royal Toxophilite Society, then the de facto governing body for archery – represented archery on the BOA Council.[24]

Theodore Andrea Cook

An oarsman and fencer, he is also a committee member of the AFA from 1904 and captain of the English fencing team. A journalist by profession, he was heavily influenced by the muscular Christianity of his headmaster at grammar school. He worked for the *St. James Gazette* (a London evening paper), of which he was briefly editor in 1900, before moving to the *Daily Telegraph* where he wrote an influential column on amateur sports under the pseudonym Old Blue (Buchanan, 2004; Who Was Who, 2007). Cook authored books and journal articles and by 1905 had published on topics as diverse as spirals in nature and art,[25] horse racing,[26] and the water-colour paintings of JMW Turner.[27]

The objects of the Association were:

(a) To spread in Great Britain a knowledge of the Olympic movement.
(b) To secure that the views of British associations shall have their due weight and influence in the organisation of the Olympic Games.
(c) To ensure the participation, both in Olympic Games and in International Athletic Congresses, of representatives properly accredited by the great athletic and sporting associations of Great Britain and by educational authorities interested in physical education; and to facilitate the attendance of such representatives.[28]

At some point between 1905 and 1908, this final part of the third objective was expanded as a distinct fourth point:

> To facilitate the attendance of such representatives by making arrangements with railway companies and hotel proprietors, and, in case of need, helping to defray the representative's expenses.[29]

---

[23]Wall, F. (1935). *Fifty years of football.* Cassell.
[24]BOA/M/1/1, BOAC Minutes, Provisional Council Meeting April 1906.
[25]Cook, T. A. (1979/1903). The curves of life: being an account of spiral formations and their application to growth in nature, to science and to art: with special reference to the manuscripts of Leonardo da Vinci. Dover.
[26]Cook, T. A. (1904). *A history of the English Turf.* H Virtue & Co Ltd. (six volumes).
[27]Turner, J. M. W., & Cook, T. A. (1904). *The water-colour Drawings of JMW Turner, RA in the National Gallery: A selection of 58 subjects reproduced in colour, comprising– Harbours of England, Rivers of England, Rivers of France: The Seine.* Cassell and Company, Limited.
[28]Cook (1908, p. 96).
[29]Cook (1910, International Sport, Constable and Co. p. 152).

Although small when first founded there were:

> directions to invite the leading governing association in each form of sport to appoint a member to represent it on their Council, the object being to secure the full information as to the views of experts in every branch of sport should be at the disposal of the Council without making that body so numerous as to be incapable of discussing in full meeting all questions which might arise.

Additional points were thus enshrined in the Association's constitution, for example, membership was open to all amateurs with a subscription rate set to be as accessible as possible, annually 5s or a lifetime subscription of 2 guineas for individuals and an annual rate of £1 1s for Associations and unions, or 10s for Clubs. Governance would be by Council, and it was proposed two-thirds should be representatives nominated by 10 significant sporting bodies: AAA, MCC, NCU, FA, RFU, AGA, Amateur Rifle Association, NSA, Amateur Swimming Association (ASA), AFA and one-third elected at the Annual General Meeting in June each year .

The structure of this new organisation seems to have thereafter been used, or at least adapted, by other countries, Bailey (1997) cites a letter from Coubertin to the BOA dated 9 February 1906, stating so and also observes how Coubertin corresponded with Laffan showing 'close interest in the progress of the new British organization'. Whether or not this was true or a form of flattery from the Baron is not clear, but as we shall see the British way of organising would be demonstrably influential at points in Olympic history.

Just one month after its formation, the BOA sent delegates to the Third Olympic Congress, held in Brussels between 9 and 14 June 1905, although given the short timescale it is reasonable to assume these BOA delegates – Sir Howard Vincent, Desborough, Laffan, Hutton, and Wall had possibly already planned to attend as members of the IOC or on behalf of their sporting associations. In an unusual moment of government involvement two representatives from the Board of Education, then the UK government department responsible for education, attended.[30] This event was postponed from 1903 when it was due to determine the regulations for the 1904 Olympic Games. However, when the Head of the Organising Committee resigned (possibly because of the problems with organising that edition of the games) it was postponed. This allowed Coubertin to shape the agenda, returning to the pedagogic themes he had raised at earlier meetings. The British Olympic movement now had a bona fide Olympic Association with which to participate at Congress, which was attended by 205 people from 21 countries, sent by 14 governments, 9 universities, and 54 sports federations. Following St Louis, it must have been encouraging that some of the delegations were from North and South America (IOC, 2021c). The congress was important for the adoption of an amateur definition that barred physical education teachers and

---

[30]National Football Museum Archive, Preston. FA Minute Book May 1903–July 1907, 'International Olympic Congress: Report of the Secretary'.

instructors from competing in sports that they taught; though they could compete in others. The principle of allowed repayment of travelling expenses was allowed, and ruled not to constitute professionalism – a necessary concession to open up international competition. The British delegation did, however, abstain from the vote over the broad definition of an amateur on the grounds that it required more discussion, a sign that perhaps Cook and Desborough, both hardline amateurs, wished to include a manual worker's clause.[31] A British Association delegation also attended in Paris, May 1906, the Conference to consider the possibility of combining art and literature with the celebration of modern Olympiads.[32]

Developments in Association Football

Outside of the Olympic movement, the sport of association football had continued to be popular and spread quickly around the world. English clubs, such as Corinthians, toured internationally, including Europe in 1897 (Booth, 2002). On 21 May 1904, the national FAs of Belgium, Sweden, Switzerland, Denmark, France, Spain, and the Netherlands established the *Fédération internationale de Football Association* (FIFA) as an international governing body under which national associations, of one per country, would be organised. To begin with, this was really a European continental governing body but the word *International* used in its title showed its ambition. We have already introduced in Chapter 3 that the four British Home Nation Football Associations representing England, Scotland, Wales, and Ireland (later Northern Ireland) were the longest established national bodies. Together they had pioneered and evolved the Laws of the Game and international fixtures between representative national teams in the 19th century. Booth (2002) identifies how international football then began to occur on the continent in the early 20th century, citing a fixture between Austria and Hungary in 1902. The sport was particularly popular in the coffee house culture of the Austro-Hungarian empire, with a more tactically aware version of the game developing in Austria, Bohemia, and Hungary (Wilson, 2014), countries which were also becoming important in the Olympic movement. Booth (2002) states that it presented an opportunity for the English FA, as the oldest and most dominant Association, 'to take the lead in establishing an international administrative body' (p. 217) but that the initiative, like that of the IOC 10 years earlier, came instead from France. Robert Guerin[33] and the Union des Societes Francaises des

[31]National Football Museum Archive, Preston (hereafter FA) FA Minute Book May 1903–July 1907, 'International Olympic Congress: Report of the Secretary'.
[32]Cook (1910, pp.145–146).
[33]Confusion exists as to his real name. Known variously as Maurice Robert, Robert-Guerin (as a hyphenated surname) or Robert Guérin, research indicates his full birth name as being Robert Clément Auguste Maurice Robert, the 'Guérin' being added from 1900 to reflect a Grandmother's maiden name used in a family business 'Robert- Guérin' that had exhibited Merino Fabrics at the Great Exhibition of 1851 (Robertson, 2022).

Sports Athletiques appear to have initiated the idea, 'inviting England to take the lead', but the FA declined the offer; FIFA 'was born, not in London as would have been logical, but in Paris' (p. 217). We must consider Booth's statement. In hindsight London does appear logical and it is possible to see the early reluctance of the English and other British FAs as a short-sighted missed opportunity. However, historical context is important; we should consider that the British associations governed not just the British Isles but the British Empire, at this point the largest in the World.

The British had not been alone in forming a National Olympic Committee, Denmark established its own also in 1905, and would be followed in 1906 by Belgium (Chappalet, 2018). The elected President of the new Belgian committee was its founder, Baron Édouard-Émile-Albert de Laveleye, a Belgian mining engineer, financier, and writer who, since 1895 was also inaugural Chairman of the Belgian Football Association, which had been a founder member of FIFA. As a football administrator he was made the first honorary member for convincing representatives of British Home Nations to join FIFA.[34] Wall's attendance at the IOC congress in 1905 demonstrates that British sport was opening up to international competition at this time – he suggested in his report back to the FA Council that English teams touring the continent 'do not fairly represent our Sport, or the Association', and that the FA should in future look for opportunities to send representative teams to the continent.[35]

The English FA officially joined FIFA in 1906. As well as being diplomatic this would validate the movement which would also benefit from their governance and organisational abilities, and geographic reach. Discussion at that meeting revealed the international federation was struggling to devise the organisational structure for European football with confusion as to what constituted 'international football', and inter-club matches being billed as international matches. The FA thus joined on the condition of several changes being formally made to the FIFA constitution. FIFA formally agreed to accept the Laws which the British Home Nations had set down as the International Football Associations Board (IFAB) and through this agreement the British and the IFAB remained the most influential lobby in international football (Gillett et al., 2022; Tennent & Gillett, 2022). Other important principles were reinforced on the advice of the English, including the concept that FIFA member associations should be those genuinely controlling all football in their country, and that only matches played between representative teams picked by those associations should be formally considered 'international' matches. The principle of control was ingrained by mandating that international fixtures could only be arranged at the annual FIFA Conferences, and that inter-club matches between clubs of different nationalities could only be arranged by the permission of the two respective associations.

[34]FA Minute Book May 1903–July 1907, Minutes of Meeting of Council, 14 April 1905.

[35]FA Minute Book May 1903–July1907, 'International Olympic Congress: Report of the Secretary'.

Amateurism was also reinforced by a rule banning the arrangement of matches that would profit individuals, and the FA's Treasurer Daniel Woolfall was elected its first president, serving until 1918.[36] The French were left with the concessions of a Vice-Presidency (alongside other officials drawn from Switzerland, the Netherlands and Germany) and that French should be the official language of the FIFA, The FA's accession to FIFA therefore represented the relative power of the FA relative to the then fledgling continental body, which had not yet worked out the mechanisms necessary to establish itself. FIFA would remain the junior partner until it was given representation on IFAB in 1913, but the reshaping of its regulations to make them acceptable to the FA. would have important consequences for the Olympic movement, setting the expectation that formalised associations would choose representative athletes, rather than self-chosen individuals or clubs competing under a national banner as had happened at Athens, Paris, and St. Louis.

This is supported by the memoires of football administrator William Pickford, a referee and FA Council member who eventually became FA President and Vice-President of FIFA. He suggests that the English FA initially thought the idea of an International Federation 'did not seem to concern us' and also cites the FAs response to an earlier letter from the French Union of Athletic Sports as being a 'monumental instance of that English insularity which puzzles our friends across the water'. Although the British nations would eventually join FIFA after 1906, and Pickford would himself be elected a Vice-President of FIFA, they did not initially know quite what to make of it, he remembers at one meeting listening to the chatter round the table for a time, and then remarking plaintively, 'Perhaps one of you gentlemen will tell me what it is all about' (Gannaway, 2009, p. 44). FIFA would emerge as the 'other' sport superpower through the 20th century. But that was probably not evident at its inception and it is not clear how, or even if, the IOC considered its formation, though the Olympic football tournament, which we will discuss more in Volume Two, was an important precursor to the World Cup (Tennent & Gillett, 2022, pp. 7–8).

As well as its increasing internationalisation, the game of association football in England continued to become more commercialised. In February 1905 the first four-figure transfer fee was paid, £1,000 by Middlesbrough to Sunderland for Alf Common. This was a significant event and the FA responded by establishing a special committee to investigate but reported nothing unlawful (Gannaway, 2009, p.46). The football referee, FA (and later FIFA) administrator and author William Pickford, writing in his memoir mentions that the issue of transfer fees was part of the question around professionalism that had been a cause of concern for the FA since the end of the previous century:

> We had some trouble in the 'nineties' about the questions of transfer fees and scratch teams. The former recurred in one form or

[36]FA Council Minutes 1903–1907. *International Conference at Bern, June 1906: Report of the Representatives of The Football Association.* National Football Museum Archive, Preston, UK.

> another for a long tie, some of the Council leaders honestly trying to check the growth of the practice, while others quite as earnest in their own views that it was a necessary accompaniment of the professional system, advocating a freer hand (Gannaway, 2009, p. 46).

Overall, by 1905, amateur clubs were dissatisfied with the FA's approach to the growth of the professional game, such as changes to laws such penalty kicks, introduced in 1891. Concerns increased when the County FAs were told by the national FA to absorb the professional clubs located within their areas. The ever-higher profile of professional football presented a challenge to the purity inherent in the amateur ethos. In an era when amateur sportsmen often dabbled in more than one discipline, the AAA ruled that participating in soccer or cricket matches involving professionals would not compromise an athlete's amateur status, even though it would not countenance this within athletics.[37] The FA for its part continued to enforce sanctions on amateur clubs who were thought to have violated amateurism – for instance, in May 1903 they had investigated Shepherd's Bush FC and found them to be employing at least one professional player, G. J. Dibsdale, who was banned from football for a year – the club's Honorary Secretary and Treasurer were also banned.[38] The contradictions of running a two tier system were starting to show. The response was that in 1906 the Amateur Football Defence Federation was formed in the South-East of England, and the movement would later create problems for the FA (Taylor, 2008, p. 84)

Internationally, British influence at FIFA was welcomed. In 1906 the founding President of FIFA Robert Guérin was replaced by the election of English FA's Daniel Burley Woolfall. During Woolfall's tenure, the sport continued to evolve, particularly in international fixtures and the English continued to influence international football through FIFA as well as the IFAB, the rules of association football being standardised globally based on the English model.

William Pickford again provides first-hand insight as to the development of the game, particularly in the evolution of the Laws of the Game. He was prominent in the Referee's Association for which he became Vice President and in 1895 had been instrumental in the production for the 1895-96 season of *the Referee's Chart*, introduced to help officials learn and apply the Laws, which he summarised in 17 points but which had become more complicated than those first agreed in 1863. He is also attributed with introducing in 1902 some innovative and long-lasting changes to the game, specifically the marking of the penalty area, penalty spot and the goal area. In 1906 he had published the book *How to Referee*[39] a guide to the laws of the game and how to apply them, to provide a more discussive and deeper account than could be captured by the chart, which was a succinct synthesis for simplicity. He was of the opinion that football had quickly become the

[37]AAA, 'Amateur Athletics Association: Constitution Rules, Objects and Lists of Officers and Clubs &c.: Laws for Athletic Meetings and Competitions, 1902, p. 9.

[38]FA Council Minutes 1903–1907. FA Council Minutes, 25 May 1903, p. 2.

[39]Pickford, W. (1906). *How to Referee.* E. Hulton.

most popular sport in England, largely crossing the boundaries of social classes and thus of amateur and professional. His book met a gap hitherto not covered by existing football writing:

> Books containing the best of how to play have been written by many acknowledged experts. The history of the game has become an attractive subject for the pens of numerous authoritative writers. Thanks to the exhaustive manner in which the Press has kept pace with the wonderful spread of Association football, its multitudinous votaries are enabled throughout the long playing months to be up-to-date and familiar with the doing of the clubs great and small, and with the legislation which is incidental thereto. In this blaze of publicity the game thrives and grows pace.[40]

Pickford could have been referring here to several books, firstly, *Football: Our Winter Game*[41] published 32 years earlier, was one of *the* first comprehensive accounts of football and its development. Alcock was a sportsman, administrator, author and editor, who had significant influence on the development of football and cricket, including important events we mentioned earlier in previous chapters. He arranged the first Test Cricket Match, England versus Australia in 1880, and as Secretary to the FA 1870–1895 is attributed as involved in arranging the first international fixtures, between England and Scotland, and as founder of the FA Cup, which he also won in 1872 as Captain of The Wanderers. In the book, Alcock traces the ancient roots and folk versions of football, and then development of association football. He outlines the laws of the game and makes the case for 'soccer' as having several advantages over other sports such as cricket, and like Coubertin, references Thomas Hughes, author of *Tom Brown's School Days*, to make his point. In 1874, the FA and its rules had been only 11 years old and other codes were still considered important, thus 'The Rugby Game' as codified and administered by the RFU is also outlined within this book, as the word 'football' was still used broadly to cover both codes at that time. Alcock also outlines other variations including those attributed to Eton, Marlborough, Cheltenham, Uppingham, Shrewsbury, and Winchester, most if not all of which were schools. Alcock died in 1907 by which time the book, although seminal, was already somewhat dated.

Secondly, Pickford's own four-volume set *Association Football and the Men Who Made it*,[42]which he co-authored with Alfred Gibson and published at around the same time as *How to Referee*[43] between 1905 and 1906. Over the four volumes, published between 1905 and 1906, eventually as a lavish hard-bound quadrillogy

---

[40]Pickford, W. (1906). *How to Referee*. E. Hulton, p. 3.

[41]Alcock, C. W. (1874). *Football: Our winter game*. Field Office.

[42]Gibson, A., & Pickford, P. (1906). *Association football and the men who made it*. Caxton.

[43]Pickford, W. (1906). *How to Referee*. E. Hulton.

contained within a slipcase, the authors' explain the roots and history of the game, club histories, player profiles, tactical advice from players themselves, and more. Lavishly bound and illustrated, the set was the most comprehensive yet attempted to chronicle the game, updating and surpassing even Alcock's work (Gibson & Pickford, 1906).

We have explained Pickford, his work and the evolution of association football in such depth because they were already important to the history of British sport and its governing institutions and would become more so in years to come.

Chapter Summary

The formation of the BOA consolidated a process of institutional development in British sport which had been gathering pace since the 1830s. The AAA through Herbert had attempted to represent Britain in the Olympic system, but there had been no central multi-sport 'clearing house' equivalent to France's USFSA to formalise and manage Britain's representation within the IOC. The BOA, at first a very lightweight organisation with no officers of its own beyond the committee or an independent budget, was built upon the distributed responsibility structure of the existing grouping of sporting associations, who's officers it represented in committee form. William Grenfell, or Lord Desborough, acted entrepreneurially in providing the leadership to facilitate this transition, and perhaps his coming as an experienced politician and administrator from outside existing organised sport was useful in providing a neutral ground for the various bodies who sometimes disputed the doctrine of amateurism to cooperate. Amateurism was central to the BOA's ethos. The organisation was at this time representative of the English (and Welsh) sporting bodies while claiming to represent Britain as a whole. Those from around the United Kingdom which had formed separately from or had broken away from the English bodies would only come to be included later. It is hard to establish that this was a deliberate policy at this time and may have been based on the pragmatics of forming the organisation. Certainly, it is hard to portray the body as lacking egalitarianism and at least a sense of philanthropy as it included the NPRS alongside the sporting associations, though an undercurrent here might have been wishing to fuel a sense of military preparedness without the intervention inherent in formal conscription. What is clear is that the body was intended to reinforce and perhaps legitimate amateurism – the Conservative background, with its preference in this period to minimise government intervention except when pragmatic, of some of its founding members meant that it could pre-empt government intervention by itself appearing authentically statesmanlike in terms of its structures and governance. This enabled the BOA to provide a diplomatic front which would remind other nations that Britain contributed the ethos of muscular Christianity to the Olympic movement and which would prove important at the next games, Athens 1906.

This chapter has also explained the foundations of another important emergent international sporting institution, FIFA, although at this time the organisation looked to the British Home Nations and particularly the London-based FA for inspiration. Indeed, the FA was still the largest footballing body in the world, an umbrella for not only the English County Associations but also those of the British Empire, where they existed. Association football had become codified and popularised quickly since inception in the 1860s although it had its own challenges regarding amateurism and professionalism. Given the significance of the game, the evolution of its governance, codification, and literature, all of which were developed to a greater extent than those of the IOC at the time, we have provided substantial detail about this and the administrators involved, some of whom are also important to the British Olympic story due to their involvement with the formation and early years of the BOA and would eventually become involved with later editions of the games.

Chapter 9

The Intercalated Games, Athens 1906

Abstract

The intercalated games of 1906 represented an attempt by the Greeks to reassert some influence over the Olympic movement by instituting a series of games fixed in Athens intercalated between the peripatetic series. The British participated though the British Olympic Association (BOA) was forced to use its networks to raise money from charitable organisations to pay the expenses of athletes. We follow the voyage of the British fencer Theodore Andrea Cook, who travelled with Desborough and others from Naples to Athens on the Steam Yacht Branwen. The event would be diplomatically important because the British used it to wrest for London the hosting rights for 1908 from Rome. We discuss the diplomatic process that facilitated this as well as the broader success of these games, which despite their intercalated nature demonstrated the established nature of the Olympic movement by this time.

Keywords: Athens 1906; intercalated games; Rome; London; sport history

Introduction

The BOA established and its Council (the BOAC) appointed, there now existed a formal institution to govern, administer, focus and promote the multi-sport British Olympic effort, coordinating the previously detached single-interest bodies. One such task for the BOA in its early days was to raise funds to send a team to the Interim or intercalated games in Athens, scheduled to happen in 1906.[1] We have already introduced the intercalated games (Chapter 5) as a compromise agreed between Coubertin and Crown Prince Constantine for a series of competitions to occur between official Olympiads. They had Coubertin's

[1]Cook, T.A. (1910).

Foundations of Managing British Olympics: Institutions through Time, 165–181

doi:10.1108/978-1-80262-095-520251009

blessing, even if that was just his diplomatic solution to the Greek suggestion that they should host in perpetuity. As such they can be considered as being 'the first truly international event held under IOC auspices .... Twenty nations sent nearly nine hundred athletes to Athens' (Baker, 2008, pp. 4–5). Before now these events had not taken place, but by 1906 Greece would be ready to proceed (MacAloon, 2006g).

Organising Athens

The Athens Games of 1906 involved a broad programme of sport, including[2]:

- Foot races – 100 metres flat, 110 metres hurdle, 400 metres flat, 800 metres flat, 1,500 metres flat, 5 mile (8,045 metres), Marathon (42 kilometres) (26 miles), and 1,500 metres walking match.
- Jumping – high jump, long jump, triple jump all 'with impetus' and long jump 'without impetus', pole jumping.
- Throwing – free disc, free Hellenic disc (which involved standing on a pedestal), free stone with impetus.
- Weight exercises – bar with two hands, dumb bell with each hand alternatively.
- Wrestling (Greco-Roman style).
- Ropes: tug-of-war, 'Climbing a smooth rope with the aid of arms'.
- Hellenic Pentathlon (comprised long-jump without impetus, Hellenic throwing of the discus, spear throwing, Olympic stade race (192 metres), Greco-Roman wrestling match.
- Gymnastic – pentathlon (parallel bars, horizontal bar, rings, vaulting-horse, long and high jumping combined), movements in unison (team-based synchronised gymnastics).
- Fencing (individual foil, sword, sabre, and team sword and sabre).
- Association football (which followed more or less the Laws of the Game of the English FA including use of a referee and two linesmen which by now was the agreed method to officiate games), no use of hands, no hacking or deliberately charging goalkeepers, and scoring goals under the cross-bar.
- Lawn tennis (singles and doubles, although doubles could involve a duo vs a single player).

These events were overseen by a sophisticated but convoluted system of sports authorities. At the practical end of this spectrum were medics and a health office, timekeepers, measurers, inspectors of machines, and starters. The potential for confusion, inconsistencies, and bias is obvious though when considering the system of creating, interpreting and enforcing rules, which involved; a system of ephors (Stewards), a jury, honorary general managers, a general manager, commissaries (managers), and secretaries of the jury. This system brought into contact

[2]Buckinghamshire Archives, Aylesbury UK (hereafter BA), D/86/13B/1-33 International Olympic Games at Athens Regulations Part 1, Committee of the Olympic Games at Athens.

representatives from participating countries, of the sports undertaken and of the Olympic Committee (presumably the Greek committee for this intercalated edition of the games rather than the IOC, but that was not specified). Some of these roles were dedicated to sports inside the stadium and some were solely for sports outside the stadium.[3]

The Amateur Fencing Association (AFA) of Great Britain and Ireland was involved with the arrangements for a special trophy, to be modelled from an original in the British Museum at a cost of £20, considered part of Lord Desborough's personal contribution.[4] Early in 1906, the trophy was commissioned to be made by Mappin and Webb, a famous engraving and metalwork firm which had warrants as silversmith to Queen Victoria and the Russian Imperial Household (Mappin & Webb, 2024).

Despite the various interesting ways in which Britain was involved in the tournament, the intercalated games of Athens tend to be overlooked in British Olympic history. Perhaps this is because the planned intercalated series never really got off the ground, 1906 being the first and last of its kind. Perhaps it is because they were outside of the official international Olympic series and less reported than later games. Only one photographer, Messrs. Bowden, 'went out specially from England to the Athenian Games'.[5] Another factor was that the Amateur Athletic Association (AAA) again declined to finance its athletes' participation, with a motion put forward by H. W. G. Haslegrave of Blackheath Harriers to allow £150 expenses for a representative team being voted down by the General Committee on 20 January 1908. At the same meeting, the IOC's offer of 5,000 Francs towards athlete expenses was not taken up, probably because it would be in violation of the AAA rule 10(f) that the promoters of a competition should not provide expenses.[6] Llewellyn (2011) again puts this down to conservatism and a belief that the AAA Annual Championship was the premier athletics competition, but the organisation's most powerful advocate for the Olympics, the Honorary Secretary Charles Herbert, who was also an IOC member had tragically fallen from the top of a London horse bus just ten days earlier. Herbert suffered severe injuries forcing his retirement, and the AAA appointed Percy L. Fisher as Honorary Secretary in his place before electing him representative to the BOAC.[7]

---

[3]BA D/86/13B/1-33, International Olympic Games at Athens Regulations Part 1, Committee of the Olympic Games at Athens.

[4]BA D/86/13B/33, Letter to Messrs Mappin and Webb, 6 Feburary 1906; An AFA sub-committee appointed Mr Edward Godwin to have all artistic control in reproduce the statue. It asked the firm to sign an 'undertaking that the right to reproduction of this design is strictly reserved to ourselves alone". In return, the committee offered to communicate the role of the form to the Press of Europe and the United States and credit it in every photo.

[5]Cook (1910, p. xiv).

[6]ATH/AAA/1/2/2/4, AAA General Committee Minutes, 20 January 1906, Amateur Athletic Association. 1897. *Constitution Rules, Objects and Lists of Officers and Clubs &c.* London, AAA, p. 9.

[7]'Athletics'. Daily Telegraph, 10 January 1906, p. 6.; AAA General Committee Minutes, 20 January 1906; 27 October 1906.

At the IOC Lord Desborough took Herbert's place (Kent, 2008). It seems likely that Herbert's absence removed advocacy but the continuing financial weakness of the organisation was also a factor. The AAA had not run a surplus since 1900,[8] and the General Committee, mindful of its fiduciary duty to member clubs seems to have considered the 1906 games an indulgence too far.

The BOA was able to scrape together a little money for British athletes to attend – Laffan was able to work his city connections to source contributions from the City of London's Livery Companies, charitable institutions. He raised £50 from the Goldsmith's Company, and £10 from each of the Grocers, Salters, and Clothworkers Companies, while the Greek government gave a contribution of £80.[9] The BOA sent a total of 40 athletes from England, Scotland and Wales, who mostly travelled by rail and sea, leaving London on 16 April and arriving in Athens already tired from their journey on the 20th. The Irish AAA meanwhile conducted an appeal in the pages of the *Irish Field,* sending three athletes who attended in the green caps and blazers of the IAAA but were told by the Greek Crown Prince presiding that as Ireland was not a country recognised by Greece, that they would have to compete alongside the British, triggering protests in Ireland (Llewellyn, pp. 653–657). British efforts were thence largely supported by philanthropy and the Greek wish to attempt to legitimate the intercalated games with the participation of several countries by contributing to their expenses.[10]

Despite their organisation the British were thus starting to fall behind in the financing of sport, because of their belief that it should be self-sustaining with no government subsidy or public subscription. The US team raised £5,000 ($24,300) through philanthropy, while the Swedish government donated 5,000 krona directly to their team, and the French team were given 10,000 Francs (£515), with a further 3,000 (£155) from the City of Paris. The Norwegian gave their team 3,000 krona (£167), while the City of Vienna gifted the Austrian team 1,000 krona ($200), and the German team received 12,000 marks (£588) from their government. Most were able to raise further funds from the public, though 19 German athletes also self-funded.[11]

Nonetheless, we make the case that the significance of these games for what happened in competition and in the corridors of power, are worthy of detailed explanation from a British perspective. In the words of one BOAC Member Theodore Andrea Cook, who stated the preparations made for Athens 1906 'were in reality the beginnings of our Olympic Games in England'.[12] Cook, a strong enthusiast for muscular Christianity and a journalist for the *Daily Telegraph*

---

[8]See ATH/AAA/1/5/2/2 AAA Balance Sheets and Accounts, 1900–1906.
[9]Cook (1908b, pp. 95–96).
[10]Sullivan, J. E. (1906). *The Olympic Games at Athens.* American Sports Publishing Company.
[11]Cook (1910, p. 95); Sullivan (1906, pp. 50–51). Officer, L.H., & S.H. Williamson (2024). "Computing 'Real Value' Over Time with a Conversion Between U.K. Pounds and U.S. Dollars, 1791 to Present", Measuring Worth. Unfortunately it was impossible to derive a conversion for the Swedish kronen figure.
[12]Cook (1910, p. 18).

where he wrote a column on sport called 'by an Old Blue', served on the AFA committee from 1904 until his death in 1928.[13]

Fortunately, detailed first-hand accounts are provided by both Cook and Lord Desborough who competed as fencers. In Cook's case, we draw upon two main sources: Firstly he wrote at length about his journey to and from the games, as well as of his experiences at them, in a privately circulated publication which although scarce, was re-issued soon after as chapters within his book International Sport.[14] Secondly, some years later, he condensed this prose, with additional reflection, in his memoirs *The Sunlit Hours*.[15] Additionally, we draw upon Lord Desborough's archived documents and personal correspondence with his wife and his colleagues, in the form of letters and Telegrams. There are also official reports of the 1906 Athens Games which provide further insights, for example, the US perspective.

An Athenian Adventure

Thoedore Andrea Cook, a member of the BOA and captain of the English fencing team, first heard of the Athens Games in 1905, from Mr Marinaky,[16] of the Greek Legation, and secretary to the Greek Olympic Committee in London. Cook thought it a great opportunity to take out a British Fencing Team as he had two years earlier, in 1903, captained the first such British fencing team visit to an open competition abroad, in Paris.[17] The event had the support of the Greek establishment, and the British Government was invited by the Greek Government to send representatives to these intercalated Olympic Games, which would begin in Athens on 22 April 1906. For this purpose, the Foreign Secretary Sir Edward Grey appointed Lord Desborough as the first representative,[18] and

[13]Buchanan, I. (2004). 'Cook, Sir Theodore Andrea'. *DNB*. https://doi.org/10.1093/ref:odnb/55483.

[14]Cook (1910).

[15]Cook, T. A. (1925). *The Sunlit Hours: A Record of Sport and Life*. Nisbet & Co.

[16]Although Cook (1910, p. 20) gives the name as 'Marinaky' a contemporary source gives a different spelling, explaining a committee existed for England's (presumably representing the United Kingdom) involvement at the Intercalated Games which comprised Honorary President the Duke of Argyll, and Honorary Secretary M.C. Marinary of the Royal Greek legation, London (International Olympic Games at BA D/86/13B/1-33, Athens Regulations Part 1, Committee of the Olympic Games at Athens).

[17]That 1903 team was composed of men who would mostly eventually become members of the British Olympic Association Council when it formed, namely: Lord Desborough, Sir Cosmo Duff Gordon, Edgar Seligman, Charles Newton Robinson, Lord Howard de Walden and Theodore Andrea Cook Cook, 1910, p. 20.

[18]BA D/86/13B/1-33, Letter to Lord Desborough dated 14 March 1906. Lord Desborough was first approached in writing about this matter around a month before his departure to Athens, in a letter dated 14 March 1906. Two reasons are given, firstly that he was attending anyway, and secondly Sir Edward Grey thought he was the best person forth is important role, although specific details of the exact duties it would involve at the time were still not known.

Mr R.C. Bosanquet, Director of the British School in Athens, as the second. At some point in the preparations King Edward VII, The Queen and Prince and Princess of Wales also decided to attend.[19]

Theodore Andrea Cook attended the games as a member of the BOA and as captain of the English fencing team and within this role he was responsible for making and circulating at least some of the travel arrangements for his team members. For Cook, Newton Robinson, and Seligman, travel began on Thursday 14 April 1906 when they set off from Victoria Station[20] although they appear to have parted at some point in the journey. Cook made his way to Naples, from where he travelled with three other members of his other fencing team, Lord Desborough, Cosmo Duff-Gordon, and Lord Howard de Walden, on de Walden's steam yacht, S.Y. Branwen, R.Y.S. (Royal Yacht Squadron).[21] Their journey was by sea to Athens, and back again, by way of Ithaca, Corfu, Ragusa, and Spalato, to Venice.[22] The Branwen was made of steel with decks, skylights and fittings made of teak[23] and the 'smallest craft of her kind that had ever made the trip'.[24]

Cook admits to being 'no sailor' and that this was his 'first cruise of any real length' and he took great interest in the basic setup, with charts in deckhouse, the Captain had traced the route, and kept 'the condensed literature of the *Mediterranean Pilot* at his elbow'.[25]

Lord Desborough had a sore arm upon his departure, possibly from a recent game of golf, having not played for a while, and expected this would be his last fencing expedition. He did not expect to beat the French or Belgian teams anyhow,[26] although this injury would soon feel better.[27] Desborough arrived in Naples on 15 April[28] the day before Cook, to see the aftermath of the eruption

[19]Cook (1910, p. 22).
[20]Cook (1910, pp. 27–28).
[21]BA D/86/13B/1-33, 'Olympic Games at Athens: Journey of the English Team'. Theo Cook as captain circulated a travel itinerary for all team members. They did not all travel together and it involved getting different people through different countries by different modes of transport, several of the meeting to travel together from Naples, others meeting in Athens: Duff-Gordon (Gibraltar, Marseilles, arriving in Naples on 15 April), DeWalden (Monte Carlo to Naples arriving on 16 April) Newton-Robinson and Seligman (France to Italy, arrive to Athens Friday 20th). Lord Desbrough, Cook and Duff-Gordon joined de Walden in Naples on his yacht the Branwen. Cook advised Desborough to book his travel with Messrs Cook travel agent ('no relation, I regret to say'). Details such as steamer-berths were paid by Theo Cook who asked the team to re-imburse him, but the larger costs such as First-Class rail from London to Rome he should pay himself and settle between 2 and 7 April.
[22]Cook (1910, pp. xi, 23).
[23]Cook (1910, p. 39).
[24]Cook (1910, p. xi).
[25]Cook (1925, pp. 226–229).
[26]Hertfordshire Archives and Local Studies, Desborough collection (hereafter HALS)D/ERVC1159/365, Letter from Lord Desborough to Lady Desborough dated 13 April 1906.
[27]HALSD/ERVC1159/367, Letter dated 15 April 1906.
[28]HALSD/ERVC1159/366, Letter from Lord Desborough dated 15 April 1906.

of Mount Vesuvius which had occurred around a week earlier, on 7th April. In the city of Naples, on the coast a few miles to the West of the volcano, the situation was not as bad as they had expected to see, although the entire town was covered a foot (30 centimetres) deep in fine ash and the authorities had discovered 'that some of the volcanic dust was so heavy that it broke through any flat roof that was insufficiently supported'. Cook describes that the whole of the conical top of Vesuvius was blown off and 'fragments were being distributed for some weeks all over Italy'. The wind changed suddenly one day and other parts of Europe were affected, notably a brown fog descended on Paris and the Black Forest. Inland, towards the volcano things were much worse. There had been a lot of rock showers and also 'white hot sand and vapour'. Many people were homeless and landless, and the vineyards were destroyed probably for many years. Cook describes walking on lava ten feet thick, which was still red-hot at the length of his walking stick. In Ottajano, South East of the volcano, from a population of 18,000 only 500 people had survived. Here, powdered lava three feet thick covered everything, no house with a flat roof had survived. The army had been brought in to keep order, working in on-and-off daylight to distribute bread and water where possible and pulling down some of the most unsafe buildings. People had been driven out of these houses but then had no protection from the red hot stones that had rained down. Bodies of people injured and killed by collapsing buildings were being pulled out by troops and 'It was impossible to move about in comfort without motor-goggles to protect the eyes and a respirator over the mouth, and all the time the thin drift of heavy dust just kept falling'.[29] Elsewhere, North-East of Mount Vesuvius, in Boscotrecase, Cook tells of houses covered in lava and still smoking. Here though there was not as much death, and mainly the elderly and bed-ridden had died, mostly 'showers of bursting stones and red hot rocks' had killed or wounded a few people.[30]

Cook tells that in the aftermath, The King of the Independent Kingdom of Italy banished a priest who had silently deserted his congregation, for the safety of his own home, while they prayed. Most of the two hundred worshippers had died. Politicians did not like Royal interference, but the Pope supported the King, saying he would have done the same thing.[31] According to the dates in Cook's account, they were only in the Naples area for one day. Some of these details, such as the bodies being brought out of homes he saw himself, other were told to him by Sir Thomas Lipton, who had visited as soon as it was possible to travel by train. Lipton also made available to them the steamer the Erin for their journey across the Bay of Annunziata.[32]

The following afternoon, at 2.30 p.m. on 17th April the swordsmen set off from Naples for Greece, passing southern Italy on the afternoon of the 19th. Cook waxes lyrical in his description of the journey, finding corroboration between the

[29]Cook (1910, pp. 30–34).
[30]Cook (1910, p. 32).
[31]Cook (1910, pp. 35–36).
[32]Cook (1910, p. 34).

scenes and natural features he experienced and those described by Homer[33] and used comparisons from classical Greek literature in his written account:

> We might indeed have been the comrades of Odysseus, judging by the stern welcome old Poseidon gave us in our voyage to the shores of Greece.[34]

Cook even compares the size and speed of their yacht to the boat of Odysseus, and the locations such as Capri to how they must have been during the time of Greek poet Homer, author of the Odyssey.[35] In his later chapter, Cook manages to condense some of this, summarising 'In so small a boat with on pilot but our captain we were nearer Homeric conditions of navigation than most modern seafarers'.[36]

On the 21st April Cook, Desborough, Cosmo-Duff, de Waldren, and crew members went through the Corith Canal, coast of Attica, finally dropping anchor in the Bay of Phalerum at 5o'clock that afternoon[37]. Arriving 'battered'[38] from bad weather which had drenched the yacht's cabin,[39] they travelled to Athens by rail, finding that in their carriage 'was an enthusiastic young footballer from Smyrna who was anxious to know what we thought of the chances of his team ... I hope he won. He had no English teams to beat'. Arriving in Athens, they went to their accommodation, the Hotel Imperial, close to the central square of Athens. Here they met the team members with whom Cook had started his journey, Newton Robinson and Seligman. Also waiting was a message that the team's captain must attend the club (Cook, 1908a, p. 59). This proved to be an influential moment as we shall explain later.

Upon arrival at the meeting at the club, Cook found an 'animated meeting' discussing the fencing rules 'for hours'.[40] He later reflected 'the mere preliminary arrangement of the rules and conditions gave me some of the hardest work and most difficult diplomacy I had ever faced'.[41] Overall, Cook claims to have got as many of the British amendments agreed as possible 'until sheer hunger drive me back to dinner, carrying numbers of tickets, invitations, and free passes for everything to my companions'.[42]

---

[33]Cook (1925, pp. 226–229).
[34]Cook (1910, p. 42).
[35]Cook (1910, pp. 38–40).
[36]Cook (1925, p. 226).
[37]Early in March 1906 the British Minister advised Cook 'that Phalerum would be a better anchorage for the yacht than the Piraeus, and we found he was entirely correct' (Cook, 1910, p. 26).
[38]HALSD/ERVC1159/369, Letter date 22 April 1906.
[39]HALSD/ERVC1159/368 Letter date 'Wednesday'.
[40]Cook (1908, pp. 59–60).
[41]Cook (1925, p. 231).
[42]Cook (1908, pp. 59–60).

Athens was overcrowded, and while some of the fencing team slept in the hotel,[43] Cook and de Walden preferred to sleep onboard the yacht, which was moored close to the English second cruiser squadron, off Phalerum.[44] This was despite the fact the Greek Government had provided The Zappeion for competitors' accommodation, and today this is claimed to have been the first Olympic Village (Zappas.org, n.d.) although Cook's account provides a perspective that suggests this was much more basic than the modern idea of an Olympic village:

> [...] a kind of common hostelry for all competitors in the Zappeion, a fine white building in a park near the stadium, But this kindly plan did not prove a practical success. Men who had finished their contests came home late and made a noise. Men who still had their work before them could not get enough sleep. The necessary arrangements for feeding so many persons at once did not always suit competitors who had any little idiosyncrasies of appetite or health.[45]

The American competitors shared a house under supervision, while the English swimmers stayed at the Aktaen Hotel at Phalerum, close to where they competed, and were joined by other British athletes 'who thought it wise to leave the Zappeion'.[46] Reflecting on these events, Cook later suggested that if more intercalated games were to be held, then all British athletes should travel there by boat and anchor in Phalerum Bay, budgeted at half a guinea a head for the whole trip, £200 minimum towards reasonable expenses.[47]

The first 'Great function' of the games was the very next day, on Sunday 22nd April[48] a formal welcome of competitors in the marble horse-shoe shaped stadium.[49] Desborough first lunched at the Legation to meet the King and Crown Prince of Wales, before moving on to the event, where Cook and Desborough estimated at least 50,000 people were crowded.[50] The British were led by Lord Desborough, wearing top hat and frock coat, as official chief and representative[51]

---

[43]BA D86/13B/11, Letter Cook to Desborough dated 'Friday'. Theodore A. Cook organised hotel rooms for Duff-Gordon and Lord Desborough, foreseeing Desborough may have ceremonial duties to attend.
[44]Cook (1908, p. 60).
[45]Cook (1908, p. 95).
[46]Cook (1908, p. 95).
[47]Cook (1908, p. 95).
[48]Cook (1925, p. 231).
[49]BA D86/13B/25 and Lord Desborough had a busy schedule of functions to attend in his roles as competitor and as an official representative, and he retained several of his invitations which indicate the dates, venues and occasions of at least some of them.
[50]HALSD/ERVC1159/369 Letter from Lord Desborough to Lady Desborough dated 22 April 1906, and Cook (1910, p. 64).
[51]Cook (1910, p. 63).

and processed with the other competitors and with the King and Queen of the United Kingdom, Prince and Princess of Wales, and the King of Greece.[52] After the official opening by the King of Greece at around 3pm, gymnastics exhibitions took place.[53]

The games had begun with due pomp and ceremony, and with impressive crowds. But practically, problems emerged. As well as the long and frustrating negotiation of rules on the eve of the games, Cook observed 'the beautiful marble stadium' had 'been built with a keener eye for sightseeing and magnificent architecture than for the sterner necessities of sport'.[54] Indeed, Lord Desborough's first impressions were quite scathing:

> The Greeks, I have come to the conclusion, know nothing whatever about the management of any form of athletic sports. I am scratching this with the most awful row going on.[55]
>
> I broke a strength machine on the yacht which these idiots sent to me all done up, at dinner with a sham Greek inscription, and Duff-Gordon[56] spreads about most ridiculous tales of destruction caused by me.[57]

A day after the welcoming ceremonies, the competitions began. Monday 23rd was notable for Cook and Desborough who attended preliminary rounds of fencing, and there were also cycling competitions, for Britain, Bouffler of the Regent Street Polytechnic reached the final of the bicycle race.[58]

An Opportunity for London?

Although no clue as to a date is given other then 'Monday' it was probably on or before Monday 23rd that Lord Desborough was first approached about the possibility of London, rather than Rome, hosting the forthcoming International Olympic Games of 1908. This is because he mentions having spoken about it to the King, presumably the English King, who left Athens before the following

[52]HALSD/ERVC1159/369, Letter from Lord Desborough to Lady Desborough dated 22 April 1906.
[53]Cook (1910, p. 64).
[54]Cook (1925, p. 231).
[55]HALSD/ERVC1159/369, Letter from Lord Desborough to Lady Desborough dated 22 April 1906.
[56]Sir Cosmo Edmund Duff-Gordon, 5th Baronet, DL (22 July 1862–20 April 1931) was a prominent Scottish landowner and sportsman, best known for the controversy surrounding his escape from the sinking of the RMS Titanic.
[57]HALSD/ERVC1159/369, Letter from Lord Desborough to Lady Desborough dated 22 April 1906.
[58]Cook (1910, p. 65, 1925, p. 231).

Monday. There was still much to consider, but Lord Desborough was immediately thinking of what might be required to create a grand Olympic spectacle:

> I hear that the Roman Games may fall through, so we shall have I think to hold them in London in 1908. I spoke to the King about it this morning and he highly approved – we could [indecipherable but presumably play tennis] at the Queen's Club, Fence at Olympia, row on the Thames, Swim at Highgate Ponds – and I think are able much more business like arrangements than they have here, but it would give one a good lot to do as President of the Olympic Committee – we have no stadium, which is simply glorious, with the Acropolis above you in the sun, but could make a fine show at Olympia to wind up with; massed bands and crown the Victors – I shall propose it tomorrow and undertable the management – if they cannot bring it off at Rome.[59]

Reasons for the Mooted change from Rome are provided by Kent who claims:

> Arrangements got off to a bad start when two committees were formed and started bickering almost from the start. One of the committees was headed by Prince Colonna, the Lord Mayor of Rome and a member of an ancient aristocratic family. Its decisions were disputed persistently by a second organisation, called the Municipal Board, supervised by Count de San Martino. Both groups came under an almost continuous fusillade of sniping fire from the city of Milan, which considered itself 'the moral capital' of Italy and was jealous that Rome had been selected to host the Games. There were also complaints from the city of Turin, which regarded itself as the centre of national sport. (Kent, 2008, p. 30)
>
> Ominously, the Italian government constantly refused to contribute funds to their Olympiad. (Kent, 2008, p. 30)

Kent (2008, p. 31) explains how the Italian government made 'the expected token protests' about losing their right to host the 1908 Olympiad, and soon after faced the tragedy of Mount Vesuvius, which provided 'face-saving excuse' when it was announced officially that funds intended for the Rome Olympics were being diverted to the relief of the victims and so Rome was reluctantly withdrawing from its patronage for the 1908 games.

The choice of London as a possible short-notice replacement host is explained by Baker (2008, p. 9) who highlight the British reputation for their ability to organise large-scale sporting events 'such as the Amateur Athletic Association

[59]HALSD/ERVC1159/376, Letter from Lord Desborough to Lady Desborough dated simply 'Monday'.

(AAA) Championships, Wimbledon and the Henley Regatta' as well as the reputation of Lord Desborough, the Chair of the BOAC, and his friendship with Coubertin (to which we add that of others such as Laffan, his historic friendship with Dr Brookes, and admiration of British sport and education generally).

Tuesday 24th was the first heat of fencing, with Greek and British Royals watching.[60] The Greek Crown Princess at this time was sister to the German Kaiser, and Cook remembers fondly how King Edward had a bet with her as to the outcome of the British versus German International Fencing Teams. The British beat the Germans by 9 to 2 and King Edward was so pleased that he 'graciously consented to become Patron of the AFA of Great Britain and Ireland, as his ancestor, King Henry VIII, had been before him'.[61] The British Royal Family left for Naples that same night.[62] Desborough was especially pleased that in front of the King he had not been struck.[63]

Other achievements by British athletes on Tuesday 24th were in swimming, with Taylor and Jarvis placed first and second respectively in the mile distance.[64] Prior to the games, hopes had been high for the British swimmers, the team's selector had intimated to Lord Desborough that they 'should win the majority of events.'[65] There was also the conclusion of the brief soccer tournament which has not been given official recognition because it featured club sides, Smyrna from the Ottoman Empire beating Thessaloniki 12-0 in the final (RSSSF, 2024).

Cook also mentions the free-style discus throw record was made by a policeman from the United States, Martin Sheridan, and that the event, newly re-discovered and little known at that time, is 'one of the most appropriate events possible for any Olympic Games'. A Greek-style event was also included for which 'the Greeks themselves provided some very curious rules for competitions in the Athenian stadium' and Cook gave similar praise to the javelin event.[66] James E. Sullivan, again serving as the American Commissioner, claimed in his report that the Greek-style event had been introduced to attempt to restore ancient styles to the competition, the American athletes having put their own their own interpretation on it while attempting to throw the discus as far as possible. Sheridan promptly had his Greek-style throw disallowed and Verner Järvinen of Finland triumphed, though Sullivan claimed that the Greek judges, wishing to avoid further protests from the confused competitors, had been lenient towards him![67]

On Wednesday 25th April British runner W.T. Pett won the 20 kilometres track race event and on Thursday 26th Lt Hawtrey won the five miles distance to

---

[60]Cook (1910, p. 65–66).
[61]Cook (1925b, p. 230).
[62]Cook (1910, pp. 22, 67).
[63]HALSD/ERVC1159/369, Telegram from Lord Desborough dated 24 April 1906.
[64]Cook (1910, pp. 67–75, 1925, p. 231).
[65]BA D86/13B/2, Letter to Lord Desborough dated 8 April 1906.
[66]Cook (1910, pp. 67–75).
[67]Sullivan, J. E. (1906). *The Olympic games at Athens.* American Sports Publishing Company, pp. 85–89.

further help the medal haul. Additionally, in épée the team qualified for the final event.[68] Earlier efforts, on the eve of the games a few days earlier, to agree rules proved to be somewhat in vain; upon arriving at the épée final, the French team insisted on changing a rule, explicit in the rule book for the intercalated games, applying to fixtures on the swords and the British agreed to it, but found that it suited the French technique more, the French winning the Gold medal by three points.[69] This re- negotiating of rules was something that Desborough and Cook would seek to overcome in future.[70] Additionally, Desborough was annoyed by the judging which he considered unfair, although he was overall pleased with his performance, having been hit just once in the fights with the Germans and Belgians put together. This is especially impressive considering it came just days after a long sea voyage and among his other role as official representative, which necessitate a busy schedule of functions with royalty and government.[71]

Friday 27th, Saturday 28th, and Sunday 29th were mainly taken with social entertainments. Cook dined at the British Legation and had 'an enormous lunch' in the Aktaen Hotel at Phalerum, given by the Crown Prince. There was a garden party in the house of the Director of the British School, and a performance of Oedipus Rex in the stadium.[72] Of the performance, Cook found it difficult to understand the modern Greek language but was disappointed that it had been 'deliberately modernised' in this way.[73] On Sunday, prior to attending the play, Lord Desborough wrote to his wife with an update on his progress with the idea to host the 1908 Olympic Games in London, financing it was his greatest concern:

> I have had several meetings about the Olympic meeting in England in 1908 but I do not see how to get the money yet – The Sports here cost £40,000 – the Gov guarantee a good lot, and get it back by a new stamp issue and various other ways – but I do not suppose that our Government would give a shilling.[74]

1 May 1906 was the last day of competitions, British athletes Leahy won high jump, and Healey came second in the hurdles. Most anticipated though was the great Marathon.[75] There were an estimated 60,000 spectators in the stadium,

---

[68]Cook (1910, p. 76).

[69]HALSD/ERVC1159/369, Telegram from Lord Desborough dated 24 April 1906; in fencing, the 'pointed arret' (button at the end of the sword) was 'obligatory' for the benefit of the jury; BA D86-13B.1, International Olympic Games at Athens Regulations Part 1, Committee of the Olympic Games at Athens, p. 36.

[70]Cook (1910, p. 27).

[71]HALSD/ERVC1159/374, Letter from Lord Desborough date Thursday 26 April.

[72]HALSD/ERVC1159/374, Letter from Lord Desborough to Lady Desborough dated 'Sunday', and Cook (1910, p. 79).

[73]Cook (1910, pp. 79–81).

[74]HALSD/ERVC1159/374, Letter from Lord Desborough to Lady Desborough, Hotel Imperial, Athens, dated 'Sunday'.

[75]Cook (1910, p. 82).

'every inch of the hill above the marble arena was packed with Greeks from every district south of Turkey, and there was a solid line of soldiers round the top against the blue sky'.[76] The winner, a Canadian, was presented with prizes of a bouquet of flowers and a goat. The Greeks had expected one of their own to win and Cook states the Canadian's victory was 'evidently unexpected and unwelcome'.[77] The day closed with a ball at the Aktaen Hotel at Phalerum.[78]

Greece's participation had again been important in continuing their own national revival. They fielded 88 athletes, at least a quarter of them coming from Asia Minor and the broader Greek diaspora. A particular flashpoint came when the Greek flag was raised to celebrate the victory of the Alibrantis brothers (Georgios in the pentathlon and Nicholaos in gymnastics), who represented an athletics club from Constantinople, drawing a high-profile protest from the Ottoman ambassador (Georgakis, 2003).[79]

Wednesday May 2nd was saved for prize-giving in the stadium, at which victorious athletes were given medals and olive branches by the King of Greece. Cook recalls being presented with a branch of olive from the Altis of Olympia which accompanied the epee teams' medals. Desborough wrote of having lunch with the Greek King and of the team being cheered by the populace as they received olive branches and 'very good' medals 'but not the First which we really won' 'We got these as second prize, and the Belgians got third – We really won without a doubt and I am very sad about it'.[80] Cook reflected that while the British might not be able to muster the resources of the Americans, they might be more organised in future intercalated games by chartering a steamer that might take the athletes directly from an English port to Greece, and provide them accommodation and board there on it.[81]

Overall, Britain did well according to the points system in place at the 1906 event, more so than Cook gave credit for in his earlier account,[82] although he updated this view favourably and provided a more factually based summary in his later publication:

> The Americans almost swept the board in the Stadium events, but they paid for specialisation by doing very little else. Scoring 5 for first prize, 3 for a second, and 1 for a third, the French won the best aggregate with a total of 92 points and thirteen first prizes. The British came second with a total of 78, nine firsts and eleven seconds. The Greeks were a close third with 76. The Americans, with eleven magnificent victories on the track and the arena, totalled 75. [83]

---

[76]Cook (1910, pp. 82–83).
[77]Cook (1910, p. 83).
[78]Cook (1910, p. 84).
[79]Savvidis, P. (1906). *Album of the intermediate Olympic games*. SEGAS, p. 39.
[80]HALSD/ERVC1159/380, Lord Desborough to Lady Desborough, 'Thursday'.
[81]Cook (1910, p. 95).
[82]Cook (1910, pp. 24–25).
[83]Cook (1925, pp. 232–233).

Cook and Desborough set sail for Venice and Rome, Lord Desborough having more fencing to do, and Olympic administrative meetings planned 'where I have several meeting with the French and Italians about the Olympic Games – and the rules for the several sports in 1908' but lamented 'There is not a man among the foreign representatives who cannot speak 3 languages fluently – I cannot, which is humiliating'. [84] They travelled more or less the same route as they had on the way there, but were able to visit Islands such as Corfu, where they arrived in the evening of the 4th May, and the Gravosa in Dalmatia in the morning of 5th May.[85] The journey was colourful, the weather 'chucked' them about 'like a cork'[86] but some members of the yacht staff could also be dangerous:

> There is one old steward to wait on us four. He was so dotty that at Corfu he was sent to see the man-of-wars doctor, who says he is suffering from incipient paralysis and mania, so I shall be glad to see the back of him. The second steward took charge one night, and got mad drunk and wanted to fight the captain. Most of the rest of the crew have their ailments.[87]

The importance Cook placed on the experiences of the locations is reflected in the way that he explains some of these travels in rich detail.[88] Indeed, enjoying the adventure seems to have been as important as enjoying the sport, and Cook also describes having been sightseeing while in Athens, such as the Temple of Zeus, Theseum, and the Acropolis.[89]

On 13th May, now in Italy, Lord Desborough had a dinner to attend, presumably one of the Olympic meetings in Italy. He planned to see Coubertin and Brunetta d'Usseaux, an Italian nobleman involved with the Olympic movement involved with Rome's 1908 bid to host and now hoping to have the games moved to London, if possible. Desborough still didn't know how to raise the required funds but hoped for help from the King.[90] The next day, 14th May, Lord Desborough wrote to Coubertin, we can therefore assume that the French Baron had not attended on the 13th as had been hoped. Desborough wrote that he is visiting Athens in two capacities, firstly to fence with the British team, and secondly as the

---

[84]HALSD/ERVC1159/374, Letter from Lord Desborough to Lady Desborough dated 'Sunday'.
[85]Cook (1925, p. 234).
[86]HALSD/ERVC1159/379, Letter from Lord Desborough to Lady Desborough dated 7 May 1906.
[87]HALSD/ERVC1159/379, Letter from Lord Desborough to Lady Desborough dated 7 May 1906.
[88]Cook (1910, pp. 124–144).
[89]Cook (1910, pp. 110–123).
[90]HALSD/ERVC1159/377, Letter from Lord Desborough to Lady Desborough dated 10 May 1906; D/ERVC1159/382, Letter from Lord Desborough to Lady Desborough dated 13 May 1906.

First British Representative to the Greek Government. He understood that he is to consult with the British committee[91]:

> and see if the Olympic Games cannot be held in England in 1908. I spoke to our King about it in Athens and he gave his acquiescence, and I think would help them.[92]

Lord Desborough knew that to make any Olympic Games in London a success he would need the backing of the establishment, in the same way as the Games in Athens that he had just attended:

> I should be very sorry to have them there unless they were a *great* success, and were taken up by all the best people from the King downwards.[93]

Lord Desborough was also aware of a meeting of the International Committee at the Sorbonne on 26th May but the timing was not right for him, having been on his intercalated games adventure already since mid-April. There was though also a meeting at The Hague scheduled for January 1907 that he thought he might go to. Lord Desborough's correspondence from this time show that his main concern at this point was about raising finance to host the games should they be moved to London, and that he was aware of how busy he would be as Chairman of the BOAC:[94]

> If the Games really come off in England in 1908 I shall have a very great deal to do being President of the Olympic Committee – but I do not know if we should be able to raise the money: one ought to have £10,000 guaranteed.[95]

Chapter Summary

Despite its intercalated, or unofficial nature in the eyes of the IOC the Athens Games were in some ways more successful than the previous Paris or St Louis

---

[91]IOCCIO/JO/LON08/CORR, 'Correspondence 1908', Letter from Lord Desborough to Baron de Coubertin, dated 14 May 1906.
[92]IOCCIO/JO/LON08/CORR, 'Correspondence 1908', Letter from Lord Desborough to Baron de Coubertin, dated 14 May 1906.
[93]IOCCIO/JO/LON08/CORR, 'Correspondence 1908', Letter from Lord Desborough to Baron de Coubertin, dated 14 May 1906.
[94]HALSD/ERVC1159/380, Letter from Lord Desborough to Lady Desborough, 'Ithaea, Thursday' aboard Branwen R.Y.S.
[95]HALSD/ERVC1159/380, Letter from Lord Desborough to Lady Desborough, 'Ithaea, Thursday' aboard Branwen R.Y.S.

meetings. They were more international, and the European location made it possible for more countries to send representative teams. The Greeks, seeking to establish a series of intercalated events that could rival Coubertin's quadrennial series, also encouraged participation through funding and diplomacy. The British lagged in enthusiasm and funding, but what was important was that the key members of the BOAC made the trip to Athens on the *Branwen* and were able to secure a diplomatic victory – doing the groundwork that would enable them to prize the 1908 hosting rights away from Rome, with London able to present itself as a sort of white knight ensuring the continuity of the games. The involvement of figures such as Desborough and Cook in 1906 was important as it allowed the BOA to consolidate its control over British participation in the Olympic Games, while the incident with the Irish athletes would also meant that the IAAA would be forced to see the BOA as the central body. The BOAC members had also had a front row seat at a successfully organised event and witnessed the sort of diplomatic opportunities that a well-run games could bring. This experience would give them ideas for 1908, and we will explore this further in Volume 2.

Chapter 10

Conclusion

Main Themes

Gillett and Tennent (2020) suggest the study of sport and project management offers a window into the development of the organisations, usually temporary, that form to plan, govern, and operate major sporting events. In this volume, we have looked at the growing interest in Olympicism in Britain and its broader influence internationally. We also have looked at the organisation and governance of the International Olympic Committee (IOC) in continental Europe and with some US influence. We have considered in detail the first few editions of the IOC's Olympic Games as well as other revivals in Greece and Britain. Some of the actors who we have identified as important are Dr Brooks in Shropshire, the National Olympic Association in the United Kingdom more widely, and Zappas in Greece, who among other names and institutions identified in the earlier chapters, played important facilitating roles in the earlier movements and revivals. All of these early sports were about physical performance and some had elements of military preparedness including the use of swords, daggers, javelins, or even firearms. Paradoxically, the Olympic movement would have connections to the world peace movement with aspirations to compete through sport rather than war. Our narrative of this volume ends with the moving of the hosting rights of the 1908 Olympic Games from Rome to London.

In tandem, we have discussed the emergence of and British participation in expositions and world's fairs which some early editions of the Olympic Games were attached to, although not without tension. For example, Paris 1900 and St Louis 1904 were held parallel to expositions which acted as celebrations of *fin-de siecle* modernity. Similarly, the Olympic revivals also looked forwards as well as backwards, but this was a facet of the movement that Coubertin had difficulty in selling to the public as people had difficulty in understanding the purpose of the revival. Even once the games were underway in 1896, the British press questioned the presence of bicycle racing, then a technological novelty, in an Olympic tournament.

We have further discussed the rise of amateurism which legitimated and cleansed sport in Britain and which was admired by Coubertin and thence adopted by the Olympic movement. This led to the pursuit of sport for the

Foundations of Managing British Olympics: Institutions through Time, 183–186

doi:10.1108/978-1-80262-095-520251010

prestige of sport alone, rather than monetary reward, despite the contradictions inherent in pursuing the model when internationalised. The AAA, a middle-class body, led by Charles Herbert, accepted the principle of expenses in cases of representative sport but avoiding resorting to philanthropic donations, they often ran out of money. In 1906, Reverend Laffan managed to attract charitable support from some of the City Companies and as British Olympism took shape he played a vital role in catalysing the movement. In this way, Laffan's role in forming the BOA was important in terms of the collaborative work involved, in a similar fashion to some of the individuals from government and football identified by Tennent and Gillett (2016) who use the analogy of a swarm of people coming together to organise sporting events.

The British traditions of amateurism and the related voluntarism in organisation further directly influenced the formation of the Olympic system, originally based on that of the Henley Regatta, as well as through Coubertin's interest in muscular Christianity and sport within education. This book has been written from a British perspective and our findings about how the institutional Olympic project evolved, and what Britain brought to it – and how it was perceived and contributed to from the British perspective.

Contributions

The first contribution that we would like to highlight is that the Olympic Games were considered as projects beyond sport from the start–indeed the term 'project' was used from the early editions of the games. Stadiums were built or renovated, financing and ticketing were given great consideration, and representative organisational committees and sub-committees were organised to plan and deliver games. Systems of distributed responsibility bringing together many actors were key from the start. While the organisations for each edition of the games were temporary, they existed with the sanction and permission of a permanent IOC, even if the relationship was at times fractious as in St. Louis. We have presented a detailed outline of the games that were delivered, and also considered some cancelled projects such as the Chicago games, or games not considered officially Olympic in retrospect such as the Intercalated games of 1906.

The motives for the revival can be summarised as fitting within Gillett and Tennent's (2017) dynamic sublimes, who built on Flyvbjerg (2014), while institutional influences affected the culture, structure, and process of organising (Thornton et al., 2012). The games had an aesthetic sublime, for example, being iconic and beautiful in the eyes of people who enjoy good design, in the sense that they drew up on the symbolic legacy of the classical Olympiad, combining it with the purity of amateurism, and encouraging the restoration of and the building of new stadiums. This re-enacted in rhetorical form (Suddaby Foster & Quinn Trank, 2010), and there were constructions of ancient Olympia which brought authenticity and legitimacy to the new concept of international sport.

The political sublime, which speaks to the political benefit to parliamentary governments, royalty, and national identity building of a project, related to the reinforcement of Greek independence and the broader justification of its dynasty within the 19th-century European political system. Generations of Greek politicians, businessmen, and royalty sought to use the games to promote Greece, and this itself gave legitimacy to Coubertin's efforts to reinstate the games. The political and diplomatic links between Greece and Britain at the time gave broader legitimacy to British revival efforts, together with an interest in classicism, starting with the Wenlock games which shared correspondence and prizes with early revivalists in Greece. More broadly, the IOC provided an arena for competing claims between the sporting politics of different nations. The 1904 St Louis Olympics in Chapter 7 provides a good example of this.

The games had an economic sublime in terms of the opportunities presented to sporting entrepreneurs. Broadly, a tension merged between the amateur thousand the need to make the events pay for themselves out of gate revenue. The Paris games in 1900 ran late in preparation and health and safety issues arose, but some sports events were well attended, and budgets were claimed to be managed successfully. A broader point was made that sports had been promoted within Paris, which would have a legacy of participation and attendance. In Chicago, there was an attempt to create a profit-making corporation with investors – which demonstrates the approaches existing in different national economic systems. It was hoped the sports would boost the attractiveness of the World's Fairs which were themselves businesses, and vice versa, and the Olympics inherited legitimacy from these World's Fairs by attempting to cover their financial costs in a similar way.

The technological sublime, which stresses the attractiveness of innovation emerging from a project, relates to the World's Fair element more than the Olympic Games. For example, at the Paris 1900 event, many scientific achievements were showcased examples, speculated in the British press ranged from the sublime to the ridiculous which we have labelled *technotainment*. This fed into the excitement and build-up of the World's Fair, perhaps helping it to gain momentum in the public interest.

We would now like to propose a fifth sublime – the educational. This we define as the informative benefit for society that a megaevent offers. This starts with the educative potential identified by Dr Brooks and the introduction of an 'Olympic Class' in Much Wenlock, Shropshire, for the benefit of the rural people. At the same time, the English public school system in corporate sport directly into its muscular Christianity pedagogy. Coubertin connected these ideas together and looked to Britain as a model upon which to improve education in France and later internationally. This educational aspect led Coubertin to seek Laffan's expertise in physical education, bringing Laffan into the Olympic movement. There was also the hope that sporting competitions would raise the profile of physical exercise and encourage the broader public to take it up – a dimension, for example, pursued by the National Physical Recreation Society in Britain.

This synthesis led to the consolidation of multiple sports from regionally varied folk pursuits to increasingly standardised, governed, and organised competitions. While sport was commercialised, for instance at Morpeth, the concept of sport for its own sake, or as the Greeks might say αθλητισμός για χάρη του αθλητισμού (*athlitismós gia chári tou athlitismoú*) was systemised first by the British and then taken up by the IOC after 1892.

The Games Come to England

Tennent and Gillett (2016) and Gillett and Tennent (2017) stress the prevalence of changing plans in the mega-event preparation process. Following the decision to move the 1908 Games from Rome to London, there was a need for quick thinking on the part of the British representatives, most significantly Lord Desborough who had the ultimate decision. The approach from Coubertin was made at the Intercalated Games of 1906 in Athens, where Desborough was captaining the British *épée* participants. Desborough recognised the importance of gaining the endorsement of Edward VII to host the games and moved quickly to secure this. A stadium would also need to be built, and everything would have to be ready in two years' time. The pressure was on.

References

Acheson, G. G., Campbell, G., Turner, J. D., & Vanteeva, N. (2015). Corporate ownership and control in Victorian Britain. *The Economic History Review, 68*(3), 911–936.

Acrkill, M., & Hannah, L. (2001). *Barclays the business of banking 1690–1996*. Cambridge University Press.

American Battlefield Trust. (2013). *The reasons for secession: A documentary study*. Retrieved January, 24, 2025, from https://www.battlefields.org/learn/articles/reasons-secession

Andrews, T., & Burke, F. (2007). What does it mean to think historically. *Perspectives on History, 45*(1), 32–35.

Anthony, D. (1997). Coubertin, Britain and the British: A chronology. *Journal of Olympic History, 5*(3), 18–21.

Anthony, D. (2007). Honorary members of the Wenlock Olympian Society. *Journal of Olympic History, 15*(1), 19–21.

Arnold, A. J. (1988). *A game that would pay: A business history of professional football in Bradford*. Gerald Duckworth & Company Limited.

Ashrafian, H. (2005). William Penny Brookes (1809–1895): Forgotten Olympic Lord of the Rings. *British Journal of Sports Medicine, 39*(12), 969.

Bagwell, P., & Lyth, P. (2002). *Transport in Britain 1750–2000: From Canal Lock to Gridlock*. Hambledon and London.

Bagwell, P. S. (1968). *The railway clearing house in the British economy, 1842–1922*. Allen & Unwin.

Bailey, S. (1997). A noble ally and Olympic disciple: The Reverend Robert S. de Courcy Laffan, Coubertin's 'Man' in England. Olympika-London Ontario, *6*, 51–64.

Bailey, S. (2012). *Laffan, Robert Stuart de Courcy (1853–1927), sports administrator and Church of England clergyman*. Oxford Dictionary of National Biography. Retrieved December 4, 2024, from https://www.oxforddnb.com/view/10.1093/ref:odnb/9780198614128.001.0001/odnb-9780198614128-e-104187

Baker, A. (1995, August 19). 100 years of rugby league; From the great divide to the Super era. *The Independent*.

Baker, K. (2008). *The 1908 Olympics*. SportsBooks Limited.

Barker, P. (2005). The British Olympic Association 1905–2005 – A chronology. *Journal of Olympic History, 13*(2), 64–72.

Barker, P. (2012). *Five rings over Britain: The IOC sessions in London and Birmingham*. Cotinos Books.

Bayle, E., & Chappalet, J. L. (Eds.). (2018). *From Olympic administration to Olympic governance*. Routledge.

Beale, C. 2011. *Born Out of Wenlock William Penny Brookes And The British Origins of The Modern Olympics*. DB Publishing.

Beckett, I. (2012). *Grenfell, William Henry, Baron Desborough (1855–1945), sportsman and politician*. Oxford Dictionary of National Biography. Retrieved December 11, 2024, from https://www.oxforddnb.com/view/10.1093/ref:odnb/9780198614128.001.0001/odnb-9780198614128-e-33566

Bonython, E., & Burton, A. (2001). *The great exhibitor: The life and work of Henry Cole*. V&A Publishing.

Booth, K. (2002). *The father of modern sport: The life and times of Charles W. Alcock*. The Parrs Wood Press.

Boughey, D. (2009). British overseas railways as free-standing companies, 1900–1915. *Business History*, *51*(3), 484–500.

Britannica. (n.d.). *World's Columbian exposition fair, Chicago, Illinois [1893]*. Retrieved January 24, 2025, from https://www.britannica.com/event/Worlds-Columbian-Exposition

British National Buffalo Bill Archive. (n.d.). *The programme, 1904*. Retrieved November 28, 2024, from https://bnbba.co.uk/programme_1904.html

Brownell, S. (2008). *The 1904 anthropology days and Olympic Games: Sport, race and American imperialism*. University of Nebraska Press.

Bryant, M. (2020). *Jackson, Clement Nugent (1846–1924), sports administrator*. Oxford Dictionary of National Biography. Retrieved January 24, 2025, from https://www.oxforddnb.com/view/10.1093/ref:odnb/9780198614128.001.0001/odnb-9780198614128-e-50371

Bryson, B. (2011). *At home: A short history of private life*. Black Swan/Transworld.

Buchanan, I. (1993). Cricket at the 1900 games. *Journal of Olympic History. International Society of Olympic Historians*, *1*(2), 4–5.

Buchanan, I. (2004). *Cook, Sir Theodore Andrea (1867–1928), journalist and sportsman*. Oxford Dictionary of National Biography. Retrieved December 13, 2024, from https://www.oxforddnb.com/view/10.1093/ref:odnb/9780198614128.001.0001/odnb-9780198614128-e-55483

Budd, C. (2017). *Sport in urban England: Middlesbrough, 1870–1914*. Lexington Books.

Cain, P. J., & Hopkins, A. G. (1987). Gentlemanly capitalism and British expansion overseas I. The old colonial system, 1688–1850. *The Economic History Review*, *39*(4), 501–525.

Carter, N. (2021). *Cycling and the British: A modern history*. Bloomsbury.

Chandler, A. D. (1977). *The visible hand: The managerial revolution in American business*. Harvard University Press.

Chandler, R. (1776). *Travels in Greece: Or an account of a tour made at the expense of the Society of Dilettanti*. Clarendon Press.

Chaney, E. (2014). *The evolution of the grand tour: Anglo-Italian cultural relations since the renaissance*. Routledge.

Chappalet, J. L. (2018). From Olympic administration to Olympic governance. In E. Bayle & J. L. Chappelet (Eds.), *From Olympic administration to Olympic governance* (pp. 3–15). Routledge.

Chappalet, J. L. (2023). The governance of the Olympic system: From one to many stakeholders. *Journal of Global Sport Management*, *8*(4), 783–800.

Chatziioannou, M. C. (2019). Greek sovereign debt and loans in 19th-century public discourse. *The Journal of European Economic History*, *48*(2), 21–55.

Chicago Tribune. (2021). *Flashback: White City, Chicago's first amusement park mixed family friendly joys with sensationalism*. Retrieved January 24, 2025, from https://www.chicagotribune.com/2021/07/09/flashback-white-city-chicagos-first-amusement-park-mixed-family-friendly-joys-with-sensationalism/

Cleophas, F. (2024). *Who were the first Africans at the Olympics? The disturbing story of two 1904 marathon runners*. The Conversation. Retrieved December 5, 2024, from https://theconversation.com/who-were-the-first-africans-at-the-olympics-the-disturbing-story-of-two-1904-marathon-runners-234429

Cooke, C. A. (1950). *Corporation, trust and company: An essay in legal history*. Manchester University Press.

Corker, C. (2023). The Sheffield innovation system 1860–1914: Steel, armaments, metallurgy and education. In J. Wilson, C. Corker, & J. Lane (Eds.), *Industrial clusters: Knowledge, innovation systems and sustainability in the UK*. Routledge.

Country Life. (2005, June 22). *The true home of Tennis*. Retrieved January 24, 2025, from https://www.countrylife.co.uk/out-and-about/sporting-country-pursuits/the-true-home-of-tennis-41091

Courtin, N. (2016). *L'ancêtre des expositions universelles*. Retrieved January 24, 2025, from https://histoire-image.org/etudes/ancetre-expositions-universelles?i=232

Crotty, M. (1998). 'Separate and distinct'? The manual labour question in nineteenth-century Victorian rowing. *The International Journal of the History of Sport*, *15*(2), 152–163.

Decker, S. (2013). The silence of the archives: Business history, post-colonialism and archival ethnography. *Management & Organizational History*, *8*(2), 155–173.

Dickie, M. W. (1984). Fair and foul play in the funeral games in the "Iliad". *Journal of Sport History*, *11*(2), 8–17.

Declercq, R. (2022). A return ticket to the world market? The Leipzig fur industry, internationalism and the case of the International Fur Exhibition (IPA) in 1930. *Business History*, *64*(3), 610–625. https://doi.org/10.1080/00076791.2020.1736045

Dixon, P., Garnham, N., & Jackson, A. (2007). Shareholders and shareholding: The case of the football company in late Victorian England. *Business History*, *46*(4), 503–524.

Driega, A. W. (1997). Olympics before Pierre de Coubertin. *Journal of Olympic History*, *5*(2), 20–27.

Elbech, S., & Stokkermans, K. (2024). *Intermediate games of the IV. Olympiad Football Tournament*. Retrieved December 18, 2024, from https://www.rsssf.org/tableso/ol1906f.html

Evans, E. J. (1996). *The forging of the modern state: Early industrial Britain 1783–1870*. Longman.

FA.com. (n.d.). *Preliminary round, FA Cup, 1900*. Retrieved January 24, 2025, from https://www.thefa.com/competitions/thefacup/results-archive#

Ferzoco, G. (2000). The changing face of tradition: Monastic education in the Middle Ages. In F. Ferzoco & C. Muessig (Eds.), *Medieval monastic education*. Leicester University Press.

Findling, J. E. (2004). Chicago loses the 1904 Olympics. *Journal of Olympic History*, *12*(3), 24–29.

Finer, H. (1934). *English local government*. Columbia University Press.

Flyvbjerg, B. (2014). What you should know about megaprojects and why: An overview. *Project Management Journal*, *45*(2), 6–19.

Foreman-Peck, J., & Hannah, L. (2012). Extreme divorce: The managerial revolution in UK companies before 1914. *The Economic History Review*, *65*(4), 1217–1238.

Friedman, W. A., & Jones, G. (2011). Business history: Time for debate. *Business History Review*, *85*(1), 1–8.

Frost, W. (2002). Heritage, nationalism, identity: The 1861–62 England cricket tour of Australia. *The International Journal of the History of Sport*, *19*(4), 55–69.

Gallardo-Albarrán, D., & De Jong, H. (2021). Optimism or pessimism? A composite view on English living standards during the Industrial Revolution. *European Review of Economic History*, *25*(1), 1–19.

Gannaway, N. (2009) *William Pickford: A biography*. Hampshire Football Association Limited.

Georgakis, S. (2003). Sporting Links: The Greek Diaspora and the Modern Olympic Games. *Modern Greek Studies (Australia and New Zealand)*, 11.

Geppert, A. C. T. (2010). *Fleeting cities. Imperial expositions in Fin-de-Siècle Europe*. Palgrave Macmillan.

Gibson, A., & Pickford, W. (1906). *Association football and the men who made it* (Vols. I–IV). The Caxton Publishing Company.

Gillett, A. G., & Tennent, K. D. (2017). Dynamic sublimes, changing plans, and the legacy of a megaproject: The case of the 1966 Soccer World Cup. *Project Management Journal*, *48*(6), 93–116.

Gillett, A. G., & Tennent, K. D. (2020). Sport and project management: A window into the development of temporary organizations. In *Handbook of research on management and organizational history* (pp. 169–191). Edward Elgar Publishing.

Gillett, A. G., Tennent, K. D., & Tomlinson, A. (2022, August 31–September 2). *From gentleman's pastime to global consumption: Exploring the emergence of soccer as an entertainment product during its first hundred years* [Working Paper]. British Academy of Management Annual Conference, Manchester.

Gøksyr, M. (1990). 'One certainly expected a great deal more from the savages': The anthropology days in St. Louis, 1904, and their aftermath. *The International Journal of the History of Sport*, *7*(2), 297–306.

Gourvish, T. R. (1972). *Mark Huish and the London & North Western Railway: A study of management*. Leicester University Press.

Govett, L. A. (1890). *The King's book of sports: A history of the declarations of King James I. and King Charles I. as to the use of lawful sports on Sundays*. Elliot Stock.

Grenfell Family History. (n.d.). *William Henry Grenfell (1855–1945)*. Retrieved January 24, 2025, from https://grenfellhistory.co.uk/biographies/william-henry-grenfell

Guttman, A. (2002). *The Olympics – A history of the modern games* (2nd ed.). University of Illinois Press.

Haddon, C. (2004). *The first ever English Olympic games*. Hodder & Staughton.

Halladay, E. (1990). *Rowing in England: A social history – The amateur debate*. Manchester University Press.

Hammersley, P. (2016). The other Upton Park – The forgotten Olympic champions. *Journal of Olympic History*, *24*(1), 28–37.

Hannah, L. (2007). The 'divorce' of ownership from control from 1900 onwards: Re-calibrating imagined global trends. *Business History*, *49*(4), 404–438.

Harvey, C., Maclean, M., & Suddaby, R. (2019). Historical perspectives on entrepreneurship and philanthropy. *Business History Review*, *93*(3), 443–471.

Harvey, C., & Press, J. (1990). The city and international mining, 1870–1914. *Business History*, *32*(3), 98–119.

Heller, M. (2008a). Work, income and stability: The late Victorian and Edwardian London male clerk revisited. *Business History*, *50*(3), 253–271.

Heller, M. (2008b). Sport, bureaucracies and London clerks 1880–1939. *The International Journal of the History of Sport*, *25*(5), 579–614.

Hill, C. R. (1996) *Olympic politics*. Manchester University Press.

Holt, R. (1990). *Sport and the British: A modern history*. Oxford University Press.

Hornby, H., & Inglis, S. (2007). *Uppies and downies: The extraordinary football games of Britain*. English Heritage.

Howarth, P. (1951). *The year is 1851*. Collins.

Hughes, G. (2009). *A Develyshe pastime: A history of football in all its forms*. Sportsbooks.

Hulley, R. (2010). John Hulley – An Olympic innovator. In D. Day (Ed.), *Sporting lives* (pp. 126–141). MMU Sport and Leisure History.

IOC (International Olympic Committee). (n.d.). *Pierre de Coubertin*. Retrieved January 24, 2025, from https://olympics.com/ioc/pierre-de-coubertin

IOC (International Olympic Committee). (2020). *The "Red Devils" at the top of world football at Antwerp 1920*. Retrieved January 24, 2025, from https://olympics.com/en/news/the-red-devils-at-the-top-of-world-football-at-antwerp-1920

IOC (International Olympic Committee). (2021a). *Welcome to the ancient Olympic games*. Retrieved July 6, 2023, from https://olympics.com/ioc/ancient-olympic-games

IOC (International Olympic Committee). (2021b). *II Olympic Congress – Le Havre 1897*. Retrieved January 24, 2025, from https://olympics.com/ioc/le-havre-1897-olympic-congress

IOC (International Olympic Committee). (2021c). *III Olympic Congress – Brussels 1905*. Retrieved January 24, 2025, from https://www.olympics.com/ioc/brusels-1905-olympic-congress

IOC (International Olympic Committee). (2023a). *Olympic games Paris 1900*. Retrieved January 24, 2025, from https://olympics.com/en/olympic-games/paris-1900

IOC (International Olympic Committee). (2023b). *Edgar Syers biography, Olympic medals, records and age*. Retrieved January 24, 2025, from https://olympics.com/en/athletes/edgar-syers

Irish Independent. (2012). *The amazing tale of Ireland's greatest-ever Olympian*. Retrieved December 5, 2024, from https://www.independent.ie/life/the-amazing-tale-of-irelands-greatest-ever-olympian/26885886.html

JDP Economics. (n.d.). *London, England 1851: The great exhibition of the arts & industries of all nations*. Retrieved November 5, 2021, from http://jdpecon.com/expo/wflondon1851.html

John Hulley Memorial Fund. (n.d.). *National Olympian Association*. Retrieved January 24, 2025, from http://www.tiger2.f2s.com/JohnHulleyMemorialFund/national_olympian_association.shtml

Jones, P. (2013). *The 1848 revolutions*. Routledge.

Jutta, B., & Leuiten van Zanden, J. (2024). MPD version (2023): Maddison style estimates of the evolution of the world economy: A new 2023 update. *Journal of Economic Surveys*, 1–41.

Keeling, D. (2008). Shipping companies and transatlantic migration costs: the case of cunard, 1880-1914. In *Economic Business History Association Annual Conference*.

Kellett, J. R. (1978). Municipal socialism, enterprise and trading in the Victorian city. *Urban History*, *5*, 36–45.

Kelly, D. (2020). *The Red Taylorist: The life and times of Walter Nicholas Polakov*. Emerald.

Kent, G. (2008). *London's Olympic Follies: The madness and mayhem of the 1908 London Games*. The Robson Press.

Koliopoulos, G. V., & Veremis, T. (2009). *Modern Greece: A history since 1821*. Wiley-Blackwell.

Lane, J. (2023). Knowledge, identity and cooperation in an early industrial cluster: The potteries in 1775. In J. Wilson, C. Corker, & J. Lane (Eds.), *Industrial clusters: Knowledge, innovation systems and sustainability in the UK*. Routledge.

Leapman, M. (2001). *The world for a shilling: How the great exhibition of 1851 shaped a nation*. Faber & Faber.

Llewellyn, M. P. (2011). Lighting the Olympic flame. *The International Journal of the History of Sport*, *28*(5), 648–668.

Llewellyn Smith, M. (2004). *Olympics in Athens 1896: The invention of the modern Olympic Games*. Profile Books.

Lucas, R., & Emsley, C. (2010). *Vincent, Sir (Charles Edward) Howard (1849–1908), politician and police administrator*. Oxford Dictionary of National Biography. Retrieved December 4, 2024, from https://www.oxforddnb.com/view/10.1093/ref:odnb/9780198614128.001.0001/odnb-9780198614128-e-36660

Lundvall, S. (2015). From Ling gymnastics to sport science: The Swedish School of Sport and Health Sciences, GIH, from 1813 to 2013. *The International Journal of the History of Sport*, *32*(6), 789–799.

Lupson, P., & Lerwill, J. (2011). *The inspirational William McGregor: Father of the football league and all football leagues*. A&J L Solutions.

Lupson, P. J. (2006). *Thank God for football!*. Azure.

MacAloon, J. J. (2006a). Preface to original edition. *The International Journal of the History of Sport*, *23*(3–4), 336–340.

MacAloon, J. J. (2006b). The Olympic idea. *The International Journal of the History of Sport*, *23*(3–4), 483–527.

MacAloon, J. J. (2006c). The vision at Rugby Chapel. *The International Journal of the History of Sport*, *23*(3–4), 393–445. https://doi.org/10.1080/09523360600639204

MacAloon, J. J. (2006d). The mighty working of a symbol: From idea to organization. *The International Journal of the History of Sport*, *23*(3–4), 528–570. https://doi.org/10.1080/09523360600639261

MacAloon, J. J. (2006e). Noble works, glorious examples, generous sacrifices. *The International Journal of the History of Sport*, *23*(3–4), 350–392. https://doi.org/10.1080/09523360600639154

MacAloon, J. J. (2006f). Preface to second edition. *The International Journal of the History of Sport*, *23*(3–4), 331–335.

MacAloon, J. J. (2006g). An indescribable spectacle. *The International Journal of the History of Sport*, *23*(3–4), 571–645.

Maclean, M., Harvey, C., & Clegg, S. R. (2016). Conceptualizing historical organization studies. *Academy of Management Review*, *41*(4), 609–632.

Major, J. R. (2007). *More than a game : the story of cricket's early years*. HarperPress.

Mappin and Webb. (2024). *Our history*. Retrieved December 19, 2024, from Our History | Mappin and Webb.

Matthews, G. R. (2005). *America's first Olympics: The St. Louis Games of 1904*. University of Missouri Press.

McClaughlin, L. (2024, July 17). How Great Britain claimed Olympic cricket glory in Paris 124 years ago. *The Guardian*. Retrieved January 24, 2025, from https://www.theguardian.com/sport/article/2024/jul/17/great-britain-olympics-cricket-castle-cary-paris-france-the-spin

Meethan, K. (2010). Touring the other: Buffalo Bill's Wild West in Europe. *Journal of Tourism History*, *2*(2), 117–13.

Merriman, J. (1996). *A history of modern Europe from the renaissance to the present*. W. W. Norton & Co.

Mollan, S. (2018). The free-standing company: A "zombie" theory of international business history?. *Journal of Management History*, *24*(2), 156–173.

Morrell, J. B., & Watson, A. G. (1928). *How York governs itself: Civic government as illustrated by the county of the city of York*. George Allen & Unwin Ltd.

Moseley Society. (2018). *Moseley wins silver at the Olympics!*. Retrieved January 24, 2025, from https://moseley-society.org.uk/wp-content/uploads/2018/11/Moseley-won-silver-at-the-Olympics.pdf

Nix, A., Decker, S., Kirsch, D. A., & Venkata, S. K. (2023). Archival research in the digital era. In S. Decker, W. M. Foster, & E. Giovannoni (Eds.), *Handbook of historical methods for management* (pp. 156–172). Edward Elgar Publishing.

Olympia London. (2025). *A Journey through 130 Years*. Available online: https://events.olympia.london/our-story [accessed 25 April 2025].

Owen, G. (1999). *From empire to Europe: The decline and revival of British industry since the Second World War*. HarperCollins.

Parezo, N. J., & Fowler, D. D. (2007). *Anthropology goes to the fair: The 1904 Louisiana purchase exposition*. University of Nebraska Press.

Parkar, U. (2023). *Cricket in Olympics: Great Britain stumps France for gold at Paris 1900*. Retrieved January 24, 2025, from https://olympics.com/en/news/why-cricket-olympics-1900-paris-games-commonwealth-athletes-cricketers

Parker, C. (2001). The rise of competitive swimming 1840 to 1878. *Sports Historian*, *21*(2), 54–67.

PBS.org. (n.d.). *Summing up, looking forward, and the Paris Exposition*. Retrieved January 24, 2025, from https://www.pbs.org/wgbh/americanexperience/features/1900-forward-exposition/#:~:text=As%20a%20tribute%20to%20technology,and%20boosterism%20was%20evident%20everywhere

Pickford, E. (1940). The psychology of the history and organization of association football Part 1. *British Journal of Psychology. General Section*, *31*(1), 80–93.

Platt, D. C. M. (1977). *Business imperialism, 1840–1930: An inquiry based on British experience in Latin America*. Clarendon Press.

Polley, M. (2011). *The British Olympics: Britain's Olympic heritage 1612–2012* (Vol. 10). English Heritage.

Popp, A. (2006). Governance at points of corporate transition: Networks and the formation of the United Alkali Company, 1890–1895. *Enterprise & Society*, *7*(2), 315–352.

Popp, A., & Fellman, S. (2017). Writing business history: Creating narratives. *Business History*, *59*(8), 1242–1260.

Pugh, M. (2008). *Fisher, William Hayes, Baron Downham (1853–1920), politician*. Oxford Dictionary of National Biography. Retrieved December 11, 2024, from https://www.oxforddnb.com/view/10.1093/ref:odnb/9780198614128.001.0001/odnb-9780198614128-e-53101

Radford, P. (2012). The Olympic games in the long eighteenth century. *Journal for Eighteenth-Century Studies*, *35*(2), 161–184.

Randall, D. (2011, November 6). Winter 1893: Greece is bankrupt. Summer 1896: It hosts the first modern Olympics. *The Independent*. Retrieved January 24, 2025, from https://www.independent.co.uk/life-style/history/winter-1893-greece-is-bankrupt-summer-1896-it-hosts-the-first-modern-olympics-6257912.html

Reid, D. A. (1996). Weddings, weekdays, work and leisure in urban England 1791–1911: The decline of Saint Monday revisited. *Past & Present*, *153*(1), 135–163.

Robertson, A. (2022). *The mystery of Robert Guérin, the man who founded FIFA*. Retrieved January 24, 2025, from https://www.scottishsporthistory.com/sports-history-news-and-blog/the-mystery-of-robert-guerin-the-man-who-founded-fifa

Rozmiarek, M., Gleaves, J., Malchrowicz-Mośko, E., & Włodarczyk, A. (2023). Pseudo-Olympics in California: From circus shows and local sports competitions to a mass statewide event. *The International Journal of the History of Sport*, *40*(6–7), 533–552.

Ruhl, J. K. (1997). The Olympic games in Athens in the year 1877. *Journal of Olympic History*, *5*(3), 27–34.

Rutterford, J., & Maltby, J. (2007). "The nesting instinct": Women and investment risk in a historical context. *Accounting History*, *12*(3), 305–327.

Sanders, R. (2010). *Beastly fury: The strange birth of British football*. Random House.

Schofield, J. A. (1982). The development of first-class cricket in England: An economic analysis. *The Journal of Industrial Economics*, *30*(4), 337–360.

Scottish Football Association (SFA). (n.d.). *History of the cup*. Retrieved November 12, 2021, from https://www.scottishfa.co.uk/scottish-cup/archive/scottish-cup-history/the-history-of-the-cup/

Shanks, M. (2003). *The classical archaeology of Greece: Experiences of the discipline*. Routledge.

Shaw, B. (1904). *The common sense of municipal trading*. Archibald Constable & Co.

Sheard, K. (2004). *Hill, Sir (George) Rowland (1855–1928), rugby administrator*. Oxford Dictionary of National Biography. Retrieved December 11, 2024, from https://www.oxforddnb.com/view/10.1093/ref:odnb/9780198614128.001.0001/odnb-9780198614128-e-50400

Sieveking, A., & Lock, J. (2004). *Hutton, Alfred (1839–1910), swordsman*. Oxford Dictionary of National Biography. Retrieved December 11, 2024, from https://www.oxforddnb.com/view/10.1093/ref:odnb/9780198614128.001.0001/odnb-9780198614128-e-34078

Smith, R. A. (1988). *Sports and freedom: The rise of big-time college athletics*. Oxford University Press.

Solem, D. (n.d.). *'S/S St Louis, American Line'. Norway Heritage: Hands-across-the-sea*. Retrieved January 24, 2025, from https://www.norwayheritage.com/p_ship.asp?sh=stlou

Spivey, N. (2005). *The ancient Olympics*. Oxford University Press.
Stokes, J. (2019). Chapter 10 – Men, women and horses: Public spectacle in 1887. In P. Fielding & A. Taylor (Eds.), *Nineteenth century literature in transition: The 1880s* (pp. 200–222). Cambridge University Press.
Stone, D. (2022). *Different class: The untold story of English cricket*. Repeater.
Storey, R. (2004). *Montagu, John Walter Edward Douglas-Scott-, second Baron Montagu of Beaulieu (1866–1929), promoter of motoring*. Oxford Dictionary of National Biography. Retrieved December 11, 2024, from https://www.oxforddnb.com/view/10.1093/ref:odnb/9780198614128.001.0001/odnb-9780198614128-e-32879
Suddaby, R., Foster, W. M., & Trank, C. Q. (2010). Rhetorical history as a source of competitive advantage. In J. A. C. Baum & J. Lampel (Eds.), *The globalization of strategy research* (Vol. 27, pp. 147-173). Emerald Group Publishing Limited.
Tait, J. (1917). The declaration of sports for Lancashire. *English Historical Review*, *32*, 561–568.
Taylor, H. (2002). Play up, but don't play the game: English amateur athletic elitism, 1863–1910. *Sports Historian*, *22*(2), 75–97.
Taylor, M. (2008). *The association game: A history of British football*. Pearson Longman.
Tennent, K. D. (2013). Management and the free-standing company: The New Zealand and Australia land company c. 1866–1900. *The Journal of Imperial and Commonwealth History*, *41*(1), 81–97.
Tennent, K. D. (2021). Management and business history – A reflexive research agenda for the 2020s. *Journal of Management History*, *27*(1), 80–98.
Tennent, K. D., & Gillett, A. G. (2016). *Foundations of managing sporting events: Organising the 1966 FIFA World Cup*. Routledge.
Tennent, K. D., & Gillett, A. G. (2022). A brief history of the FIFA World Cup as a business. In S. Chadwick, P. Widdop, C. Anagnostopoulos, & D. Parnell (Eds.), *The business of the FIFA World Cup* (pp. 5–27). Routledge.
Tennent, K. D., & Gillett, A. G. (2023). How to research in an archive. In S. Decker, W. M. Foster, & E. Giovannoni (Eds.), *Handbook of historical methods for management*. Edward Elgar Publishing.
Tennent, K. D., & Gillett, A. G. (2024). Conceptualising historical project studies: A complementary partnership. *International Journal of Project Management*, *42*(4), 102601.
Tennent, K. D., Gillett, A. G., & Foster, W. M. (2020). Developing historical consciousness in management learners. *Management Learning*, *51*(1), 73–88.
The Rec.Sport.Soccer Statistics Foundation (RSSSF). (2024). *Intermediate Games of the IV Olympiad*. Available online: https://www.rsssf.org/tableso/ol1906f.html [accessed 25 April 2025].
Thornton, P. H., Ocasio, W., & Lounsbury, M. (2012). *The institutional logics perspective: A new approach to culture, structure and process*. Oxford University Press.
Torkildsen, G. (2005). *Torkildsen's sport and leisure management*. Routledge.
Torres, C. R. (2005). What was Pierre de Coubertin concerned about in 1889? A view from an Argentine contemporary source. *The International Journal of the History of Sport*, *22*(3), 344–364.
Turner, D. A. (2013). *Managing the "Royal Road": The London & South Western Railway 1870–1911* [Ph.D. thesis, University of York].
Turner, D. A., & Tennent, K. D. (2021). Progressive strategies of municipal trading: The policies of the London County Council Tramways c. 1891–1914. *Business History*, *63*(3), 397–420.
V&A (Victoria and Albert Museum). (n.d.). *The first Christmas card*. Retrieved January 24, 2025, from https://www.vam.ac.uk/articles/the-first-christmas-card
Vamplew, W. (2004). *Pay up and play the game: Professional sport in Britain, 1875–1914*. Cambridge University Press.

Van Nijf, O. (2000). Athletics, festivals and Greek identity in the Roman East. *The Cambridge Classical Journal*, *45*, 176–200.

Van Nijf, O. (2004). In M. A. Kaila, et al. (Eds.), *The Roman Olympics* (pp. 186–215).

Van Nijf, O. M. (2023). *The civic world of professional associations in the Roman East*. Brill.

Vogel, R. M. (1961). Elevator systems of the Eiffel Tower, 1889. *United States National Museum Bulletin*, *228*, 1–37.

Walker, S. P. (2024). Being unbusinesslike. Financing strategy at the Great exhibition. *Business History*, 1–24.

Wall, F. (1935). *Fifty years of football*. Cassell.

Walton, J. K. (1981). The demand for working-class seaside holidays in Victorian England. *Economic History Review*, *34*(2), 249–265.

Walvin, J. (1994). *The people's game* (Rev. ed.). Mainstream.

Watson, N. J., Weir, S., & Friend, S. (2005). The development of muscular Christianity in Victorian Britain and beyond. *Journal of religion and society*, *7*(1), 1–25.

Westby, M. (2018) *A history of Sheffield Football 1857–1889 '…speed, science and bottom'*. England's Oldest Football Clubs.

WHO'S WHO &WHO WAS WHO. (2007a). *Cook, Sir Theodore Andrea (28 March 1867–16 Sept. 1928), Editor-in-Chief of the Field since 1910*. Retrieved December 13, 2024, from https://www.ukwhoswho.com/view/10.1093/ww/9780199540891.001.0001/ww-9780199540884-e-194961

WHO'S WHO & WHO WAS WHO. (2007b). *Desborough, 1st Baron (William Henry Grenfell) (30 Oct. 1855–9 Jan. 1945)*. Retrieved December 12, 2024, from https://www.ukwhoswho.com/view/10.1093/ww/9780199540891.001.0001/ww-9780199540884-e-224636

WHO'S WHO &WHO WAS WHO. (2007c). *Downham, 1st Baron (William Hayes Fisher) (1853–2 July 1920)*. Retrieved December 11, 2024, from https://www.ukwhoswho.com/view/10.1093/ww/9780199540891.001.0001/ww-9780199540884-e-195744

WHO'S WHO &WHO WAS WHO. (2007d). *Hill, Sir G. Rowland (21 Jan. 1855–25 April 1928), Past President of the Rugby Football Union, for which he was for many years Hon. Secretary*. Retrieved December 11, 2024, from https://www.ukwhoswho.com/view/10.1093/ww/9780199540891.001.0001/ww-9780199540884-e-197881

WHO'S WHO &WHO WAS WHO. (2007e). *Hutton, Captain Alfred (1840–17 Dec. 1910)*. Retrieved December 11, 2024, from https://www.ukwhoswho.com/view/10.1093/ww/9780199540891.001.0001/ww-9780199540884-e-187423

WHO'S WHO &WHO WAS WHO. (2007f). *Knowles, Sir Lees (16 Feb. 1857–7 Oct. 1928)* Retrieved December 11, 2024, from https://www.ukwhoswho.com/view/10.1093/ww/9780199540891.001.0001/ww-9780199540884-e-198942

WHO'S WHO & WHO WAS WHO. (2007g). *Montagu of Beaulieu, 2nd Baron (John Walter Edward Douglas-Scott-Montagu) (10 June 1866–30 March 1929)*. https://www.ukwhoswho.com/view/10.1093/ww/9780199540891.001.0001/ww-9780199540884-e-214281

WHO'S WHO & WHO WAS WHO. (2007h). *Vincent, Sir (Charles Edward) Howard (31 May 1849–7 April 1908), JP, Senior DL of London; ADC to the King; Colonel Commandant Queen's Westminster Volunteers, 1884–1904; Hon. Colonel; MP for Central Sheffield (Conservative and Industrial) from 1885*. Retrieved December 11, 2012, from https://www.ukwhoswho.com/view/10.1093/ww/9780199540891.001.0001/ww-9780199540884-e-191854

Wilkins, M. (1988). The free-standing company, 1870–1914: An important type of British foreign direct investment. *Economic History Review*, 259–282.

Williamson, M. (2012). *The ignorant Olympians*. Espncricinfo. Retrieved January 24, 2025, from https://www.espncricinfo.com/story/rewind-to-1900-cricket-at-the-olympics-571936

Wilson, J. (2014). *Inverting the pyramid: The history of football tactics*. Orion.

Wilson, J., & Popp, A. (2003). *Industrial clusters and regional business networks in England, 1750–1970*. Ashgate.

Wilson, R., & Mackley, A. (2000). *The building of the English country house: 1660–1880: Creating paradise*. Hambledon Continuum.

Wimbledon.com. (n.d.). *About the AELTC*. Retrieved July 4, 2023, from https://www.wimbledon.com/en_GB/atoz/about_aeltc.html

Winn, W. E. (1960). Tom Brown's schooldays and the development of "Muscular Christianity". *Church History*, *29*(1), 64–73.

Young, D. (1996). *The modern Olympics – A struggle for survival*. Johns Hopkins University Press.

Zappas.org. (n.d.). *Abridged biography of Evangelis Vasileiou Zappas (1800–1865) founder of the modern Olympic games*. Retrieved December 18, 2024, from https://www.zappas.org/zappas.shtml

Index